BY WAY OF LUCK

how chance shaped a storied life

by Jim Perkins

A Work In Progress Book

Library of Congress Catalog-in-Publication Data
2015905867

ISBN 9781495152566

Copyright © 2015 Jim Perkins

All Rights Reserved.

Manufactured in the United States of America

First Edition

Acknowledgment

The QWERTY keyboard: without which the speed of communications advances over the last one hundred years may not have been possible.

Dedication

To the women in my life: My wife, Judith. My daughters Susan, Karen and Elizabeth. My sisters Nitsa and Pamela. My granddaughters Hannah, Shannon and Maddy. My nieces Lydia and Sarah. And my aunt Catherine.

And to the men: Jon, Julio, Bruce, Jim, Mike, Robert, Brendan, Max, Andy and Alex who are lucky to have them in their lives.

By Way of Luck

Prologue

John Wayne, the actor and biggest box office film star of his time, walked into my office, whapped my shoulder with a solid thud, stopping me at my work, and said in a cadence familiar to 60s movie fans, "C'mon, kid…Let's go to the Polo…We can both use a drink."

The afternoon was late. I was hunched over a Remington typewriter at work on a screen play at Batjac Productions, a West Hollywood studio just off Sunset Boulevard that Wayne, directors John Ford and William A. Wellman and producer Bob Fellows had started only a couple of years earlier. I was a beneficiary of their first film, "The High and the Mighty." Based on an Ernie Gann novel and released in 1954 it starred Wayne as the resolute pilot who guided an about-to-crash passenger plane to safety and saved everyone aboard. Its surprising success kicked the start-up into passing gear, money was rolling in and the partners were spending it on new properties. I had gotten swept up in their spending spree.

That I was there at all and getting a palsy-walsy invite to belly up to the bar with a famous Hollywood hero was pure luck. It was the sort of thing that happened only in the movies. I was a barely published writer — a couple of articles in *The Saturday Evening Post*, one each for the *Reader's Digest* and *Field and Stream* my highest achievements — and as green as the money Batjac was paying me. Introduced to the studio by my collaborator, a friend and writer whom you'll read about later, I had never before written a screen play and typed with just two fingers, my nuisant pecking

By Way of Luck

an annoyance to everyone within earshot. Nor was I sure how to address Mr. Wayne. Or was it just John? Or, as I learned when we got to the Polo Lounge at the Beverly Hills Hotel, he expected to be called Duke. I took the safer choice. I called him Mr. Wayne.

From his films — my favorites: "Red River" directed by Howard Hawks and "Stagecoach" directed by John Ford — Mr. Wayne did not fit his movie image. Noticeably missing: a sweat-soiled Stetson, brim badly bent, high-heeled, plains-drifter boots, and a holster hanging off a hip, filled, and strung to his thigh. A gruff guy in rough gear, how I had always seen him in his movies. Except for a face that was mostly cheeks and chin yet easily identifiable by most pre-adult American movie goers, he seemed the typical Malibu resident in an open collared shirt, a jacket of blue cotton and loose double-pleated chinos with a simple, unadorned cowhide belt.

Seeing me still sitting and struck silent by his invitation, he roared "How about now!" I scurried to catch up with him as he left the building.

The Beverly Hills Hotel during the 1950s, I learned from stories I'd heard and pictures I'd seen, wasn't much different than it was in the 1930s. The war had slowed business, film making was recovering though barely and the hotel, grand as it had been, looked and felt old lady-ish. Prime space, a bungalow, was going for $40 a night, tops. Yet the bar at the hotel's Polo Lounge was still Hollywood's oasis of choice, attracting a rowdy mixture of actors, directors and writers, names and faces I'd seen on theater posters, mostly men and the occasional woman who could handle the rough talk at the bar.

As the crowd milled about I saw a social ritual at play. The drinks and the crude remarks that followed were offered up only by friends, and friends of friends, people with tight ties and loose talk, their quick jokes a currency that bought them a place in the mix, people who could call Mr. Wayne, the film star, Duke and who could not. The not's, as in not invited, soon knew who they were and ambled off to the tourist tables in a far corner of the room.

That I had walked through the door in the wake of Mr. Wayne, thunder claps greeting him, cherry-cheeked imbibers at the bar

III

pushing each other aside to make space, deferential waiters setting up chairs in whatever direction Mr. Wayne looked to sit, being off-handedly introduced by the Duke as a writer from back East working at Batjac, the bartender giving me a nod, as if he were keeping a list and noting, kid with the Duke OK. For the moment at least, I was deemed acceptable. Yet acceptance did not diminish my awkwardness. Weak at the knees and timid, mingling with icons of the film industry and humbled by their celebrity, I tried not to be seen the young fool. But it wasn't to happen. Unaware that a customer was expected to wave off the bartender's pouring of a drink, as in "enough", my first and only Scotch went easily four maybe five ounces. I could not push it aside, the bartender eyeing me critically. I chose to nurse it instead, the minutes passing. By then the story telling and the laughter had moved on and I might just as well have been sitting with the tourists.

How is it, a reader might ask, that a 22 year old "kid", still a work in progress, can find himself in the right seat of an ages-old Chevrolet on his way to an iconic watering hole with a movie giant behind the wheel talking through his frustrations producing "Blood Alley," a film he'd just wrapped, at the last minute having to stand in for Robert Mitchum who arrived on location drunk and was promptly fired, delaying production, and co-starring with an indulgent Anita Ekberg who, in an unscripted scene, taunted the crew by frolicking in the rain clad only in an extra-large men's T-shirt and bringing the shoot to a halt?

The answer will come in the opening chapter of this book.

Which brings me to "this book." Beginning as a simple autobiography, or memoir if you wish, it has become much more than that. Reading through my notes, outlining my recollections and reconstructing what I considered notable, personal events, I saw that my life has unfolded in continuing yet totally unpredictable events that over the years have served me well and from which I have mightily benefitted. And for which there is no reasonable explanation except, somewhere along the line, someone or something, mathematically or by chance, decided I would be the recipient of what I can only define as luck.

By Way of Luck

Forks in the road taken and leading inexorably to pleasurable and profitable happenings may be a fanciful supposition, perhaps, but I am given to fantasy, though largely as an entertainment, when in real life there are no other viable alternatives of merit. Accepting these conclusions, however imaginary they may be, I write here how all this may have come about.

Born to working parents in a hardscrabble New Hampshire village just miles south of the Canadian border, the eldest child and only boy and younger than others in my school class, I was left alone much of the time and feeling isolated. On the playground when sides were picked I'd be the last chosen. Winters were long and sub-zero cold. The sky seemed perennially dark. Walking by myself I thought perilous. I sought light and warmth and an answer to my beginnings — only eight to ten years old at the time and already searching for the consequence of life and, for me, how it might turn out.

There was no way I could surely know, so I concocted a fantasy that comforted and stayed with me until it faded in my adult years, and I am only now just recalling it. I pretended I was in a movie. That all around me, unseen, there were cameras and a director and actors readying to play their roles, all of them in support of me, the player with the most lines, the most scenes, and with an appreciative audience looking on.

I had an ensemble; I would be the character to whom good things happened, lucky things. Assuredly, my story, if not my life, would have a happy ending.

The pretense came easily. My eldest uncle built and managed a chain of art deco movie theaters, the nearest, the Palace, just around the corner from my grandparents' house in St. Johnsbury, Vermont. When visiting, as we frequently did — my parents, uncles and aunts and an occasional cousin, gathered in the living room and distracted by their chatter — I would slip away unnoticed, enter the theater wrong-way through an exit door and hunker down in a front row seat where I might not be seen. The ushers knew I was there. I didn't need a ticket, but felt I'd gotten away with watching a lot of movies for free.

V

Sitting so close to the stage — I could reach it with the toe of my shoe — and hidden from the paying customers, I felt joined to the cast, whether playing in a film or in a live vaudeville show. Western star of black and white films Gabby Hayes once appeared at the Palace live. Standing alone on stage, lit by a single spot, all else dark, with one foot anchoring a manual bicycle pump, he blew up a balloon and by squeezing its neck with both thumbs and fingers he allowed the escaping air to emit a squeaky but acceptable rendering of "My Old Kentucky Home." The audience turned giddy with surprise, in its astonishment laughing and applauding. Gabby bowed regally, sweeping his cowboy's hat across the boards, and left the stage, as he strode away tossing me the exhausted balloon as if I'd played a role in his act. Of course, I had.

While my fantasy was but a device to help a child with questions adults were not prepared to answer, my actual life, now lived large, has played out as an enactment of my make-believe life, with me — as I once pretended — a central character.

Despite what the reader may draw from what I have just described, the story that follows is not fanciful. Rather, it is a telling of tales that actually took place, embedded in the narrative a continuance of events that, lacking any other definition, were just plain lucky. I'm not referring to one-time luck, winning a sweepstakes or scoring at the slots, surviving unscathed an accident that should have been fatal or simply being at the right place at the right time. Nor the kind of luck that shows up when it's least expected, the accidental encounter, a sudden awakening, an ephemeral incidence short-lived and likely of little importance. It is far more than that. For me it has been a special kind of luck, the repetitive appearance of it occurring over and over, a door closing, another door opening, a person at the threshold extending a hand to guide me through the next portal. The luck has been most times good, sometimes not, yet happening so often I sometimes think I truly am in a movie, that my fantasy has somehow flopped over into reality, or is it the other way around, leading me to believe there is a director out there, that there's a script that reads **give the guy some luck,** and someone with a megaphone

By Way of Luck

hollering, you over there, ***with the spot, put it on him, you know, the guy with the luck.***

This book could have begun almost anywhere. So to start I've chosen a moment in time, when lucky events hit me in rapid fire, when I was young, naïve, and unaware of the phenomenon I was caught up in and accepting.

1

The Curtain Rises

How often can fifty or more years zip by and unexpectedly something emerges from the past, punches you in the gut and leaves you teary-eyed and emotionally spent? Couldn't happen to me, I would tell you. But it did. In November of 2010.

I was living in rural Connecticut a hundred miles north of New York City in the town of Kent, a rural community that time had passed by, with large open hay fields on the approach to the village, in the distance white church steeples piercing the horizon, a commercial center with but a handful of stores, and a local history embedded in the revolutionary war when its iron foundries were making cannon balls for George Washington's army.

I had walked up the hill to our mailbox to collect the usual mixture of bills, advertisements and magazines, and perhaps a note from one of our kids, and right away saw an envelope with a return address that read

Department of Defense
Washington, DC 20301

I had served in the U.S. Air Force in the late 1950s, the latter two years of a three-year tour stationed in the Pentagon, an assignment that had come about through a series of orders that no military

By Way of Luck

manual could have ever published. Or no ranking officer might have condoned. What could this be about?

Curious and anxious, I tore open the envelope and sat down on the grass to read the letter inside.

"Dear Mr. Perkins," it began.

"An out-of-the-blue letter from the U.S. Air Force."

"I am an historian with the U.S. Air Force Historical Studies Office in Washington, D.C., and am researching the history of USAF conservation and environmental programs."

What came next stunned me.

"I am not certain if you are aware of the impact that your research and proposal had on not only the U.S. Air Force, but later all military conservation programs and ultimately all federal agencies' conservation programs, but it has endured."

My proposal? Endured? Had I done something wrong?

The letter, signed Jean Mansavage, Ph.D., went on:

"...today the Department of Defense manages 30 million acres of land on which there exists the highest density of threatened and endangered species..."

Not wrong. Incredible!

I went on reading. Thirty million acres! That a land conservation program I had suggested and later promoted had by 2010 encompassed such a massive area was staggering, its size alone today putting it easily in the ranks of the Sierra Club and The Nature Conservancy. From a simple proposition and perhaps two years' work, how could this have happened?

I was overwhelmed. I stopped reading. I could barely see the print on the letter through the tears that were swiftly coming.

Dr. Mansavage's letter was asking whether she could come to Kent to interview me. Her assignment was to document how the program had come about, she wrote, and during the intervening years how it had fallen to the United States Air Force to be its steward. Left unsaid, I assumed she also had to determine how a junior officer got into the Pentagon in the first place and whether he was a credible resource.

Still sitting by the open mail box, the entire episode came rushing back. Not all at once, but in bits and pieces as I was later to relate to Dr. Mansavage.

I was fresh from training at Ellington Air Force Base in Houston, Texas, naïve to military protocol, uneasy in my new job and cautious not to make a mess of it. In Washington but two weeks and following my first staff meeting, brashly I made a recommendation to my immediate superior, Major Tim Dunn, on how the Air Force might solve a problem our division head, Major General Ben LeBailey, had described in his office on the 4th floor, D ring, of the Pentagon.

There's a bill in a House committee that would open military land to exploitation by agricultural, mining, and logging interests, the General had said, as much as I can recount. We can't run an Air Force, he went on, with a bunch of civilians and bulldozers crossing our runways and fucking up the mission. The boys upstairs in Legislative Liaison asked us to think of what they might do about it.

(Legislative Liaison was one of many Pentagon links to the Congress.)

I was in an assembly of a dozen or so officers, Colonels and Lt. Colonels and a Major or two. All were World War II and Korean War veterans, most of them combat pilots, wearing their wings proudly, given to action and fearless, and by their posture stiffly resolute. But Legislative Liaison's request had them shifting in their seats and looking about the room as if choked for air and seeking help. There was none. The General kindly ended the meeting. Let me know next day or two if you have any ideas, he said.

In my mind's eye, with Jean Mansavage's letter in my hand, still sitting on the grass by the mail box, I could see that office, the men at the meeting, the hopeful look on the General's face and much of what came afterward.

That evening, leaving the Pentagon's River Entrance parking lot and driving home to Falls Church, I thought of a plausible answer

By Way of Luck

to the General's question. Sleep on it, I told myself, thinking how presumptive a lowly lieutenant might be seen offering a suggestion his superiors were reluctant to make. Yet I thought my thought a good thought, coming from a junior or not. What risk was I taking? The following day, on my way back to the Pentagon, I decided to try it out on Tim Dunn.

I had come quickly to trust Tim. He had once been a lieutenant himself, he reminded me, a navigator-bombardier serving in the Pacific theater aboard a B-29, the model of aircraft that dropped the A-bomb on Hiroshima. His assignment in the Pentagon was in stark contrast to his combat experience. His PIO (Public Information Office) responsibility was Magazines and Books, standing by to answer questions and assist writers and reporters covering USAF matters and, aggressively, to define and pursue projects that might reflect favorably on the service. Smartly, and looking for an early promotion, he had eased into a very visible desk job.

On my first day, he said call me Tim, no salutes, no "Yes sir, No sir," We're working together here. We could wear civilian clothes, he went on. That way no one can stand on rank. We're grownups. Fuck-ups don't get to the Pentagon.

Tim wasn't running a training squadron, I realized, my only experience with rank. He was in command of his office and I was a crew member and, unless I fucked up, valued and respected. And I respected him, proof lying in my recollection now many decades later of his extended very Irish name: Mathew Timothy James Edward Dunn III.

I went straight to Tim's desk. Six of us were elbowed into a crowded office — everything gray, the desks, the chairs, the paint on the walls — among them Major Jim Sunderman; Bill Mack, a captain, and secretary Virginia Waugh — and offered an idea that might spark the General's interest. Characteristically, I later came to recognize, Tim tilted onto the back legs of his chair, locked his hands behind his head, and said, "Talk to me."

We could designate all Air Force lands as conservation districts, I told him, with well-defined land, water, wildlife and timber management programs and make it work in ways without interfering with operations. He nodded an understanding nod. Then I added the thought that had come to me in a half sleep the night before: And encourage powerful conservation groups such as the National Wildlife Federation and the Wilderness Society, whose interests might also be served, I went on, to lobby against the bill.

I wasn't expecting Tim's reaction. Ranking Air Force officers, flight operations their life-time experience, generally chew on administrative decisions before pushing them along. Yet Tim literally jumped out of his chair. "Great," he said, grabbing my hand like he didn't want me to go away. "Just great. Give me a one-pager I can talk from. I'll take it right to General LeBailey."

Startled by his swift response, I was slow to say, "Yes, sir." Oops. Uncertainty settled fast upon me. I imagined the unintended consequences of my recommendation, hearing the General laughing, Tim coming back to the office humiliated and flushed with anger and me being the putz.

Nonetheless, this soldier had taken a position. There was no backing away.

In several agonizing minutes, on a worn Underwood, I banged out a brief memo for Tim that went as follows:

> "Designate all domestic U.S. Air Force bases as conservation districts for the protection of wildlife and the management of soil, water and timber resources. Issue guidelines. Require base commanders to designate a field grade officer to be responsible for inaugurating and managing the program. Promote the program widely. Attract the attention of conservation-minded agencies and organizations such as the National Wildlife Federation and the U.S. Fish and Wildlife Service and ask for their support of the program and their opposition to turning over public lands to private interests for their exploitation."

As I hit the last key, Tim, now standing next to me, yanked the memo from the typewriter. How could you know to write that? he questioned.

By Way of Luck

Before I could answer, he disappeared across the hall.

Waiting for him to come back, I rationalized what I had done and why I had done it and prepared for the argument, if there was to be one, of why I had chosen to make the suggestion, write the one-pager and, in the end, to justify how I might be qualified to offer up such a reply to General LeBailey's request.

It was a question that Jean Mansavage was also to ask sitting in the living room of my Kent home. What were my qualifications for making such a proposal? She waited for a reply, patiently, as might a concerned sister. Based pretty much on what I had told Tim 54 years earlier, I wrote her the answer that follows:

As the minutes passed, waiting for Tim's return, I saw myself the youngster in a small New Hampshire town, population 3000, just a few miles from the White Mountain National Forest, living on a hillside with a sweeping view of the Presidential Range, from Mt. Lincoln to Mt. Washington, during the 30s and 40s. And I'm eight to twelve years old, school but a diversion, and too young to be drinking beer and chasing girls, the local rural pastimes.

The nearest radio station is WBZ Boston, 175 miles away. I could pick up its signal on the Philco after sundown and through the static listen to 15 minute segments, Lowell Thomas and Gabriel Heatter with the news, the Green Hornet and Jack Armstrong, tales of crime and adventure. The daily Boston Globe arrived same day by train usually after six pm. I had to walk a mile to get our copy. The local weekly reported soft news, weddings, births (sometimes not in that order), visitors to town, break-ins and arrests, and the like. Talk at the counter of my dad's restaurant, the White Mountain Café, men mostly, ladies sat in the booths, chatting about local "goings on," jobs at the Saranac Deerskin Glove Factory and Norton Abrasives, high school sports, dancing at Art's Ark with music by Win Wright and the Ramblers, but mostly about hunting and fishing. This was my world, small and distant.

I see myself back there now, sitting at my desk in the Pentagon, waiting for Tim to return, my brow popping with perspiration, growing ever more uneasy, bringing up pictures from the past to fill my head and calm me, seeing bird season coming on as the leaves begin to turn, the first flakes of snow flitting through the trees, a single barrel, single shot Sears shot gun cradled against my chest, with chums Bob Rowe and Boyd Cole, walking the alders, alert to the electric burst of a woodcock or partridge, and feeling good about myself. Not about the shooting, but about the doing.

Bob and I skied Cannon Mountain, the site of the first aerial tram-way constructed in the United States. There were no open slopes, only narrow trails. There were no grooming machines, the sharp winds blowing the runs bare, rock and ice part of our race downhill. Our clothes like our skis were used, home-sewn of heavy wool that caught the snow and froze hard, by the end of the day melting wet as we drank cocoa waiting for one of our moms to pick us up. Freezing and unfreezing, skiing or going to school, or just beating home through the woods in the dark, was how our winters went.

Hiking through the short summer and early fall, not hunting, not fishing, just walking and climbing was for me and Bob, Boyd and his cousin Sandy, and Pinky Towle, the police chief's son, not sport but a ritual. The near slope of Parker Mountain was my backyard. We spent hours, days and years hiking it, building tree houses, following streams, climbing giant pines to see where we were. We figured once that from the top of Parker Mountain we could draw a straight line to the North Pole and it would never hit a single city or town on its way.

But the more adventurous trails we walked were in the National Forest, from Franconia Notch, beginning at Mt. Lafayette, across from Cannon Mountain, to Mt. Guyot and to Mt. Garfield; from Crawford Notch, Mt. Adams and Mt. Jefferson. Irregular paths, early legs of the Appalachian Trail, were not well marked, some so steep we'd be crawling on hands and knees. Our stretch of the Trail some hikers thought as the toughest section for hikers going either way.

By Way of Luck

We first learned about the National Forest not from neighbors but from the CCC boys, a troop of them one day descending on our town to build a playground in our public park. Clad in work clothes and ankle-top boots, city kids from the Boston area, others from the Bronx and Brooklyn, they jumped at the task, involving us, their enthusiasm catching, a spirit of togetherness surfacing, learning names, where they were from, putting up swings and chinning bars, and listening to their stories at lunch break.

From distressed neighborhoods, they had discovered a different life of incredible vistas, pines higher than a five-story walk up and craggy hilltops, living in lean-to's, building roads and harboring ponds and waking mornings to the sounds that come from the forest, so different from the ell's roaring above the streets back home. Bob and I, and Sandy, too, probably decided then that we had to learn what the CCC boys had learned.

We learned both from hiking and from reading. During WW II our local library as a way of encouraging kids to read held a contest. Entrants would be buck privates at the start. For each book read there'd be an advancement in rank, a promotion. The first reader to become a four-star general would receive a prize, my goal. I took out three of the shortest books I could find, returned them the next day, each with a brief report, hoping I'd become a sergeant. The librarian shook her head, dismayed. She wouldn't let me get away with it. She might have sent me home. Instead, she led me to a section labeled Nature Books.

Now I was dismayed. For an outdoors boy, nature was for girls, like horses and Home Ec. Thinking back on it, I couldn't see the forest for the trees, literally.

The first book she handed me was no *Walden Pond*, but a tattered tome about trees, their names and identifiable characteristics. My report, submitted the next morning, got me the grade of private first class. From then on, I stuck to the nature section, worn volumes about fish, farming, rivers, growing apples, personal journals and the like, some of them published in the late 1800s when the United States was raw, the librarian promoting me all the way to my four stars and a win!

The war years were fundaments for a youngster too young to fight but of an age ready to grasp bigger meanings. With uncles and cousins in uniform and overseas, one a marine captured at Wake Island, another a ferry pilot delivering aircraft and munitions across the south Atlantic from Brazil to North Africa, patriotism and the American flag were more than symbolic; they were proof of who we were, "of a God given nation in the defense of a greater good" I recall reading somewhere. Gold stars pasted on the windows of houses next door told stories of both sorrow and pride. Letters received and sent by V-mail, back yard victory gardens and ration stamps for gas and butter demonstrated a resolve not only to win, but to be victorious. How much I wanted to be a part of that, to this day I still recall.

In a small farmhouse down the street, where the Houle family — French Canadians from Quebec — kept chickens and goats, Conrad Houle, a year or two older than I, wanted what I wanted but couldn't get, being in the war. So we settled for much less. We built a mock airplane frame out of pine branches and slash, with seats and a dashboard, deep in a patch of trees where no one could see us. When he could, Conrad would dig into the paper scrap pile for copies of *The New York Times* that carried front page stories of the war, with maps. We'd take the papers into our make-shift airplane and read aloud to each other while climbing our B-17 to altitude, crossing the Dover cliffs on bombing missions, or in a P-38 flying low over the Sahara seeing Montgomery's tanks chasing Rommel across the sands. We were warriors and the woods were where we lived and fought.

Escape, adventure, challenge, and just plain fun was for us in the outdoors — sleeping out, cooking out, hiking out, playing ball and horsing around, learning to swing an ax, drive a fence post, tie a fly, walk a pasture, identify trees, seeing them come back in the spring, every spring, their buds just beginning to show. So close to the land, we could feel the world in rebirth.

Chronologically, by this account, as I sit there waiting for Tim, I am not more than 15 or 16 years old, away at school, contemplating college, and recognizing that ahead lay the changing years. But I

By Way of Luck

don't want it all to change, not the mountains and hillsides, the rivers and the streams, the wildlife and the woods, but I was fearful it would.

I learned about change, maybe in 1948, when Mr. Elliot came to the door with some bad news. Mr. Elliot was a local farmer who delivered raw milk to our back porch in quart-sized bottles, cream on the top, and during winter, the freezing cream pushed the paper cap two or three inches high above the rim. Can't deliver no more milk, Mr. Elliot said, and went on to tell us about bovine tuberculosis. "The gub'ment gonna shoot all my cows." The gub'ment did. After that we had to buy our milk at the local A&P.

I was distressed, not about having to walk to the A&P, but by the image of some blank-faced gub'ment official putting a pistol to a cow's squarish forehead and pulling the trigger. One cow after another crumpling in Mr. Elliot's pasture. Rural small town kids know cows. Benign animals you can hug, feel their warmth, and learn from: watching a calving and discovering how babies are born long before mom and dad deal with the subject, if they ever do. We also know about critters: porcupines and woodchucks, skunks and beavers, bear and deer, partridges and woodcocks, pigeons and hawks, telling one from the other, where they nest, where they feed, how they come and go, and how we get along in that small part of the world where we all live. The images are etched into our memories.

Now I'm 18 or 19 and I hear talk, from game and tree wardens (later to be designated conservation officers) and foresters, and it sounds like they're losing the fight to poaching and clear cutting, to dumping and well contamination and, most of all, to ignorance.

And I'm going to Dartmouth College in Hanover, New Hampshire. In the class room, Professor Herb West's courses on the Nature Writers, his insistent railings against polluters, bull dozing, over development and trash in the streets and along the roads, and his teachings of the Humanities, books whose writings could bring out the moral best in his students. Author and outdoorsman Corey Ford, his nurturing, his friendship and generosity, his introduction to me of Hugh Grey, writer and outdoorsman Dan Holland, *Field and Stream's* fishing editor. Pan Am pilot and heralded Dartmouth skier of the late 1930s, Everett Wood, a statuesque man, a hunter and fisherman with hair like straw drawn straight back into a rush of curls. Parker Merrow of West Ossipee, a publisher, his ramblings against deer jackers, clear cutters and sluice miners coming out of the soil. Together joined for drinks by a warming fireplace at One North Balch Street, Corey's house in Hanover, NH, their talk of conserving wildlife and protecting the land working into me like seepage.

So there is no Aha! moment. Just a day when some kid whose elders have helped him think like a man and hears a General say, "a bill in committee...threatens Air Force land...what can we do about it?" simply responds, almost like he's programmed to be there, with a suggestion that could answer the General's question and lead to the protection of vast acreage, some of it for recreation, some of it for habitat, and much of it just to look at and be proud that it's there.

I could hear Tim coming down the hall, his clipped steps already familiar. Was I about to become the fuck-up or the grown up, I'd soon know.

Tim gushed his way through the doorway of our office suite, beaming.

I told Jean Mansavage all this. She had a canvas bag chocked full of folders and loose pages and while we talked she spread them out on the coffee table where we sat. A dogged researcher, her interest in environmental and U.S. Air Force history led to her Department of Defense assignment, concluding at the time no one involved with the program in the Fifties would still be alive. She had questions to ask of me, and documents to either prove or disprove what I might tell her, wanting to be sure, as she hinted, whether I was the real thing, that a young officer was in that place at the time and had witnessed what he said he had witnessed and done the things he said he had done.

The others, Tim, Ben LeBailey, and everyone I knew back then

By Way of Luck

working in the Pentagon had long since died. She hoped in me she had a reliable source.

She asked for names. As I gave them to her, she searched through the pages in front of us, copies of orders, meeting minutes, published articles, marking them as we talked, looking for evidence that could correlate the events I was describing. She was thorough, surgical in her manner.

Originally from Wisconsin, she had earned her doctorate at Texas A&M and among her earliest efforts for the Department of Defense had successfully documented cases of missing in action (MIA) American combatants, first in the Korean War, later in World War II, and in 2005 provided MIA research protocols for the Vietnamese. Evidence of her unique skill had been framed prominently on the walls of a Pentagon corridor. She was a super star at what she did.

Jean's probing questions went on, stopping only when she got a hint of what she was looking for. I answered what I could, pausing often while mentally thumbing through a 54 year old recollection of people and events, places and times. When I told her that a Lt. Colonel Ben Royal from the Provost's Office had been assigned to the "conservation program" to help me write the regulations and to keep me out of trouble, Jean, by then each of us comfortable using first names, pulled a page from her pile.

It was a copy of the orders issued in May 1956 assigning Lt. Colonel Benjamin Royal to the conservation program and unmistakably confirming what I had just told her.

Jean's questioning stopped. She had what she needed proving me definitively real. She shoved her papers back into her bag and hugged me a grateful hug.

Tim was a happy man, and for a few minutes so was I. The General had bought the proposal, had called his opposite in Legislative Liaison who endorsed the idea, and given Tim the responsibility for making it happen. Ben LeBailey wanted a detailed proposition, the what, when and how that could answer whatever objections that might arise as the proposal made its way through the approval process. The "it" part Tim passed on to me. How long will it take you to get "it" done, I recall Tim asking.

I hadn't a clue. The one-pager had exhausted my competence.

Lieutenants are rare in the Washington, DC, military mix, rarer still in the Pentagon. I was the lowest ranking Air Force officer in a building of 32,000 employees, all of them military or government personnel, and in that company, truly, I was of no apparent importance. Yet Major Tim Dunn did not question that what he had asked of me I might be incapable of producing, assuming that behind the one-pager lay a greater knowledge. Unnerved, I began to think of what to do next. Tim had so far treated me like a grown-up and I had to act like one.

I couldn't know then, nor could Tim, but he and I were about to trigger an event years in the making. And in the weeks to come, absurd but real, I would be explaining myself to three of the highest ranking generals in Air Force history: the Air Force's Chief of Staff, General Thomas D. White; the Chairman of the Joint Chiefs of Staff, General Nathan Twining; and World War II's foremost air war strategist, the U.S. Air Force's first chief of staff, retired General Carl "Tooey" Spaatz, warriors all and, as this Lieutenant discovered, ardent environmentalists.

Was it purely coincidental, I have since asked myself, that I was assigned to the Pentagon, that a General had a question I could answer or was it something bigger, a stroke of luck?

I still do not know, but it all began with a series of linking events that began in the fall of 1952, the start of my sophomore year at Dartmouth College.

I closed the mail box at the top of the hill and walked down the road to the house to show my wife Jean's letter.

2

The College on the Hill

That I was accepted by Dartmouth College, looking back on it, strikes me as lucky. Pure luck. I had been suspended from Williston Academy — a New England preparatory school founded in 1841 in Easthampton, Massachusetts — in the spring of my senior year, reporting late and barely sober to my dorm master on a Saturday night and arguing caustically that being drunk was a matter of opinion.

Dartmouth's Admissions Office had to be advised, Headmaster Phil Stevens said as I sat with him in his office watching him dial Dean Al Dickerson in Hanover. Waiting for the call to go through, he eyed me critically, the Head of School, sitting at a desk deep and wide, of old oak rubbed worn, judging me. Was I about to be stripped from Dartmouth's pending list of applicants? If not Dartmouth, I was thinking, then where? I had taken no entrance exams and applied to no other school.

Headmaster Stevens held the receiving end of the phone away from his head, just enough so I could piece together their conversation. Dean Dickerson asked whether as a result of my conduct the Headmaster was withdrawing the personal recommendation he had appended to my application. Stevens said "No." In fact, he went on, Jim has handled the incident "decently." Apparently, Stevens had not conferred with my dorm master.

Dickerson replied that no note of my suspension would be made. It would be treated as though it had never happened. Phil Stevens suspended the suspension and two weeks later I received an acceptance letter from Dartmouth, signed by Al Dickerson.

Never happened? How unlikely. How bizarre. Who gets a pass like that? A reprieve, a total exoneration. Where was it written that this could have occurred? The odds against it so great. There was no coincidence here. I saw it, simply, as a stroke of luck.

In September of my freshman year, just days after matriculation, and becoming officially a member of the Class of 1955, I found my way to Dean Dickerson's office curious to learn why he decided to ignore my suspension. Certainly, he was aware of his decision, but he appeared indifferent, welcoming me to Dartmouth and abruptly eyeing the door as a signal I should leave.

At Williston, I had been a competitive swimmer and a member of the glee club. At Dartmouth, I had to choose between the two if I were to devote sufficient time to my studies. I auditioned for glee club director, Paul Zeller, and gave Karl Michael, the swimming coach, a summary of my prep school times in the 50 yard and 100 yard free style. Each gave me a thumbs up.

I chose swimming, a lucky choice as it turned out. Clad in a bathing suit, I concluded, singly responsible for what I might achieve, seemed preferable to dressing in a tuxedo, collar starched and black bow tie, and trying to look casual blending into a chorus of thirty or more boisterously performing voices. That my choice might lead to some greater experience I could not have predicted.

The decision to swim instead of sing — believe this — eventually led to Tim Dunn and Ben LeBailey and all that happened afterwards, one link after another, to the day I am writing this chronicle.

Fraternities at Dartmouth could not recruit new members until their sophomore year, although by then fraternities had pretty much decided which students they might invite, the students which house they might join. I had been wooed by the AD's (Alpha Delta Phi) and the Dekes (Delta Kappa Epsilon), in the annals of the college

By Way of Luck

both notorious for their rowdiness, indifference to campus rules and blatant challenges to both faculty and administrative standards of conduct. I could have been at home with either.

Joe Migley from Winnetka, Illinois, made the difference. A junior, a Deke, both of us rooming in Wheeler Hall, Joe invited me to meet a newly appointed advisor to the Deke house, Corey Ford, a writer who had that summer moved to Hanover, New Hampshire. That's all he knew, except that Corey had been a Deke at Columbia University.

Corey was a celebrity in the State, living in Freedom, a blip of a town hard on the Maine border, and knew Dartmouth only from tales told him by Parker Merrow, Dartmouth '25. Parker had sensed Corey's growing discomfort with Freedom and suggested a trip to Hanover for a drink with Sid Hayward who, like Corey, hunted with an English setter.

Corey was taken by Sid's dry wit, practiced though it was, and told Sid he'd seriously consider a move to Dartmouth. (His only reservation, he told me sometime later, was Sid's parsimonious nature, most evident when ladling out the scotch, a bare sip at a time.) Sid suggested that Corey might find more going on in Hanover than in Freedom. Settle in with friends, Sid said, perhaps be an advisor to student publications, and maybe a fraternity.

Sid's suggestion did not linger long. Do you have a DKE house? Corey asked. He'd been a Deke at Columbia.

At Corey's house for cocktails, Joe had gathered six or seven potential pledges, I among them, to meet the new Deke house advisor, an off-campus event clearly against the College's fraternity rushing rules. Joe knew it. I knew it, as did the other sophomores, but we were so thoroughly taken by the prospect of meeting a widely published writer, we ignored the possible penalties of breaking the rules and through the evening drank freely from glasses that appeared to fill by themselves.

In Corey's den, paneled in wide, rough-cut mid-19th century barn siding, opposite the fireplace a massive, mounted Rocky Mountain Sheep's head, Corey seemed one of us, youthful and eager, engaging at every level, whether about our studies, families, athletics, our hopes for a career and so on. He was real in a way that young men wished their elders to be. He was an Air Force Colonel, someone said, and a war hero.

We all pledged Deke.

At the time, there was no evidence that Corey would become a lifelong ombudsman for Dartmouth undergraduates and a revered supporter of college rugby. Nor that he would become my close friend and mentor through my early years and set me on a course marked by a string of exotic happenings.

A Committed Life

By the time he died in 1969, Corey had written thirty-two books, over 300 magazine articles and columns, and a handful of theatrical plays and movie scripts. He was a prodigy, prominent from his days as editor of the *Jester*, Columbia's humor magazine, writing the lyrics for "Roar, Lion, Roar", Columbia's fight song, hired as a stringer for *The New York Herald*, and building lasting friendships with classmates Bennett Cerf, later the co-founder of Random House, Richard Rodgers who connected with Oscar Hammerstein in a legendary musical partnership, and Gardner Rea, a *Jester* cartoonist who drew *The New Yorker* cover of the foppish squire that has been a featured cover each year since. (Corey supplied the squire's name, Eustace Tilley.)

Corey dropped out of Columbia at the end of his junior year in 1923, expecting to work his way up at the *Herald*, but soon jumped to *The New Yorker*, a start-up that few culture critics thought would survive. Harold Ross, the magazine's editor and founder, gave him a job writing subscription ads and press releases and found a place in "Talk of the Town" for Corey's short, humorous pieces.

Corey's literary output for *The New Yorker* surged quickly, his witty commentaries piling up on Ross's desk to such an extent that Ross suggested he slow down, mawkishly threatening him if he didn't.

There was a deeper message behind Ross's suggestion. He was assembling a core of established editors and contributing writers that included Wolcott Gibbs, Robert Benchley, Alexander Wolcott,

By Way of Luck

S. J. Perlman, E.B. White, James Thurber and Dorothy Parker, all of them demanding more of Ross's attention, more assignments, and more space in the magazine. Corey, not long out of college, could wait. He was seen by the magazine's new and better known staffers as the "kid", a writer of talent perhaps, but certainly not of their crowd, at the end of their work days ambling off to the bar at the Algonquin Hotel, informally recognizing themselves as the Algonquin Round Table, and pointedly leaving Corey behind.

Corey was indifferent. He adopted a nom de plume, John Riddell, and under that name wrote for another start-up magazine, *Vanity Fair*, gaining recognition for his stinging parodies of notable writers and performers. While Corey toiled in anonymity for Ross who published no writer credits, and was ignored by his *New Yorker* colleagues, as "John Riddell" Corey Ford became a popular by-line, touted by New York City newspaper columnists F.P. Adams, Ring Lardner, Brooks Atkinson and Walter Winchell, a must-invite at mid-town parties, and a favorite at most bars in the theater district. Books and anthologies followed. Broadway, too.

Not surprisingly, Hollywood found him out as well. Director Norman McLeod, known largely for directing W.C. Fields and Danny Kaye, offered him a job. Corey wrote two of McLeod's Topper films, becoming fast friends with both Norman and Bill Fields. During the 1930s, his high paid screen play and magazine assignments piled up like Times Square spectators on New Year's Eve. Ford flourished.

Meeting Corey at his home was for me an awakening experience, my young life so different. My references were small town. His were worldly. I wore jeans. He wore twills. He didn't have a job. He sat at a desk and wrote. And somehow got paid for it. To me, that didn't seem like work. It was like staying in college forever, writing term papers. I saw him as coming from some other planet. Certainly not the one I lived on.

I grew up in Littleton, New Hampshire. My parents were WW I refugees, my father, Nick Pisperikos, coming to the United States from Greek Macedonia in 1910, the Balkan Wars having ravaged most of southeastern Europe, and arriving at Ellis Island at age twelve, by himself; my mother, Lucia Tegu, coming at age ten in 1920 with her mother, a sister and two brothers.

They were from villages mere miles apart in the Pindus Mountains and from the same ethnic group: Vlachs they were called, nomadic sheepherders. They met in the United States. Neither had any more than a rudimentary education. They spoke not Greek but an arcane Roman dialect, Vlahica, my first language.

My father, whose name was changed from Pisperikos to Perkins by a judge at his naturalization hearings, had bought a failed restaurant in Littleton, 13 stools and seven booths. My mother's father and older brother who had come to the U.S. in 1912 and had built several motion picture theaters in Vermont lived in St. Johnsbury not 18 miles across the Connecticut River from Littleton. I was the first born of their marriage and only son. I have two sisters. (Had my parents not emigrated to the United States, had they met on familiar ground where they were born, my sisters and I might have been born there as well. And not survived World War II. Their towns were over run and destroyed both by Italian and German troops.)

My mother decided on my education. I remember clearly, in her native language, when I was in the eighth grade, she told my father, "Nick, the boy can't talk." Speaking Vlachica at home, four-year olds of New Hampshire parents had better communication skills than I.

Somehow, possibly from friends who'd shown her ads clipped from a *New York Times* advertisement featuring private schools, she learned of Williston Academy in Easthampton, Massachusetts, drove me there for an interview, and negotiated a full five-year scholarship, repeating the eighth grade. I see her now in the admissions office pleading with a tall, gaunt, mustached man named Philip Shepardson who seemed cowed by her directness. I think he took me in to rid her from his office.

Until I enrolled there, I didn't know my mother had agreed I would take a part time job as kitchen helper and dining room waiter.

Nor did I think it odd that I was the only student at the Academy who had a similar scholarship.

At Williston my English improved rapidly, although I made several memorable mistakes. One in particular, when serving coffee to a table headed by an instructor's wife, she said it was exceptional and asked what changes had the kitchen made to improve it. My mind chased the word urn, because the kitchen had installed a new one, but all I could come up with was urinal. Shocked by what she thought a crude attempt to be comical, the instructor's wife ordered me to leave the dining room. My growing vocabulary needed to grow still more.

In my junior year, an English teacher and Dartmouth alumnus, Alan Hall, who later taught at St. Paul's School in Concord, NH, encouraged me to write and not be afraid of making mistakes. Which I did. One paper he returned to me with a grade of 100. I was astonished. No one at Williston had ever gotten 100 on an English paper. News of it swept through the school and for a day my fellow students rewarded me with hand slaps and knowing nods. My English had gotten good enough to earn me friends.

By then, local Dartmouth alums, there must have been a dozen or more in the Littleton area, many Dad's restaurant customers, had found some amusement in seeing an eight, then ten, then twelve year old boy taking cash, waiting table, handling the counter during lunch and dinner rush hours — or taking over in the kitchen when the short order cook stumbled in drunk.

One local alumnus, veterinarian Dick Hill, whose brother Carl later became Dean of Dartmouth's Tuck School of Business, prodded my father endlessly: "Nick, your boy has to go to Dartmouth." Still another alumnus set up an appointment for me with his classmate, the College Registrar. I was twelve. We met in Hanover and I signed a letter of intent. I had no idea of its implications, my adolescent outlook measured in days if not hours yet haplessly agreeing, as it turned out, to a life-defining decision, lasting friendships and experiences I could not have predicted.

In the fall of my senior year at Williston I met with a one-man Dartmouth screening committee, Littleton businessman Ambrose P. McLaughlin, later Director of Development for the College. In those days, a yea or nay from a screening committee could mean you were in or you were out. I was tense. Where was the committee? I wondered. I had applied to no other college. The interview lasted ten minutes, maybe five. Ambrose P. McLaughlin, with no other committee members present, told me I was accepted.

Not knowing for sure, until eight months later receiving the Al Dickerson letter, that I was.

In September 1951, I borrowed a pick-up truck from a sawmill operator in Littleton, threw my clothes and bedding into the back, and when I reached Hanover dumped it all in a room at Wheeler Hall. I drove back to Littleton, returned the truck, and hitch-hiked back to Hanover. The easy part was over, now came the decisions, what courses to take, what extracurricular activities to sign up for and, perhaps the more elusive decision, who to be.

Course selection was simple, most of it required of freshmen and, surprisingly, not much advanced from what I had studied at Williston. With the draft looming and high school kids I'd grown up with heading to Korea, I joined the Air Force ROTC, selecting it over the Army and Navy programs because my uncle Steve was a WW II Army Air Corps pilot who had also had flown the Berlin airlift in 1949. Within a week or so, I had my first USAF uniform and Dartmouth had become my home

Next find a job, which I did, at the Golf Side Restaurant, run by a couple that could cook but couldn't run a dining room. Learning of the years I had worked for my Dad, they suggested I manage the dining room when I could get away from my studies. They'd pay me $1.00 an hour and meals. What a break. With tips, I could make maybe $30 a week, this at a time when married couples could raise a family on $30 a week and Dartmouth's tuition for a semester was but $400.

Jumping ahead and following an uneventful first year, except that I'd won my freshman's swimming numerals, we go to...

...December 1952, after a brief Thanksgiving recess, the Dekes had a holiday party, not unusual because for partying Dekes most weekends played as holidays. Karl Michaels was there. He'd pledged DKE when he was a Dartmouth undergraduate, class of 1929. I was the only swimmer in the Deke House, so he took me by the arm to

By Way of Luck

introduce me to the new fraternity advisor, a writer who'd gone to Columbia and a Deke himself, Corey Ford. I couldn't explain that I had already met Corey, that I had been illegally "rushed."

Did Corey Ford remember me? If he did, I had no way of knowing.

"Hi yah, guy," was the first thing Corey said. "How yah doin'?" And he was shaking my hand, smiling broadly as though he were genuinely glad to see me which, I learned later, was true. But clearly, that evening, I was another fresh face in a crowd of fresh faces.

Asking about Christmas vacation plans, he heard Coach Karl Michaels say that his swimmers would get but a brief holiday break. A day. Maybe two. Dartmouth's opening meet on the first Saturday of January was against Harvard.

The following Monday at swimming practice, Coach Michael said Corey was trying to reach me. Here's his number, give him a call. Corey had learned that dormitories would be closed through the holidays, that cots would be set up on the gym floor for varsity swimmers. Corey thought such spare accommodations a disgrace, he said, and invited me and teammate Gene Elsbree to stay at his house at One North Balch Street until the dorms reopened. He had an extra bedroom and a sleeping porch. Gene and I moved in, sheepishly grateful that Corey's invitation included breakfast and dinner prepared by Corey's housekeeper, Kate Townsend, who also made our beds. No greater Christmas gift could Gene and I have received!

We lost to Harvard. By then, Corey had learned a bit about me, awkwardly youthful, yet a willing punster, ripe for his challenges in word games, with a sufficient foundation in English grammar, punctuation and paragraphing, and a vocabulary to go with it, my Williston learning, with some acceptable evidence as a writer, who'd hunted and fished and knew the outdoors, in fact, could walk the woods for hours busting birds, grouse and woodcock, and easily find his way back to where we'd left his Jeep. Albeit ROTC, I was also Air Force.

Interested, though at times wary, during the ten days we stayed at his house Gene and I observed Corey's comings and goings, not nosing about, just noticing. He had rituals, we saw right away, not like religious rituals, but positive living and working rituals. At breakfast every morning at 7, juice, toast, coffee and a soft-boiled egg, after thumbing through the morning edition of the *New York Herald Tribune* he'd head upstairs to his desk at 7:45 and not break away until 12:15 for lunch. Afterwards a brief nap, then two to three hours of physical leisure, hunting or fishing, packing for a trip, shopping, or follow-ups on the commitments he'd made to Sid and the college. In the evening before dinner, he read through and edited what he had written earlier in the day.

He had a dog, Cider, an English setter with an instinctive nose for birds, a gracious cook and housekeeper, Kate Townsend; a secretary, Norma Bouchard, who typed the various iterations of his manuscripts, handled his mail and paid his bills; and a New York City literary agent, Dorothy Olding of the Harold Ober Agency, who managed his career. And no apparent wife or family, leaving him free to write, to travel, to visit friends, call on editors, go to theater and during the period 1942-1945, to accept a commission in the Army Air Corps and participate in the air battle over Europe and later in Korea.

At the Deke house, Corey was seen as too country in his dress, yet a sportsman who liked to party and tell stories. And obviously masculine, no one of us ever questioning why, soon to turn fifty, he'd never married, didn't have a girlfriend and didn't seem particularly interested in finding one. He was a guy's guy, we concluded, committed to a regimen that worked for him. He had exceptional discipline, but unlike us, our discipline coming from parents, teachers and coaches, he did it by himself.

I didn't know about Gene, but I was struck by that, by someone taking responsibility for himself and living independent of wider support, family, company, social group, as examples, instead creating a structure that suited him and imposing it upon himself. In contemporary terms, he was "inner directed."

Only years later, after his death, did I fully understand Corey. He was an idealist and would likely have been as much at home in the 18th century as he was in the 20th. If his country was at war, he

By Way of Luck

fought. He eschewed institutions, he was not a joiner. He wasn't a father or a brother or a son or a husband. That was for other people. He was a writer. He wrote. He made friends. Friends led him to stories he could write about, to places that might stir his imagination, to events he could influence and, unselfishly, to people he could help. But his life was not as rigidly structured as it seemed to be.

For the outgoing and gregarious — Ford was both — writing can be a lonely occupation. The intrusiveness of interviews, the meetings with editors and publishers, the big city lunches, the laudatory reviews and the notoriety are invigorating and provide a sense of fulfillment, but in the end the writer must confront a blank sheet of paper — or today a blank screen — and put his talent to work.

Corey was all too aware of this, and the occasional dread of writing that might sometimes sweep over him — by himself, at his desk, a few scribbled notes, at his elbow a bottle of Black and White — might put him into an inactive funk. His discipline would ebb and soon, as Corey once told me, he would ignore the first rule of writing: apply seat of pants to seat of chair. From time to time, he needed help.

With no family, a choice deliberately made, keeping friends at a distance and seeing the possibility of wife, kids, relatives and sweethearts as detractions from his work, he had few emotional underpinnings that could support him through what he called his occasional "slough of despair."

As a pastime, or as therapy, he was never quite sure, he took up fishing and hunting, travelling to New Hampshire — a train to Portland, Maine, then by car to Freedom, NH — more often during the Fall of the year when he could work the streams with a fly rod or roam the hills with a side-by-side 20-gauge shotgun and a pal, his English setter, busting ruffed grouse and migratory woodcock. The outdoors — what we now call the environment — was a diversion that led him to writing for the sporting magazines *Field and Stream* and *True*.

Corey's lifestyle was far from original; it was of a mien common to people with a peculiar genius and an unflinching commitment to personal achievement. He saw himself as the best at what he did, as a humorist and biographer, but most as a supportive friend to people he admired and respected. My good fortune: I was one of those people. He was my teacher. From him I learned to acquire information, to search for the right answers, to question authority and how to distinguish myself from the crowd.

Dartmouth did not recognize his quiet brilliance when he was invited into its midst. The faculty saw him as it would a B student, a producer of pulp stories for magazine publication, intellectually insufficient and undeserving of serious recognition as a writer. Or as a person. He hadn't even finished college, my gahd! That he had by then published a remarkable, well-reviewed history of OSS activities during WW II entitled, "Cloak and Dagger," — followed by "Klondy," a historical account of the settlement of Alaska — was ignored, as were subsequent histories and biographies whose writing consumed most of Corey's final years. He was an intruder, the faculty tacitly concluded. That he was also a flag waving patriot, a far right conservative by any one's measure, and accepted being addressed as "Colonel", nettled the college's anti-military left-leaners even further.

Much of the college's faculty and administration were against money and moneyed people, against corporations and the people who worked for them, against mixing with members of the student body, and most of all against creative people who did not fit their profile of the educated elite. Their actions were petty.

I give you two examples. Corey's closest faculty friend and confident was Professor Herb West, Chair of the Humanities Department, brusque, nerveless and quick to speak out against any administration indignity that might befall a student. He was resented by his colleagues and beloved by his students, a stand-off that lasted for years until, under sad circumstances, the administration won out. Herb's son, Herb, Jr., in his sophomore year was kicked out of the College. Campus police had burst into his dormitory room, found an open bottle of scotch and charged him with drunkenness. Whether true or not, and given that drinking on campus was permissible under most circumstances, expulsion was totally unfair,

By Way of Luck

a punishment too great to be levied against any student. Professor West bellowed loudly, the bear in defense of his wounded cub, yet his emotional appeals to the college were ignored, lifelong associates turned away from him. Herb and his wife Karren were stricken with a grief that overtook the rest of their lives in Hanover, an undeserved and cruel condemnation.

On another occasion, again a drinking episode, in October of 1954, two freshmen were expelled without recourse, their apparent misconduct, sharing a beer in their dormitory rooms with two, under age local high school seniors, all childhood friends. How the college became aware of the event was not disclosed, nor did the announcement add any detail. The college administration said simply that the students had been expelled for "Conduct unbecoming Dartmouth men."

The day after the college newspaper, *The Daily Dartmouth*, reported the event, I turned in a paper to a humanities professor — not Herb West — raising the question, how long does it take a student to become a Dartmouth man? The expelled students had been on campus a little more than five weeks. Time enough, my paper asked, to qualify? What were the criteria? Were the students informed of the requirement? I concluded my comments, semi-serious by any measure, suggesting that matriculating students should be advised of all circumstances under which they might be expelled, a contract as it were that would avoid any similar future confusion.

At a following assembly of the humanities class, the paper was returned to me with the professor's notation in the upper corner: "This is as irresponsible a statement as I have ever heard from a Dartmouth student." I thought his response also semi-serious until I noted the grade. He had given me an F.

By early 1953, I had moved out of Wheeler Hall and into Corey's house, sharing space with two other Dartmouth students.

During spring break, Corey and I went bone fishing in the Bahamas. Corey had loaned me his Rollei reflex camera and a soft-cover instruction book. Learn to use it, he said. He'd told Hugh Grey, editor of *Field and Stream*, I was a photographer! Off we went. My photos weren't great, but they were good enough to earn my travel expenses, as were my shots on a later trip quail shooting in Mexico.

That summer, packing fly rods and reels borrowed from the Orvis Company, we took an extended trip across Canada from New Foundland to Hudson's Bay to the Canadian Rockies and Vancouver Island researching a three part series for Field and Stream covering hunting, fishing, and Canada's wildlife conservation and land management practices. I was the photographer on the trip, and on return I also wrote parts of the series.

(Corey rarely took notes, only addresses and phone numbers. He could be deftly precise, leaning on others when a fact or incident had skipped by him.)

At Corey's prompting and with his help I wrote a separate piece for the *Saturday Evening Post* on my catch of a king salmon in the Vancouver Straits just off the mouth of the Campbell River. The teaching had started, a writing collaboration had begun.

There were other stories, other trips, while still an undergraduate — fishing for salmon in Ireland's chalk streams; hunting the auerhahn in Germany's black forest — most expenses covered by the airlines bartering for publicity — and in the meantime I had taken a crack at a solo piece suggested by Hugh Grey who'd been considering a *Field and Stream* series on vanishing species: My subject, the eastern heath hen, once a ubiquitous game bird, not seen since the 1930s. Hugh bought it. Corey and I celebrated with a couple of deep-dish juniper berry pies, his sobriquet for a stand-up gin martini, along with a steak heavily salted, charred on the outside yet blood rare inside.

When I needed school time to make the trips, we'd figure a vacation week with perhaps another week tacked on if needed. I'd call on Joe McDonald, Dean of Students, for permission to skip whatever days I might need, and not ever did he say "No". Once he remarked I was probably getting a better education on the road than I was in Hanover. At one poignant moment, at commencement, handing out diplomas to the graduating members of our class, Dean McDonald slapped a rolled up diploma into my hand and said, wryly, "You were

By Way of Luck

gone so much I wasn't certain you'd be here."

In 1954 Corey and I began talking Air Force, the ROTC curriculum in general and, in particular, one issue that had been brought up by my ROTC instructors — the falling retention rate of ROTC-trained Lieutenants who chose not to re-up at the end of their committed tour. It was our instructors' way of letting us know that our Air Force service might be the start of a career.

I was scheduled to spend four weeks during the summer at Otis Air Force Base on Cape Cod in a familiarization program for ROTC cadets beginning their last year of college. I didn't complete the four weeks. Corey had other ideas.

Roughly mid-way through the third week, Corey called, told me he was in uniform and had set up an appointment for us to meet the Commanding General of the Air Force Training Command at Maxwell Air Force Base in Montgomery, Alabama. The retention thing, he said.

Within hours, in my ROTC uniform, I was in a twin-engine C-45 on my way to Maxwell, to meet Corey and the General, a Ford fan from war-time days. From there we visited five additional bases — our first, Lackland AFB in San Antonio, Texas, making the trip in a reconditioned World War II B-17 — where I interviewed perhaps twenty Lieutenants, hearing repeatedly the common complaints, low pay, sub-standard housing, little health care and, occasionally a reference to the many WW II and Korean War senior officers ahead of them sucking up the promotions and dulling junior officers their chances of advancement.

The ease with which the trip had come about escaped me. That Corey had, as it appeared, simply donned a uniform and commandeered an Air Force twin-engine aircraft for his own use didn't seem unusual, so naïve was I.

We took several side-trips: to White Sands, New Mexico, to assess whether there might be a story on Major Paul Stapp, riding a jet propelled sled on rails at body slamming speeds, testing the physical effects of G-force acceleration. No, we concluded. There was little to be told. Stapp's story had already been widely published.

To Colorado Springs where we met three Congressmen and two Air Force officers surveying a possible site for the Air Force Academy. Yes, the coming birth of another major military academy that would rival West Point and Annapolis was a good story.

Corey wrote the Academy story. I did the retention piece for the *Post*: "I'll Stay in the Air Force, Maybe..." It ran in the spring of 1955 and caused a generally favorable stir among my fellow Dartmouth students, with one exception, an administration favorite, who asked, dismissively, each of us standing on the steep outside steps of the gymnasium, why I had lowered myself to be published by a popular magazine.

Corey and I went on to Offutt AFB in Omaha and a meeting with General Curtis Lemay who headed the Strategic Air Command (SAC), and a half dozen staffers including Col. Reade Tilley, his Public Information Officer. Lemay was a powerful presence: he didn't stand, he loomed. His speech was punctuated with grunts and nods, guttural commands in place of periods and exclamation marks. Corey had known Lemay in England when they were both part of 3rd Air Corps, thus the meeting was affable, to a point. He didn't have many re-up problems, Lemay said. (Rewarding performance with spot promotions and cash bonuses, a practice peculiar to SAC, was obviously effective.) Lemay broke off the dialogue and demanded, What's your college major? I told him Sociology and Political Science. He went nasty. "Shit, you're no damn good to me. I need engineers!" End of meeting.

In 1958 Lemay made a non-stop record flight to the Washington National Airport from Rio de Janeiro in a C-135, bringing with him a stack of same-day Brazilian newspapers that he wanted "run over to the White House," and calling ahead to set up the delivery. Real evidence of the trip, he reportedly said. Second Lieutenant Perkins was the delivery boy.

As the C-135's jet engines were whining down, I scampered up the gangway and into the cockpit. Lemay was sitting left seat, during the eleven hour flight his shirt stained dark from sweat, a dead cigar butt notched in the corner of his mouth. "Newspapers,

By Way of Luck

sir?" I recall asking. He threw a thumb in the direction of a nook directly behind. For a moment I thought he recognized me. Not a chance. I grabbed the papers, jumped into a staff car, got to the White House and handed them to Jim Hagerty, Eisenhower's Press Secretary who appeared bewildered by my visit. "That's it?" Hagerty questioned, obviously unimpressed. "Just newspapers?

That evening at Offutt Air Force Base Corey and I crammed into a B-47 heading to Castle AFB in California, on the way the crew making a practice bombing run on an electronic target in downtown Denver.

Compared to Corey's tough and unyielding tutorials, my college classroom assignments were a novelty. I'd join Corey in his office when I had an assignment to write, whether a paper or an idea for a magazine article, or he sought a comment from me, an opinion, an observation, perhaps an off-hand remark that might reawaken an idea for an article he'd abandoned sometime back. Routinely, he'd sit me on a stool, puppet like, in front of a typewriter stand and ask an opening question, like, what does your reader want to know? Or offer a critique, like, you can find a better word, a better phrase, look for it. He'd sit there patiently, waiting for me to hit the typewriter keys, seconds then minutes might pass, my face reddening as I sought his help, looked for his approval. Corey was undeterred by my artlessness.

Abruptly, he might say, let's swap places. He'd sit at the typewriter, I would take the chair at his desk and he'd coax from me words that might be sifting through my mind. If I offered something acceptable, he'd type it in, then read aloud the sentence or paragraph we'd just composed. He kept pushing me.

Writing, I came painfully to realize, could come easily but more often it was a grind, building a sentence, a paragraph, telling a story, setting a pace, sequencing the material in readable order. And so on it went, Corey practicing his genius for words, with me learning the craft one ouch after another.

When we returned to Hanover and Dartmouth College from Castle Air Force Base, a WW II pal, a former OSS operative, Dave Olds, by letter and by phone to Corey, was insisting there was a story to be written about the American pilots who had flown in China with Claire Chennault's Flying Tigers. At war's end, what had happened to them? Olds told a romantic tale, the Flying Tigers fighting for Chaing Kai Chek during China's 1946 civil war; smuggling precious stones and opium out of the interior and into Shanghai and south to Singapore; supporting the French in French Indo China; and later flying for China Air Transport (CAT), a CIA funded airline, a cloaked organization serving as an extension of American diplomacy in the Far East.

The detail was rich, the story promising. Corey relished the proposition. Olds an authentic source, all hesitation aside, Corey told me, we're going to Hong Kong. Wow! I was as taken by it as was he, should it prove real.

But I had to say No.

In the coming college year, my last at Dartmouth, with my ROTC summer travels as well as a pending marriage keeping me away from home, I felt the summer of 1954 might be the last time I could spend a week or more with my parents, something I might always regret.

I thought Corey would be upset. He wasn't. He understood and instead asked Jim Hall, who would that Fall room at Corey's, to accompany him. Jim, like many other Dartmouth men who learned to hunt and fish growing up, had become part of Corey's sporting coterie. Jim unhesitatingly said yes.

Weeks later, upon their return, Corey was a mess. The trip had not gone well, he'd had little sleep, the interviews had been confusing, the facts spotty, the May 1954 fall of Dien Bien Phu creating an uncertainty if not fear that apparently undermined his efforts to get the story he thought he was there to get. Worse, he had promised a two-parter, maybe even three, to *The Saturday Evening Post*. He had a deadline and no idea how he would make it. He was, in his own terms, in the slough of despair. He looked to me for help.

So we did what we had done when collaborating on an article, with a difference. I took Corey's role, interviewing him, persistently pulling the story out of his clouded recollections, sitting at his

By Way of Luck

Underwood, pounding away, a paragraph at a time, with no real idea of where the story might go yet hoping it might get there, wherever there was.

I was in my senior year, yet still very much Corey's student, coaxing along a writer whose stories had been published in dozens of magazines. Somehow it worked. Corey began reading my typed notes, aloud as was our working custom, amused by some of my conclusions, his sensibilities gradually returning, and on a morning he took over my seat and the two-parter was on its way. The story he wrote was a good one and happily received by Ben Hibbs, editor of the *Post*.

Right away, the articles attracted attention, actor Bill Holden calling Corey and suggesting a meeting. Holden was in New York City with his wife actress Brenda Marshall staying at the Pierre Hotel. Holden had won an Academy Award for his role in *Stalag 17*, and starred in *The Bridge on the River Kwai* and *Network*. Could Corey meet him? He wanted to talk about adapting the *Post* articles into a film.

Corey and I drove to New York that night — we took rooms at the Gramercy Park Hotel — and met Holden the next day. Over a pleasant lunch served in his suite at the Pierre Hotel, he talked roughly how the film might be constructed, taken by his own early enthusiasm and looking for some direction from us. When the last cup of coffee had been poured, he confessed to needing more time to think through what he had in mind, asking whether we could give him an option, just for a few weeks he said, and maybe meet for more talk in Los Angeles.

Less than a month later, we were on our way west. Holden had pulled together several backers, had a lead actor standing by and wanted more talk. We got his message when we were in Washington, DC, where I was interviewing for the CIA. Corey called Colonel Jim Sherrill at the Pentagon. Got any flights heading for LA? he asked. You bet, Sherrill responded. If you want a ride, be at National Airport in the next two hours. We scrambled, packing bags and flagging down a cab.

The ride Sherrill offered was in a distinctive, triple-tailed, prop-driven, four-engine Lockheed Constellation, the Columbine,

President Dwight D. Eisenhower's personal aircraft, a predecessor to Air Force One, and fully crewed. Corey and I were the only passengers. We ate and drank our way to California, served by two stewards in white, tight-waisted "Eisenhower" jackets.

The plane was on loan to Bob Hope. It would transport Hope, comedian Jerry Colonna, actress Faye Emerson and a supporting cast of singers and dancers on a USO holiday entertainment tour of military cases in the Pacific. Landing at Burbank Airport, the pilot, a full colonel, told us the President had requested the Columbine be formally delivered to Hope. The Colonel was to meet Hope at the Hollywood Masonic Temple where Hope was rehearsing his troupe. Why don't you come along with me, the Colonel suggested.

Of course, we'd come along. Corey called Holden, told him where we'd be. Holden said he'd meet us there. During the evening hours that followed, standing on a bare gym floor, we watched a masterful performance, Hope rehearsing his players, full of comedy, full of vulgarity and full of hardnosed, unrelenting direction, a one-of-a kind recital with but a handful of spectators, me, Corey, the Colonel and Bill Holden, all of us included in Hope's torrent of jabbing criticisms and off-color cracks.

We were so invigorated, when Holden told us he couldn't pick up the option our agent had given him, we were unable to express any disappointment. Not a trace. We thanked him for his interest, and after Hope told everyone to go home, we sped off to Chasen's for dinner.

Months later, in the spring of 1955, the *Post* articles brought an unexpected reward: Batjac Productions the film production company launched by producer Bob Fellows, legendary film directors William A. Wellman and John Ford, and actor John Wayne, was flush from the success of one of their first productions, "The High and the Mighty". Searching for new properties, they bought the screen rights to the *Post* articles, not for a lot of money, but for a writing contract.

While the *Post* articles carried only Corey's by-line, he insisted that I be included in the Batjac agreement as a co-writer. And so I was.

By Way of Luck

Working for Oscar Winner William A. Wellman

In 1927, the first year of the Hollywood Film Awards, Bill Wellman won the Oscar for his direction of *Wings* — which won the Oscar for Best Film. *Wings* set the bar high and for its time no director or producer came close to reaching it. Even Cecil B. DeMille's epics almost a generation later were shadowy imitations of what Bill accomplished. Bill took movie making to new heights, eliminating the vaudeville and road show mentality that gripped pre-World War II movie makers and legitimizing film as both entertainment and art.

Wings was followed by *A Star is Born, The Ox-Bow Incident* and *Good-Bye, My Lady,* classics all. He directed 45 full-length films. Reviewers John Andrew Gallagher and Frank Thompson recently wrote, "Wellman's incredible career is ripe for reevaluation. He was as experimental as Scorsese, as audacious as Tarantino, as sentimental as Spielberg — but he was eternally, irrevocably, himself."

For our introductory meeting with Wellman, in October 1955, Corey and I again flew to Los Angeles — this trip in a United Airlines DC-3, stopping in Chicago and Denver. We met once, at Batjac's office, talked script and story line, seemingly in agreement, Bill nodding as I made notes of our conversation, or interjecting when he thought we were getting off-track, and after no more than two hours, he simply left, that is, with no more than a wave as he went out the door.

We were there a week expecting some acknowledgement that our talks had gone OK, which finally came from Harold Ober's Hollywood affiliate, agents Rosenberg and Coryell. Waiting for a response from them, the delay was uneasy, but memorable. Corey called old friends, and for four days I saw the glittering side of Hollywood:

Dinner with director Norman Z. McLeod and his wife Bunny at their home beside Toluca Lake; lunch with Humphrey Bogart at Romanov's; dinner at Chasen's with Dave and his wife Maud introducing us in his salon abutting the restaurant's bar to Charles Laughton and his wife Elsa Lanchester, famed jockey Eddie Arcaro, and Fred McMurray and his wife, June Havoc; and dinner at the home of Milt Bren and Claire Trevor, Academy Award winner for her supporting role in *Key Largo*.

At Romanov's Restaurant, Corey and I having a drink at the bar and waiting for a table, Nat Benchley, son of Robert Benchley and author of *The Russians Are Coming, The Russians are Coming*, came by and said, Don't order. Frank is putting together a party to screen his new film, *The Tender Trap*. You're invited. We'll be gathering in the lobby in a few minutes.

The minutes went quickly. Nat introduced Corey and me to Frank Sinatra and we mixed fast with his crowd, recognizing Spencer Tracy, Humphrey Bogart and Lauren Bacall, Noel Coward, Mike Romanov, Nat, and Elizabeth Taylor. Limos were waiting on the street and Sinatra took charge of assigning who rode with whom. He gave me a seat next to Elizabeth Taylor.

(My daughter, actor Elizabeth Perkins, starring in the role of Wilma in the first full-length film version of *The Flintstones*, had Elizabeth Taylor as her on-screen mother, the two Elizabeths forming a fast friendship.)

Rudy Vallee invited us to dinner and to one of his performances at a local Los Angeles night club. We'd seen *How to Succeed in Business* in New York, Rudy co-starring with Robert Morse. Backstage, he said, Next time in LA give me a call. We did. The evening started with drinks at his house on Mulholland Drive — once Mary Pickford's commodious home — other guests: Rudy's boyhood chums from Maine, all of us wandering around the house, cocktails in hand, listening to the music boxes, one in each of six bedrooms, another in a den, others scattered about on side tables, each of them a unique recording of a song that Vallee had composed or performed during his long career. We then went to the club for a dinner-theater evening, Rudy introducing us from the stage as friends from back East. Corey told me that Rudy sent him occasional checks, payment for lines lifted from Corey's comic writings and fitting in nicely with Vallee's stand-up routines.

By Way of Luck

With a contract in hand, Corey and I went to work in December 1955, Wellman showing up for our first story meeting mid-morning at our Beverly Hills Hotel bungalow, walking through the front door without a knock and into the kitchen looking for orange juice, vodka and ice. There was none there. Annoyed because he'd called ahead with his order, he shouted at room service over the house phone, Two fifths of Smirnoff, he demanded, fresh squeezed orange juice and bags of ice. And fruit, and muffins, and cheese and pastries, yelling angrily into the phone but assuring us calmly that the Studio would be paying all the bills. With the phone back in its cradle, he turned cuddly, and for the next hour or so, we talked flying.

Without question, Wellman redefined for me the word "unconventional." He was a renegade, every idea, every decision, I sensed, he started from scratch, as if he were rediscovering the world and his place in it. He was determined to be brave. He had flown in France during World War I for the Lafayette Escadrille, a French Air Force squadron of youthful, quixotic, multi-national pilots who held aerial combat less risky than, say, playing football, their perception of engaging German ace Manfred von Richthofen, the Red Baron, pure adventure, and outwardly indifferent that they were part of an actual war. Wellman only understood that fully, he said, when he returned home.

Wellman's tales were engrossing, his narrative unmatchable, and as the morning's orange juice and vodka went on, he led us through his decision to produce "Wings", having come face to face with the realities of war and his determination to depict it.

He kept company with pilots, his people, he called them, one of them Col. Robert L. Scott, author of *God Is My Co-Pilot* who arrived at our bungalow one morning during a story conference. Scott had flown P-40's with the Flying Tigers in China, but hadn't been one of them. He was 25th Air Corps and assigned by Army Air Corps headquarters, if not by General George Marshall himself, to bring Claire Chennault and his mercenaries "into the loop." Scott's book still stands as one of a handful of masterful stories of flight, alongside the works of Ernest Gann and Antoine de St. Exupery.

Scott was a story teller, his talk a slow, cruising drawl with an inflection common to pilots, affably mixing flair and fantasy in long, seemingly important rambles. Some, we concluded, were actually true. We lost an entire morning of work, at first listening attentively and finally just being polite.

The Mahurin Story

We had another bungalow visitor, Air Force Colonel Walker "Bud" Mahurin, a veteran of WW II and Korea and for a time very much in the news. He was stationed just miles away at March Air Force Base in Riverside, California. Bud was a fighter pilot. At age 24, by 1944, he had 22½ kills in the European Theater of Operations (ETO) — where Corey met him — an ace and member of the 56th Fighter Squadron, 3rd Air Corps, flying P-40's and P-51's. Shot down over France and parachuting safely, he connected with the French Resistance and found his way back to England by way of Spain. He could not fly in the ETO again. By Convention, once on the ground, were he to land again in enemy territory, he could be treated as a spy and shot.

Bud transferred to the Pacific theater, where he flew P-38's against the Japanese, scoring four kills and, again, was shot down, this time over water. He was picked up by an American submarine and spent three weeks aboard the sub before it returned to its home port. Bud said trapped inside the sub was scarier than having a German ME-109 on his tail.

In 1951, when the Korean "police action" broke out, Bud led a squadron of F-86 D's, dogs they were called. In an aerial fight over the Yalu River, he was again shot down.

Like most pilots who had to squeeze into the short-sheeted cockpit of a WW II fighter aircraft, Bud was not a big man, yet he stood big, his brow prominent like male actors Humphrey Bogart and Spencer Tracey, and he had an actor's bravura. He performed. He joked, told stories, laughed easily and made others laugh with him. He was "manic constant", always on stage, with poking, nudging commentary, quick tongued, yet able to move easily from the comic to the serious.

By Way of Luck

Still, he was a killer. In combat — his ordinance: 50-caliber machine guns or 20 millimeter cannon lodged under his seat or under a wing — he was a lethal weapon and among the best at what he did.

Reader, think for a moment when Bud appeared at our bungalow, how I reacted, this kid too young to fight a pilot's fight during WW II, with Conrad Houle in the woods piloting our make believe airplane, acting out a war we could only read about and longing to play the warrior's role. And here, in a Beverly Hills hotel, where Wellman, Corey and I were working, came the warrior I once strove to be. He appeared magnificent. When we shook hands, I swear, he glowed.

While an armistice was being negotiated in Pyong Yang for the cessation of the conflict between North Korea and the United Nations, all American POWs were eventually returned home, but the war was still on for Bud. He had been captured and imprisoned by the North Koreans, a high ranking officer, a prize, and for fourteen months subjected to cruel indoctrination, brain washing it was called, food and sleep deprivation, beatings and blaring music, and incessant questioning, unending threats. He fought to keep his sanity by recalling or composing limericks, storing them in a far corner of his mind where North Korean torture could not reach, and retreating to them as consciousness drifted away.

(He recited several of them in that Beverly Hills bungalow, among his favorites: "A mathematician named Hall, had a single octagonal ball, the measure of whose weight, plus the penis plus eight, equaled half the square root of fuck all"…and "A habit both strange and bizarre, has fastened its grips on Papa, he fetches home camels and other large mammals, and gives them a go at Mama.")

But Bud's sense of humor would undo him. Finally and inexorably he gave in to methodical torture, admitting in a signed confession that he had invaded North Korea illegally under orders from American general officers with comic book names, assuming that his signature on a farcical document would never be taken seriously.

Yet it was, North Korean propagandists churning out both

cheerful declarations and damning accusations — and describing their own version of what Bud had put his name to — that made truth of Bud's action.

Guilty or not, Bud had been branded, his loyalties made suspect and, the Pentagon concluded, could never again be a credible military leader. There was no celebration on Bud's return to the United States, no ceremonious presentation of medals won, no hand shake thanking him for his service. He was knocked back in rank and left to drift. Within a year, he resigned his commission and went to work for one of Chennault's former Flying Tigers, Johnny Allison, president of North American Aviation and Bud's steadfast friend. Bud died at age 91 in 2012.

Corey and I saw the story in Bud's horrid sufferance. From a bed in the Good Samaritan Hospital, recovering from a minor auto accident in a car driven by Dave Chasen, Corey dispatched me to find Bill Wellman and talk him through it. The premise was simple: brain-washed soldier comes home, apparently recovered from his ordeal, but programmed by his North Korean interrogators to assassinate a major American political figure.

Bill didn't buy it. I had knocked on the door of his Beverly Hills home late on a Sunday morning, unannounced, figuring he might not return a phone call, and caught him in his PJ's. He was understandably surprised by my arrival, still he invited me in, poured a coffee and listened to the proposition. He saw the pieces, he said, but couldn't quite put them together, thanked me for coming and walked me to the door, not abruptly, but soon enough for me to recognize his disinterest.

(In 1962, novelist Richard Condon published *The Manchurian Candidate*, later made into a movie starring Laurence Harvey and Frank Sinatra, its premise identical to ours. A matter of timing? Or was it catching Bill in his PJ's?)

Batjac gave us an office. We finished the script in February 1956. Titled *The Saga of Earthquake Magoon*, it circulated among producers and studio editors for several years, prompted an off-spring or two, but was never produced.

By Way of Luck

Coincidence or Just Plain Luck

I went on active duty the following month, assigned to Ellington AFB in Houston Texas. Ten months later, I was on my way to the Pentagon, reporting to the Office of the Secretary of the Air Force, Office of Public Information, whose new leader, now a Brigadier General, was Robert L. Scott, the appointment earning him the star. With Scott's assistance, Corey engineered the transfer, and with the blessing of Major General Emmett "Rosie" O'Donnell, then USAF Deputy Chief of Staff, Personnel, who was anxiously looking for a Lieutenant who would accept Pentagon duty. O'Donnell's reasoning: too many generals making decisions that affected younger officers whom they hadn't seen or worked with in years. The brass wanted fresh blood in its midst. I was the sacrificial lamb.

By the time I arrived at the Pentagon, I learned the uneasy news that Scott had been fired by the Secretary of the Air Force, Donald Quarels. My sponsor was gone. Never one to waste words, and always reluctant to accept orders from civilians, Scott, his staff had it, turned his back on Quarels and stalked out of a meeting calling the Secretary an asshole. Scott's star disappeared, his old rank reinstated.

Making the transfer was a mixed decision for me. The classroom work and the flying was every bit as romantic as I had expected it to be. But to what end? The Korean War was behind us. The nation was at peace and the idea of girding for battle was no longer a priority. And the romance of flying, I had learned, could be but a young man's fleeting emotion. Further, I reasoned, a stint at the Pentagon — where serious stuff was always on the table, war or the likelihood of war a constant — was an adult assignment and couldn't be rejected.

Corey's reasoning differed: he'd lost his collaborator and wanted him back.

(I was not Corey's first writing partner. He had teamed in the 30s and 40s with Alastair MacBain whom he'd met in 1932. MacBain had graduated from Columbia College in 1929 where he sat stroke on the Columbia crew and after graduation free-lanced as a writer, attempting to get by on $50 checks from too few writing assignments. He sought out his fellow alumnus for advice at a time, as it turned out, that Corey had too many commitments and needed help. The two formed a lasting partnership and an unending friendship.)

General Henry H. "Hap" Arnold

In early 1942, with America's war effort just getting underway, Ford and MacBain called on Brigadier General Henry "Hap" Arnold, as writers asking him how they might help. Thinking he might suggest an article or two, according to Corey, they were "bowled over" by Arnold's reaction. "On the spot, he conscripted us," were Corey's remembered words.

Both Ivy Leaguers who smoked pipes and sported tweed jackets, neither of them fearsome or easily stirred to anger, they were surely among the least likely WW II combatants to put on a uniform. But they did. Ford and MacBain couldn't say "no." Nor did they want to. Arnold was a friend and fishing pal.

Corey's relationship with General Arnold was wader deep, having originated on an Alaskan salmon stream in the early 30s, Arnold then a Lieutenant Colonel in charge of the Alaskan Air Command, and continuing through the years as fellow fishermen and outspoken conservationists. At the outbreak of the war, by then a one-star general, Arnold recognized that Ford and MacBain with their access to both national newspapers and magazines could give him a direct line to his valued constituencies: the American people, the U.S. Congress and the White House. Arnold wanted them to know that the United States was not fighting a paper war, that it was real, that their sons and husbands were dying, that many more would die before the war was won, that he needed all the help he could get. Depending on newspaper correspondents for the task, as the War Department had allowed, was not an option.

He put Ford and MacBain in uniform. Their assignment, according to Corey, was "Tell the stories about the boys." That they did, primarily in the weeklies such as *Liberty Magazine, Colliers* and the *Saturday Evening Post,* their articles picked up by the wire services and reaching hundreds of local papers, setting off a cascade of reprints and journalistic commentary. Ford and MacBain gave Arnold a voice.

Airmen throughout the ETO and the Pacific read the stories. So when Major Ford and Captain MacBain showed up in a mess hall or a barracks or on a flight line, unlike most newspaper correspondents who were quartered in local hotels with private bars and fresh sheets on their beds, they were part of the Air Corps team, flying the missions, sharing the commitment and together shouldering the sorrow for the crews that didn't come back, The surviving airmen were comforted to know their stories were being told at home. Ford and MacBain had given them a voice, too.

Was this an early example of embedding reporters with the troops?

Even in GI dress, Ford stood out, a blazing smile — except when his jaw clenched a briar pipe — an extended hand and an informal greeting, a "Hi yah, guy, how yah doin', " according to MacBain, lighting up a room and relaxing even the most skeptical of enlisted men and officers. Men of all ranks, officers and non-coms, saluted Corey as one of their own.

William "Wild Bill" Donovan, Director, OSS

Seeing the war as a big story, patriots both, figuring how best both to report it and possibly participate in it, Ford and MacBain had already found their way to the Office of Strategic Services (OSS) and its director, "Wild Bill" Donovan. How Ford and MacBain may have worked for Donovan is, like most OSS WWII action, clouded, but I do know that Corey carried an OSS designation: Special Assistant to Director of Strategic Services — specific assignments took him to India, Burma and China, his activities there earning him two bronze stars; and later serving in the "Europe, African, Middle Eastern Theater" for which he was awarded a Service Medal.

Corey was but one of many celebrities Donovan recruited. Two examples, both of whom I met, actor Sterling Hayden, as an operative spending much of his time in the Balkans, and artist and humorist Hugh Troy, subject of "The Practical Joker," a book by H.

Allen Smith who recounted a string of Troy's bizarre exploits.

After General LeBailey gave Tim the go-ahead and Tim ordered me to write the plan, from my home in Falls Church, Virginia, in panic mode I called Corey in Hanover, New Hampshire, told him of the meeting and read him the memo, asking, "What do I do now?"

Physically, I was shaking. I could hear my voice rasping over an echoing hollow phone. Corey responded evenly. Once you get a plan, he said, everyone will want a piece of it, and you'll have no plan at all. There's no authority in the chain of command to act on it. The longer it takes to get it going, the greater the possibility of it dying. Let me think what next, he concluded, and signed off.

Two days later, he showed up at the Pentagon, in uniform. He had recalled himself to active duty. Again, I didn't think "calling oneself to duty" was unusual. But it was, I would eventually realize.

Orders were cut, and together we headed first to Eglin AFB — a 500,000 acre bombing range and aircraft research and test facility, its spacious lands well-managed and teeming with wildlife and exotic bird species, located in the Florida panhandle — to observe how a conservation program could be managed. From there to Matagorda Island, another near — barren bombing range, abutting the Texas Gulf Coast — and home to rattlesnakes big around as my arm and to breeding Whooping Cranes — to Wendover AFB, Utah, then returning to D.C. and meeting with various conservation professionals in the Washington area.

The officers and enlisted men we interviewed during the trip embraced the concept, in part because it added an up-beat and contrasting dimension to their duties, as in, hey, it's okay to hunt and fish on the base, the manual says; and in larger part because the older hands saw it as a potential legacy of the Cold War that would reach beyond the aircraft they were flying and the weapons they were carrying and be a welcoming and positive addition to their regular duties.

On our return to the Pentagon, we found secretarial help. I dictated a memo, a fact dump, as it were — where we'd been and what we'd discovered, including our recommendations. (Corey thought the

By Way of Luck

experience comical. I'd never dictated before and was embarrassed by my clumsiness.) The memo became the basis for a subsequent memo to General White.

What happened thereafter, I recall with bare sureness. But Corey must have talked to LeBailey who must have talked to his boss, the Secretary of the Air Force, if no more than to give them a heads-up.

But Corey was clearly in charge. From Hanover, he called and told me to have our final draft of the memo typed up, inserting his signature and mine. I was to take it directly to General White.

Virginia Waugh, our office secretary, typed the memo. She shook her head in dismay. With years of Pentagon experience, she thought the notion of a Second Lieutenant delivering a memo to the four-star General and Chief of Staff a career killer. You'll end up manning a radar station on the DEW line, she said, an Arctic outpost.

I asked Tim Dunn for his blessing then delivered the memo by hand to Colonel Jim Sherrill, General White's aide. I felt I had just taken the first uneasy step down a dark staircase.

Little time passed between my delivery of the memo and Corey's return to Washington. General White had invited us to meet with him.

I sat agog in General White's office, where he and retired General Carl "Tooey" Spaatz and General Nathan Twining, Chairman of the Joint Chiefs, had welcomed Corey with warm smiles and vigorous handshakes, war-time buddies yet talking about fishing and hunting. I was included once when Corey described our day in Bad Eschl trying to outsmart brown trout on Austria's River Traun. The meeting, lasting perhaps twenty minutes, was so casual we could have been sitting around a campfire by a Vermont trout stream.

Clearly these were not military strategists discussing cold war protocols, or assessing defensive counter measures against aerial attack. Nor were they standing on rank, who had it, who didn't. They were men in arms, Arnold's men. When they went to war, Arnold had assigned them his trust, and they delivered. Though

Corey was now a civilian with a reserve rank of Colonel, his influence was borne by Arnold's status, a five-star General of the Armies, recognized not only by his comrades in General White's office, but among both active and retired Air Force veterans throughout the United States as well. Corey was revered and respected as though, like Arnold, he actually carried five stars on his shoulders.

Only years later did all the pieces come together for me, how Corey could "call himself to active duty," how military aircraft were so easily available, how high ranking generals opened their doors to him so readily, how his proposals were so quickly approved. Until then, to this youthful observer, it was like a movie, and Corey was Gregory Peck in "Twelve O'clock High."

General White complimented us on the proposal. After asking me a few questions on how I might proceed, said he'd given the go ahead, to whom I wasn't sure, and had selected Lt. Colonel Ben Royal of the Provost's office to work with me on the administrative matters, you know, he went on, "To help you draft the regulations and issue the orders," and adding, "To keep you out of trouble."

Keep me posted, he said. The meeting was over.

Tim applauded when Corey and I returned to his office, with the others joining in. The news of White's OK had obviously travelled quickly. "LeBailey's waiting for us."

That evening, Corey and I celebrated with a round of deep dish juniper berry pies and a couple of charred steaks cooked rare.

In the morning Corey returned to Hanover and I called Lt. Col. Ben Royal.

Weeks after, General Spaatz invited me to his home in Bethesda, Maryland, for an up-date, he said. When I arrived he was sitting on the patio at the rear of his house and peering across the lawn toward shrubs blossoming red and yellow. He was penciling entries in a small notebook.

Keeping tabs on song birds, he said, pointing out the activity around the feeders.

The irony was obvious: the Air Force commander who had executed the aerial destruction of Germany, now in his retirement,

By Way of Luck

keeping track of the aerial action in his back yard. We had bourbon and talked, this Second Lieutenant and the still gallant, retired four-star General of the Air Force, a bit about the program and a bit about the weather. He thanked me for the visit and promised lunch one day, at the Army-Navy club, he said. He was lonely.

Ben Royal was a dour sort and blunt, perhaps resentful his counterpart was of a lesser rank, but much of our work together was so distinctly different, he in charge of editing the regulations and drafting the orders, I taking on the promotional and lobbying task, that the partnering on the detail we had to handle mutually went easily.

After my meeting with Ben Royal, I called Alastair MacBain, Corey's former collaborator and still best friend. He was listed in our memo to General White, not by name, but by title. He had become the Chief Information Officer of the U.S. Fish and Wildlife Service! He knew every organization I might approach. How lucky!

With his help I engaged the U.S. Forest Service and the National Wildlife Federation, later following up with the Audubon Society and the Smithsonian Institution, gathering supportive letters, finding sympathetic staffers in the House, identifying assistant secretaries in the Administration, briefing them on the program, and tracking down outdoor sports writers and published naturalists wherever I could find a name and an address. I could have set up a shuttle service to Eglin Air Force Base our visits so frequent, carrying and courting the influentials who favored our objective.

On the first trip, the Eglin tower, recognizing we were in-bound from Bolling AFB which served as Headquarters USAF, asked for a number designating highest rank aboard. I was unsure how numbers were assigned. Yet, I said to the pilot in command, unthinking and mistaken, tell the tower we have a three, calculating that a three qualified us at the Assistant Secretary level, never imagining that a three was the Speaker of the U.S. House of Representatives!

As we turned off the runway, from the cockpit I could see the reception committee on the tarmac, flags unfurled, troops at attention, a General and a couple of Colonels at the fore, and after the engines had been cut and as their noise abated, the band music coming at us in waves. My guests were thrilled to be so welcomed. One of the Colonels on hand to greet us and formerly in the Pentagon PIO office chewed my ass plenty. What could I do? I offered to pay for the drinks later; but he picked up the check.

Perhaps not surprisingly, an industry group I had not identified as a potential supporter stepped forward: the arms manufacturers, Winchester, Remington, Colt, and Smith and Wesson among them. While they were major suppliers to the military establishment, they were also manufacturers of sporting arms and, not coincidentally, practiced lobbyists.

My duty as a PIO officer narrowed quickly, encouraging coverage, from newspaper and magazine reporters and from the wire services — for TV was not then an effective news medium and radio stations played music — and creating a circle of heavy-lifters who could talk to their Congressional contacts. I sweat the work, recognizing that for me to be productive, Congressional members on the hill had to hear from their constituencies.

When a Marine Colonel came looking for me at my Pentagon office, and later a Navy Captain, seeking information that might apply to their respective services, I sensed that good words were out and positive things were happening.

Two breakthroughs propelled the project. First, Ben Hibbs, Editor of the *Saturday Evening Post*, arguably the most influential publication of the time, agreed to run an article by Corey and me, "Operation Wildlife." It gave national credibility to the program and got all interested parties, military and civilian, feeling good about it, like motherhood and apple pie.

Second, Corey asked General White to keynote an upcoming North American Wildlife Conference in Washington, DC, a gathering of the principal conservation officers of all 48 states, plus the higher ups in the U.S. Department of Interior and executives from a dozen or more conservation organizations. I wrote the General's introduction, the audience learning for the first time that General White was a naturalist, a student of nature, and had a "near professional interest" in ichthyology. Immediately, he was seen as one of them. In uniform, his blouse stacked with ribbons, four stars gleaming from each epaulet, he spoke eloquently and knowledgeably and when he asked his audience to back his program, the applause was loud and long.

When the luncheon broke, I ran up to the dais, grabbed the General's hand and shook it a congratulatory shake. He thanked me, but his raised eyebrow, given the disparity in rank, suggested I may have been out of place. When I told Virginia Waugh of my concern, she agreed I'd taken a step too far.

In the face of the lobbying onslaught coming from so many directions, the offending legislation — the bill in committee that promised commercial access to public lands — disappeared so quickly that not a single Congressional committee member would admit to having promoted it.

Done.

Thereafter, the conservation program took on a life of its own. I take little credit for its success. Though the suggestion was mine, the remarkable relationship between Corey Ford and General "Hap" Arnold, had established the ground work that allowed it to happen.

Tim Dunn was quick to remind me of my other, unattended duties.

Jean Mansavage was patently satisfied with my testimony and the fill-in's I later gave her by e-mail. I had unlocked two key events that rounded out her research: 1. She had not known about the bill in committee that energized the entire episode. 2. She had not factored in the relationship between Ford and Arnold that validated my proposal and gave me the authority to do what Second Lieutenants are not accustomed to doing.

Jean was then able to respond with conviction to the question she had been assigned to answer, why so many years later was the US Air Force in charge of conserving all military lands as well as most lands occupied by U.S. federal agencies.

Jean concluded that the conservation program was five-star General of the Army Henry "Hap" Arnold's legacy and the program was where it belonged, with the United States Air Force.

In an interim report Jean Mansavage gave me fair credit. Referring to Arnold and Ford, she defined my role as "an extension of their commitment to the environment," a peculiar description, but given the company she had put me in, wholly satisfactory.

Leaving Active Duty

Well after the conservation project was launched and safely on its way, and after I had let it known I would eventually return to civilian life, General LeBailey pitched me on making a career of the Air Force, offering a regular commission and bumping me up immediately in rank to Captain. He assured me my career would go well. With the 201 personnel file you've earned here in the Pentagon, he said, no matter where you serve or how well you do — or don't — any officer you work for would be reluctant to give you anything but the highest possible rating. He said I would be on a track to make Colonel early. His offer was a reward I appreciated even more than the Commendation Medal I later received from the Office of the Secretary.

My actual discharge bore its own excitement. With four months to go before my scheduled departure, Tim called me to his desk and in a conspiratorial whisper told me the name and number of a Major in Personnel. He's on the fifth floor. He has an idea on how you might get out early, he said. If you want.

I bolted up the stairs to the Major's office.

The time: May 1958. Professional football teams would soon begin training for the up-coming season, the Major explained. George Preston Marshall, owner of the Washington Redskins, had an Air Force Lieutenant under contract, Ralph Guglielmi, in 1955 a unanimous All-American quarterback from Notre Dame whose tour of duty was scheduled to end, as was mine, in September. By then, the season would be well underway, too late for Guglielmi to do little more than walk the chalk lines. "Marshall wants him, now," the Major said.

The Redskins enjoyed favored nation status in Washington, seats sold out for generations ahead, with Marshall holding a few tickets

By Way of Luck

in reserve for special occasions, such as springing a much needed quarterback who *Washington Post* sportswriters Shirley Povich and Bob Addie, an Air Force reservist, agreed could take the team to an NFL title. Congress obliged, passing a so-called White Charger bill that would release to civilian status active duty personnel who were declared surplus. As the bill was written, the bill would become active at midnight on May 26, 1958, and expire a minute later. On the list of personnel to be declared surplus during that one minute there was but one name: Ralph Guglielmi. If it's OK with you and Tim, the Major said, I'll add you to the list.

The May 26 date came and went and after a week of paper work and physical exams, two surplus and very lucky Air Force Lieutenants were on their way home.

In the months and years that followed, Corey and I worked together on a number of articles and books in support of Air Force issues, either with a double by-line or separately. When sonic booms presented a problem, mostly among chicken farmers who claimed booms were decimating their flocks, we flew to Edwards Air Force base, spent two days interviewing and hanging out with test pilots Scott Crossfield, Chuck Yeager, Bob White and James Jabara, and wrote a mollifying piece about the booms for the *Post*.

Unexpectedly, Corey quietly alerting him where we were, Bud Mahurin arrived at Edwards from March AFB, "to see who was the biggest liar," he said, heckling and joshing with the "guys" and in edgy but fraternal pilot-to-pilot banter questioning the danger of boosting the X-1 and X-15 rocket ships through the sound barrier, a cushy job compared to being seriously shot at. Jabara objected loudly. He had more kills and saw more combat in Korea against Russian Mig 15's than Bud.

(At Edwards, I watched an early U-2 "spy" plane taking off like a kite in a windstorm. A Lt. Colonel walking with me in the desert-dry, 115 degree heat told me not to tell anyone what I'd seen. Really top secret, he said. Much later I would find myself on a fringe of the U-2 "affair.")

When renewal of our U.S. Air Base leases in the Azores became an issue, as in, why spend the money? We wrote a piece for the *Reader's Digest*, "Our Key Bases in Spain and How We Got Them." We also did a piece on our air-breathing missile installations in Germany, with a visit to Ramstein AFB and surrounding emplacements. Cold War stuff. With appropriations needed for the redevelopment of Beale (now Vandenberg) Air Force Base as the USAF's ballistic missile center, we spent two days in Santa Maria, California, with General David Wade and wrote "With the Men Who Fire the Atlas" also for the *Reader's Digest*.

Because airmen at Beale were working in relative anonymity, Corey and I wrote a memo to General White recommending a morale boosting recognition program including the possible award of wings for qualifiers as Missile Men. The recommendation was adopted.

Before leaving the Pentagon and returning to civilian life, I received a score of job offers: from the *Post* in its Washington office, from GE and from *Time* magazine, among them, as well as a standing offer from Batjac to return to my "old job." But most interesting was from the US Forestry Service. Its Director offered me a full ride at Yale, to attend its forestry school, all the way to a doctorate, if I chose, and to make a career in the Forestry Service. Already with a wife and two children, I had to find better paying work. Reluctantly, expressing my gratitude, I had to say no.

Once a civilian, I concluded I couldn't handle the see-saw life of a free-lance writer, and I had found working alone much too solitary, the blank piece of paper always in front of me, demanding my attention and contesting every word I wrote. After completing several magazine assignments — one a story on Senator Judd Gregg's father, Governor Hugh Gregg of New Hampshire, running for another term, Judd then a pre-teen — I joined Doubleday & Company, a renowned book publisher. Perhaps as an editor I might fare better.

The Air Force had given me a platform I could build on. I had learned to fly airplanes and had proven I could get a job done. So how tough could it be, working for a publishing company?

3
Doubleday & Company

The redoubtable Louise Thomas, senior vice-president of Doubleday & Company and Director of Personnel, had her own ideas on how young hires were to be placed within the company, not by education, experience or preference, but by showing off their stuff in a training program, a few weeks in sales, a few weeks in production, a few weeks in subsidiary rights, and so on. Evaluations would be made by department heads. Assignments would follow.

The arrangement was clumsy, the assignments possibly conflicting with promises made, and added to the workload of a half dozen V.P's whose grumbling complaints could be overheard in the men's room. But Louise was not to be pushed aside, I soon realized. A stalwart and a force, her fashionable suits military in their styling, she alone was in charge of corporate pushing.

Four men about the same age, I included, were her initial conscripts:

Tom McCormack, a truly brilliant and peaceable guy and eventually Editor of Doubleday's Anchor Books division for more than a decade. He later became Editor-in-Chief, President and CEO of St. Martin's Press.

Jake Page, I recall, failed to show up one day and some months later emerged as Publications Editor at the Museum of Natural History.

Richard Snyder joined the grumblers and soon stalked out of the company, landing at Simon and Schuster as a salesman and rising by the time he was forty to President and CEO, along the way tripling the size of the company through acquisitions and internal growth, and eventually merging the company with Viacom.

And I. A productive and much appreciated Doubleday editor for nearly five years, the final year as Managing Editor of the Book Club Division, I was fired by a newly promoted executive whose long time career was in warehousing and order processing.

All of us, one way or another, had shown our stuff.

Getting to Doubleday

The late Jerry Nachman — columnist, Editor-in-Chief of the *New York Post* and subsequently Editor-in-Chief of MSNBC, a cable channel, and coincidentally a Connecticut neighbor — once referred to Ferris Mack, the Doubleday editor of his several books, as "a doughty fellow...an old school gent...a chuckly little guy with a twinkle who wore bow ties and smiled a lot."

For me Ferris Mack was generous, open-minded, dedicated, and a not-so-little publishing giant whose gritty talk set him apart from his colleagues and placed him historically among the higher echelons of Doubleday's editorial department. Coincidentally, that Ferris was also a Dartmouth alumnus as well as the "doughty fellow" who had a hand in my hiring, respecting him as I had learned to respect two-star generals, I could not speak lightly of him, chuckly or not.

With a letter of recommendation in his hand from Corey Ford, Ken McCormick, the company's editorial director, had walked into Ferris' office and asked whether he knew me, as if all Dartmouth graduates knew all other Dartmouth graduates. Ferris told him, bless his memory, he'd read a flattering article about me years earlier in the "Dartmouth Alumni Magazine." Ken needed no further input. He told Ferris to set up some interviews, which he did, with senior Doubleday management, the final one with Ken who told me he had never hired an editor with no editing

By Way of Luck

experience. But, he said, I could be an exception.

The manager interviews, vice-presidents all, must have gone well, for some days later Ferris steered me to the bar at the Drake Hotel. For lunch, he said. There was no talk at all about a job. Just Dartmouth reminiscences, mostly his. We didn't leave until mid-afternoon, both of us in 80 proof disrepair, and tripped carefully back to Doubleday's offices at 575 Madison Avenue, a half block away. Stepping out of the elevator onto the 14th floor, we made our way to Ken's office. Ken was asleep on a ratted wool chaise, snoring lightly, evidence that he had lunched as had we. A short nap, his secretary, Ursula, told us. Most days, for a few minutes after lunch. She extended a hand. Welcome to Doubleday, she said. In an absurdly round-about way, my hiring was confirmed.

Doubleday's trade division — trade meaning general, as in non-text book, non-scientific book, and so on — was then publishing roughly 600 new fiction and non-fiction titles a year, a dominant force in publishing, among its best-selling authors: Leon Uris, Herman Wouk and Allen Drury. At a Monday morning editorial meeting, I sitting in as an invitee, Ken held up the Best Seller list from the previous day's New York Times Book Review. Doubleday held eight out of the twelve spots for fiction! Ken rejoiced.

I was determined to be part of Ken's editorial entourage.

Following my first assignment from Louise, a stint writing jacket copy in the promotion department, I landed in the slush pile, an office processing thousands of unsolicited inquiries a year, manuscripts largely, and a scattering of letters. Fearing claims of plagiarism, the company had an established policy: every inquiry was to be read, a review written, and an action taken, either forwarded to a senior editor with a request for an additional reading or returned with a rejection to the writer, all of it legal evidence should it ever be needed. That a manuscript rising from the slush pile might meet Doubleday's publishing requirements was rare, the frequency of it happening measured in years.

The office was shorthanded, I discovered, staffed by one junior editor, Dick Brickner, and by a disinterested woman who opened the mail, entered the name and address of the writer, the title of the submission and the date received on a 3x5 card, and when a review was completed, noted on the margin the action to be taken. Then she filed it, first stitching it together with a dressmaker's common pin!

On my first day in the slush pile, engulfed by teetering stacks of manuscripts, some boxed, some loose, some typed, and some hand written, I sat at a worn oak table in a corner of the room and bent to the task. Not until late morning, near lunch time, did I see that Dick was sitting in a wheel chair wedged into a kneehole desk and awkwardly plunking the keys of an IBM electric typewriter. I should have noticed his palsied greeting when I first arrived. But I didn't. I was self-absorbed and distracted, too, by the enormity of the task that lay ahead.

While an undergraduate at Middlebury College, Dick had been mangled in an automobile accident and was near death when rushed to a local hospital. He lost the use of his legs; his ability to use his arms was limited; his hands hung limply from his wrists. He wished he'd been killed he said. Still he figured out how to use the electric typewriter. With his elbow on the padded wheel chair he was confined to, he could raise his forearm like a construction crane, swing it out over the keyboard, and drop a finger on the letter he wanted to hit. He was a speedy finger plunker, I soon discovered, amazingly functional, accurate and a willing worker.

Yet, how could we make a dent in the slush pile? I suggested a game of sorts. Dick, I said, let's see how many manuscripts we can process in a day. If we can do fifty or more, that will leave us time to go out to lunch. For Dick, lunch out was a treat, most often he'd order in, finding someone to guide his chair difficult. He grabbed at the idea. The first day, as if in a duel, we processed 67 submissions and wrote as many reviews. The following day at noon I wheeled him up Madison Avenue and across 57th street to a nearby Schraft's. Our shared reward.

Thereafter, we worked wildly at our devil's task, often reading aloud and laughing at a phrase or a sentence too absurd to be ignored, and each day Schraft's *maître de* holding open a table for us.

By Way of Luck

We operated on a single, high-speed premise: when the first slice of bread tastes of mold, you don't have to eat the whole loaf.

Dick had a productive career, not as a reader and editor, but as a novelist, leaving Doubleday and finding a publisher for his first work, *The Broken Year*, a poignant story based on his accident, his by-line: Richard P. Brickner. Other work followed, *Bringing Down the House* the better known. I miss him. He died young. He was truly courageous.

Within two or three months I recognized that Doubleday's editorial department was less of a meritocracy than I might have hoped for. That the slush pile had rapidly dwindled was greeted as some sort of circus trick. Harvey Epstein, an associate editor, was dispatched to audit our work.

Harvey, his visage grim, strolled into our cramped quarters, in his mind a grand exposé already drafted. Didn't happen. Our secretary, newly invigorated, confirmed she could handle the accelerated effort. Harvey riffled through the reviews, finding them both thorough and competent, a surprise, he admitted. And was impressed to learn that I had actually forwarded a manuscript to a senior editor for further review. Nice work, Harvey said, and left the room. His report went to Ken McCormick and Executive Editor Lee Barker with a voluble vote of approval and a recommendation that I be permanently assigned to the slush pile. Instead of moving on to the next stop in my training program, as Louise had dictated, my feet were nailed to the floor beneath a heap of manuscripts.

Only then did I look around at the career paths of the company's editors. I shuddered. All editors — except a new hire from G.P. Putnam & Sons and a former literary agent from England — were Doubleday veterans each having an exceptional editorial history that included the books they had already published, those under contract to be published, and their prospects for the next publishable manuscript — were well-established. And likely to stay that way.

Yet I was a committed employee, largely because of the company's editor in chief, Ken McCormick, one of the more prolific book editors of the century, a vigorous man who sought championships, the best authors, the best non-fiction, the best fiction, the best memoir and the best editorial staff. He and Barker were a team.

Lee, or I should note, Lebaron, was a former book salesman, a traveler throughout the southern states. He occasionally surfaced a writer, William Faulkner as an example, and from a distance built himself a publishing list while operating from a 1930s Chevrolet and carrying a bag of loose change for roadside payphones. Lee was a natural born publisher both as a salesman and as an editor.

Each editorial meeting Ken began with a smile, a story and an account of a victory, in his telling wanting us to feel good about what we were doing, proud of what we had done, and imbuing us with an excitement we could feel from our toes on up.

Ken's early experience at Doubleday at first seemed hardly promising. He was hired as a clerk in 1930. By 1935 he had made his way to the slush pile. Yet by 1940 he had become editor-in-chief of the company, staying with Doubleday until 1987, his latter years as a publishing consultant. Few editors are remembered in the annals of book publishing. Ken is one of them. Could my career follow a similar course? Would I wish it to?

While pondering what next to do, were I to surface from the slush pile, during the weeks and months ahead several lucky options surfaced:

- Sam Vaughan, the senior editor to whom I had forwarded the slush pile manuscript, asked me to come by to discuss it, the teacher beckoning the student.
- Guru mathematician George Blagowidow, Ph.D., sold his Doubleday boss, Leonard Shatzkin, on adopting an exotic mathematical theory as a way of managing book distribution. For George's theory to work, the company would have to issue an additional 100 titles per year. Might Ken need to add an editor?
- Harvey Epstein resigned to take the job at Putnam's that had just been vacated, taking the lid off the slush pile and opening an editorial seat. Possibly for me?
- And Douglas Black, Doubleday's Chairman, President and CEO, invited me to lunch.

By Way of Luck

In no particular order that I can recall, let me start with the lunch, the chain of events bringing it about so unlikely.

Alastair MacBain had left the U.S. Fish and Wildlife Service to manage a preserve on both private and public lands in Tuxedo Park, New York, a vast land holding once part of the Harriman estate. I visited him there on a weekend, meeting his brother Gavin MacBain, then CFO of Bristol Myers and later the company's President and CEO, who introduced me to a New York City real estate developer and Columbia University trustee who, in turn, told Doug Black at a Trustee meeting that he had met one of his company's young stars. Mr. Black apparently accepted the offhand remark as a suggestion to meet me.

Douglas Black was an attorney, a Columbia graduate, with a universal intellect that easily spanned both book publishing and the law, most notably his public defense of free speech and his legal attacks on censorship. His appointment as president of Doubleday was a result of a gap in succession.

One corporate iteration after another, there had always been a Doubleday in charge of the company, whether it was Doubleday Doran or Doubleday Page, or just plain Doubleday, until 1946 when Nelson Doubleday, Sr. chose to retire. His successor, Nelson Doubleday Jr., was at the time 13 years old.

That a lawyer should head what was by any definition the country's largest general book publishing company led to widespread dismay among New York City publishers, as in, what has this business come to? A lawyer assuming a privilege usually reserved for literary folk? When I joined Doubleday in 1958, 12 years later, the carping could still be heard.

The decision by Nelson Doubleday to hire Black was bold. Black proved it a correct. Turning over the day-to-day business to a publishing professional, A. Milton Runyon, Black then devoted his time to larger projects, among them pushing Columbia University to appoint General Dwight D. Eisenhower as President of the School and in 1951 supporting his candidacy for the presidency, influencing Eisenhower's appointment of Richard Nixon as his running mate and co-founding the Freedom to Read Committee which publishers everywhere supported.

Not so coincidentally, Doubleday acquired the publishing rights to Eisenhower's memoirs, all four volumes.

To my eye, Black was a juggernaut, and I was to meet him, worrying at once how I was to conduct myself. Accompanied by Doubleday's business manager, Bob Banker, no doubt assigned by Ken to deflect comments I might make that could redound to the discredit of Ken's Trade Division, I met Mr. Black at Coté Basque, his usual lunch hangout.

Clad in a dark grey, faintly striped three-piece lawyerly suit, ruddy-cheeked and hefty, he was seated in a banquette and waving us to his table. Waiting for drinks, he complained about his morning's commutation from his Shelter Island summer home aboard an amphibian aircraft. A bumpy ride, he said.

After the usual introductory chit-chat and a slow sip from a generous scotch on the rocks, Black posed a somberly delivered, deliberate, off-putting question: "What do you think," he asked me, "of Richard Nixon?"

I might have shuddered, but I didn't. Banker gulped, his eyebrows twitched, sending semaphoric signals that read, Be Cautious.

This was 1959, the run-up year to the Nixon-Kennedy contest. Editors, I calculated, were democrats; the moguls who hired them republicans. I had so far remained apolitical, yet I sensed the reply Doug Black might be looking for.

"We're lucky to have him," I answered. Bob exhaled in relief. Mr. Black clinked my glass. I had passed the test. The rest of lunch was like happy hour.

Ken was thrilled with Bob's report, and told me so *con brio*, asking me to recount as best I could how the dialogue had gone. It would make good office gossip. I got a pat on the back as I left his office, accepting gladly his invitation to attend editorial meetings.

My meeting with Sam Vaughan I saw equally daunting. He had been Doubleday's sales director and in a rare move migrated to the

By Way of Luck

editorial department as a senior editor assigned to the Eisenhower project. In a single swoop he had provenance. On his desk in a windowed corner office sat the manuscript I had forwarded to him.

I agree this book needs further attention, he said, but I have no idea what to do with it. The book was titled *Outdoor Camping*.

Whether wittingly or not, Sam had opened a door for me.

I had been knocking on that door for many weeks, to learn how books were published and to be seen as a person of value. Late afternoons, a time when Dick Brickner and I had exhausted our energies for the day, I stopped by editors' offices, asking for work. Invariably, someone might suggest I read or comment on a manuscript just received from a contracted writer, or follow up with a copy editor on a book already in production, and so on. This led to the actual editing of books commissioned by editors with heavy workloads.

In one instance, Managing Editor Walter Bradbury handed me a contracted manuscript he truly didn't want to publish by a writer whose best work, *I Cover the Waterfront*, was far behind him. Read it, Bradbury said, and write the author a letter for my signature telling him why we can't publish it. Instead, over a weekend, I rewrote the book, adding momentum to paragraphs that languished, polishing the gems that lay in the garbage and rescuing what the author had wanted to say but no longer had the skill to say it. Walter was surprised, and a bit testy. Read it, I suggested. Walter published the book, the rejection letter forgotten.

I drifted in and out of departments, my own training program, finding senior managers willing to talk and teach. I asked questions. Sales men and sales managers, copy editors, a production manager, an art director and a promotion manager seemed eager to tell me what they did and how they went about doing it, walking through their departments and introducing me to people I hoped one day I'd be working with.

With Bob Banker's okay, I read through contract files, learning how royalties were structured, and how subsidiary rights might contribute to the evaluation of a book's fiscal promise, in fact, called on the Vice President for Subsidiary Rights, Joe Marks, a proper

British gent in Jermyn Street attire who had upset the industry's usual practice of limiting its rights sales to other publishing entities, a book club, as an example, or paperback publisher.

Joe licensed Doubleday's Hopalong Cassidy books to a toy company and to an incentives marketing company. Over the first four years of the license, the royalties Doubleday earned from Joe's ingenuity boosted the trade division's profits by more than half.

During a summer when my wife and daughters were spending time at my in-law's farm in Vermont, I worked occasional weekday evenings in the two Doubleday Fifth Avenue Book stores, open until midnight. I wanted to see how readers bought books. I wanted to learn how I might sell books.

On one late night occasion, not long before closing time, a richly appareled couple dropping in after theater asked whether the store had a biography of Fra Filippo Lippi, the medieval friar and revered religious artist. By coincidence, I had read that very afternoon at lunch in a fresh copy of Publisher's Weekly, the book industry's trade journal, a review of a soon-to-be released volume of Fra Filippo's life and his paintings. I told the couple of the book's price and publication date and said when it was available I could arrange to have a copy sent to their home.

Thank you, the man said declining my offer, but added, Very impressive, knowing so much about a relatively obscure figure. And the pub date, too, he said. I hadn't told him about Publisher's Weekly. He took my hand, shook it and handed me his card. He was the president of I. Magnin & Company, the San Francisco high-fashion department store.

He browsed the bookstore for a few minutes then asked whether I'd like to move to San Francisco and manage his book department.

I shook my head and said I was happy working for Doubleday, adding, Would you be interested in buying a Webster's Unabridged Dictionary for your children? I managed to sell him the dictionary's wooden bookstand as well.

Senior editors saw me as a novelty, for few of them concerned themselves with the details of publishing. Their job was to acquire

By Way of Luck

a manuscript, in progress or as a finished work, to negotiate and deliver a signed contract, and hand over a professionally edited manuscript to the "downstairs" people, copy editing, design, printing and sales, located on the floor below, along the way reviewing and correcting proofs. Harvey Epstein, just before leaving the company, was confounded by my interest in how a book might travel from manuscript to market. I was equally confounded by his disinterest.

Sam Vaughan was interested. The camping manuscript, I told him, referring to my review, was quite good, its content informative but lacking illustration. So, Sam, said, How do we publish it? I had already given some thought to his question. A bestselling gun and ammo catalog, *The Shooter's Bible*, I saw as a model. Let's kick off a Doubleday series of outdoor sports books, I suggested, beginning with *The Doubleday Outdoor Camper's Bible*, to be followed by bibles on Trout Fishing, Bass Fishing, Upland Game Hunting, Deer Hunting, Outdoor Cooking, Boating, Scuba Diving and so on, even jokingly suggesting The Varmint and Crow Hunter's Bible. Which Doubleday eventually included in the series and sold especially well in the South.

How I could assemble the books, I explained: in over-sized paperback format, some titles original, some out of print to be acquired and up-dated, and some derived from magazine articles and generally available photography files. There was a trove of illustrations, maps and charts in public domain, much of it material in the storage cabinets of the U.S. Fish and Wildlife Service and previously published in bulletin format for distribution in National Parks.

"You know this stuff, don't you?" Sam said. I did. I would build on my New Hampshire and Dartmouth experience and my involvement with the Air Force Conservation Program...and what I had so far learned about publishing. And I would manage the series all the way through from manuscript to finding space on retail book shelves.

At the next editorial meeting, Sam brought up the project, not for discussion but, surprisingly, for final approval. Let's give Jim the go-ahead, he said. I was temporarily numbed, expecting there would be some sort of open commentary among the editors, already fearing the doubts to be expressed and the questions to be answered. There were none.

Good idea, Jim, Ken said, approving the project. He then turned to the next item on the agenda.

I was out of the slush pile and out of Louise's training program, given a bathtub-sized office on editorial row and the services of a secretary two half days a week. (The secretary had taken dictation for years from comic poet Ogden Nash, her ears attuned to his humorously crafted syntax and giving the transcripts of my dictation an occasional odd twist.)

Editing, compiling, assigning writers for the titles in the Outdoor Bible series, and following them through marketing and sales went smoothly, and in no time at all we had published the first four titles. Sales for the first title, the *Camper's Bible*, soared. Reorders piled up quickly and it seemed everyone involved, writers and artists and the "downstairs" department heads, enjoyed their roles in putting the books together...some of it inspirational, the best example, the cover of the *Upland Game Hunters Bible*, featuring a color photograph of two hunters walking a dirt road, back to the camera, clad in red hunting shirts, with freshly taken turkeys slung over their shoulders — Alastair MacBain and Corey Ford.

The division's vice-president, John Sargent, a Doubleday in-law who was to succeed Doug Black as corporate CEO, offered his appreciation, telling me, We need more books like your Outdoor Bibles! He gave me a $5 raise, bumping me to $105 a week.

All at once pumped up and deflated, I left his office dismayed, my head clouded in disappointment. Making money in this job would be tough. Ken could offer me no solace. I got a bigger office and a full time secretary, Shelby Elliot.

Aside: with my family in Vermont during the summer I sometimes took the D train to Yankee Stadium to watch a night baseball game. I'd buy a 50¢ bleacher seat in center field where I could have a hot dog and a beer and watch Mickey Mantle play. Shelby noticed the ticket stubs on my desk. "You don't have to buy tickets to see the Yankees," she said.

By Way of Luck

"Oh?"

"My godfather, Uncle Dan, owns the Yankees."

Dan was Dan Topping who with co-owner Del Webb did indeed own the Yankees. Throughout much of the 1960 and 1961 seasons — two of the greatest years ever for Yankee fans — lucky me, I had complimentary access to the owners' box and, for the World Series, two seats behind the first base dugout. The day after a game, as a way of thanking Shelby, I put a flower on her desk. Onlookers suspected there was something going on between us. There was, but no one would have guessed it was just about baseball.

In the meantime, I had been building my own publishing list, drawing on Washington and Pentagon contacts, writers I had come to know and manuscripts assigned to me by Ken and executive editor Lee Barker. I also kept an eye on English language books published in Australia and Great Britain that might have relevance. My working list of military books included Mel Hunter's photo illustrated book on the Strategic Air Command; a report on the U.S. Ballistic Missile program; a narrative on the development of the Minuteman ICBM entitled *Ace in the Hole* written by Los Angeles KNBC's news anchor Roy Neal whom I'd struck up a friendship with at Cape Canaveral; and *Life* magazine's Don Schanche's account of Lt. Colonel Richard Simon's record balloon ascent, *Man High*.

Other projects emerged from my monitoring of NASA's space development program, an interest spawned by being in the Pentagon when Sputnik first orbited earth, the announcement shocking the U.S. Defense establishment. I had easy access to Cape Canaveral and was on hand for several early test launches.

On one occasion, following a successful down range test flight carrying Ham, a chimpanzee, Jules Bergman, ABC TV's National Science editor, and I flew to Miami and to ABC's local affiliate to cut a piece for ABC's evening news coverage of the launch and recovery. Arriving there, because of scarcely available cable time, there were scant minutes for Jules to prepare a script. He went on camera with one page plus notes while I wrote an additional page and several lead ins, then on my knees and out of sight handing Jules the pages and Jules reading them cold. Adding taped shots of Ham's flight, ABC did a seven-minute report that evening. Jules and I watched from a restaurant bar where we celebrated with deep dish juniper berry pies and charred steaks.

Jules was a licensed pilot, owning a Piper Tri-Pacer hangared at Teterboro Field in New Jersey. I flew with him one weekend while he practiced touch and go landings, asking for my advice on each approach but in truth wanting praise and a pat on the back from a fellow pilot. Ferris Mack was the editor of his two books *Anyone Can Fly* and *90 Seconds to Space, the story of the X-15.*

(A reader may wish to know more about Jules and other personalities I write about in this work. A reader can search on-line for further biographical information. My remarks are limited to my personal involvement with the people I write about, a personal history about me and about them that could not have been otherwise captured.)

I was learning my trade, but to be successful at it, I realized, an editor must have certainty for what he or she wishes to accomplish when working with a writer and a determination to invoke it, without wavering and with as little argument as possible. I do not believe certainty to be an acquired trait. I credit my mother for having it and passing it on to me. Learning to manage content, I learned from Corey Ford. Both served me well.

How I managed my work, I learned by myself, a couple of examples follow:

In his office, Ken McCormick introduced me to Edward Stephens, a Doyle, Dane, Bernbach copy writer and a once-published novelist, his book, *A Twist of Lemon*, an ad agency story. The reviews were indifferent; the sales fewer than 3000 copies bought mostly, I guessed, by agency people figuring the book as a *roman a clef*, seeking and perhaps identifying agency colleagues as fictional characters in scantily disguised roles. There was tension in the room, aggravated by a mid-afternoon sun that cast a harsh glare. Ken was noticeably uncomfortable. Ed held in his lap roughly 500 pages of

By Way of Luck

a yet-to-be-finished novel he expected Doubleday to publish. Ken respected Ed's talent — he wrote fresh, admirable prose — but was squeamish about taking on the risk of another Stephen's book. As it was written, he told Ed abruptly, Doubleday couldn't publish it. Ed moaned, literally. He hadn't expected a flat out rejection.

But, Ken went on, immediately sympathetic, suggesting that I give it a read. Ken had passed the buck. I saw it as a compliment.

Ed's new novel, *Blow Negative*, was based on the life of Admiral Hyman Rickover, the father of nuclear submarines. Ed had served aboard submarines and was sufficiently knowledgeable to make the book an authentic read. I took it back to my office, in disassembled pages.

Two weeks later, the three of us gathered again, Ken sitting in judgment, placidly waiting for the defense to begin. Ed at the edge of his chair. And I.

I'd labored over the manuscript and knew what to do with it. The novel doesn't start until page 172! I said.

Everything written up to then Ed had dragged throughout the story, unnecessary baggage, slowing it down and making mush of a pretty good tale. What are you suggesting? Ed asked, aghast.

Ken's eyes were questioning.

Throw out the first 171 pages, I said, trash the secondary characters and write a lead-in to page 172 that positions your hero and hints at the conflicts to come. I then briefly outlined how the novel could progress from there, much of it already written. Ken nodded what I took to be approval.

Ed stiffened, as if I had asked him to abandon his first born. He wavered a mournful waver, his head gradually lowering in acquiescence. I'll do it, he said, but how do you know, you know, to suggest this?

I ignored his question. I couldn't answer because I wasn't sure how. Manuscripts had a way of opening up to me and I could easily read where the writing had gone awry, and how to bring it back on course.

Blow Negative, newly rewritten, was published within a year and climbed rapidly up the *New York Times* best seller list. Paperback rights brought a hefty sum, screen rights were sold, and foreign language and translation rights added to the books earnings.

Ed and I were friends for years after. With what he'd made on *Blow Negative* he gave up his advertising job, married a winsome ballerina and became an instructor in creative writing at Northwestern University.

On another occasion, Senior editor Elliott Shriver put a manuscript on my desk, a novel, *The Private World of Cully Powers*. It's been turned down by every publisher in town, Elliott told me. But worth looking at. Maybe you can do something with it. The author, George Bluestone, had years before written a non-fiction book, *Novels into Film*, popularly received by film school and Hollywood aspirants, and was teaching writing at the University of Washington, a stopover position for him between stints at Harvard and Boston University.

Cully Powers was an inky-black comic novel, the protagonist a delusional army grunt whose fantasies push him into a succession of Edgar Allen Poe-like episodic horrors. In spite of its grimness, the story was smoothly written and flat out funny, yet uneasy to read, as uncomfortable as sitting bare-assed on broken glass.

I wanted the book to work and told Elliott how it could, unfortunately rambling my way through an explanation. The plot sits on a satiric undercurrent, I said, that runs throughout the novel, the realities of the tale gripping. For the story to succeed, reality has to be sustained. But many of the comic episodes, I went on, are pure slapstick — which is grossly exaggerated comedy — and totally unreal, creating a conflict that results in disbelief and breaking the connection between the narrative and the reader. The certainty thing kicking in, I proclaimed, It can be fixed.

Elliott shook his head. I'm not sure what you're talking about, he said, but if you think you can fix it, I recommend you do it. Ken understood my argument and agreed. I wrote George a 5000 word commentary with specific directions, some of them line-by-line examples of the edits I expected of him, effectively ridding the story

By Way of Luck

of the slapstick episodes and popping the deftly written comic scenes too subtle to be understood.

I concluded with an offer Ken suggested: If you follow Jim's directions, Doubleday will publish *Cully Powers*. We offered a modest advance.

George accepted the offer, his letter gracious, thanking me for my editorial insight, obviously from an experienced editor he wrote, and went to work on the rewrite. On publication day, a Friday, a *New York Times* reviewer, judiciously picking it out of the clutter of books scheduled for same day release, wrote a thoughtful critique of the novel, agush with praise.

"Most extraordinary," George wrote me.

The review contained, for me, a memorable line: Bluestone's comedy succeeds, the reviewer summed up, because *it never lapses into slapstick*.

Tah, dah!

The correspondence between me and George had been entirely by letter, how most publishers transacted business in 1960. We had not met, nor had we talked by phone. Some weeks after *Cully Powers* publication, Ken and I were on our way to Portland, Oregon, a Doubleday sales conference at the Mt. Hood Lodge our destination, to present our upcoming fall titles. I returned flying home by way of Seattle specifically to meet George and his wife Natalie. Coming down the airplane's gangway I spotted a couple at the gate, assuming it was they, and made my way toward them. They looked right past me as I approached. I walked up to them and said, I'm Jim Perkins.

Never had I seen more mouth-gaping looks. George and Natalie had expected his editor to be a publishing elder, perhaps somewhat stiff in his manner and scholarly in his appearance, he said, and possibly related to famed Scribner's editor Maxwell Perkins. I've got grad students older than you, George exclaimed at lunch, laughing away his expectation.

We talked about his next book. He never wrote it. He returned to Boston and took a faculty position at Boston University. I never saw or talked to him again.

Luckily — can I say this? — Ken and executive editor Lee Barker grew comfortable with me, letting me loose with the writers they considered part of their stable, all rare and interesting people:

Mary Astor. Lee inviting me to work with Oscar winning *(The Maltese Falcon)* actress and writer Mary Astor in the editing of her autobiographical novel, a tell-all of her long affair with Jack Barrymore, introducing me at a Saturday lunch at the Laurent. Exploited financially, romantically and artistically by family, lovers, agents and producers, she had nonetheless endured. Meeting her, I was physically shaken. She was a beckoning woman, ably projecting familiarity, her facial skin creamy soft, promising comfort and quickly stirring the affection of this young editor. I pointed out a constant anomaly in her writing, sentences without verbs and oddly truncated. She touched her forehead with the tip of a finger, a theatrical gesture of acceptance. Of course, she said, and promised to correct it. The novel never emerged, shards of it appearing in subsequent books.

Francis Parkinson Keyes. Lee handing me the autobiography of romance novelist Francis Parkinson Keyes, best known for *Dinner at Antoine's* set in her native Louisiana. Needs work, Lee said. Ms. Keyes was married to a former governor of New Hampshire and had a summer home there but a few miles from my hometown. She had little interest in talking to me, but responded to the critique I wrote, amending her manuscript without hesitation, and sending me a cordial note of thanks when her book entitled *Roses in December* went to press.

Irving Stone. Lee and I in his office awaiting the arrival of author Irving Stone, *The Agony and the Ecstasy* to be discussed, a foot high manuscript on his desk. Lee felt it overwritten, with too much attention to Michelangelo's painting and sculpturing techniques, sidebar information, Lee described it, suggesting I work with Stone to slim down the book. We argued. I thought the detail added to the novel's richness, the sidebars reinforcing the validity of Stone's research, which had been considerable. When Mr. Stone arrived, we had coffee — Lee might drink as many as a dozen cups a day — chatted about

By Way of Luck

nothing for a few minutes while Stone sat expectantly, Lee deciding what to say, eventually taking my suggestion and blurting, Irving, I wouldn't change a thing. Stone was the contrarian. He disagreed. The book is just too long, he said. With Stone's permission, I was assigned to shorten it.

Louis Nizer. Ken asking me whether Doubleday should advance famed attorney Louis Nizer $50,000 for his proposed book, *My Life in Court*. One chapter had been written. I had read it. A gripping narrative that would deal with his five most famous cases. The advance was cheap, I said. Ken agreed and asked that I work with him and Nizer on the manuscript. *My Life* sat atop the best seller lists for more than 20 weeks.

Edna Ferber. Ken coming into my office, irritably red-cheeked and puzzled. Edna Ferber just called, he said. She wants to know whether you're available to work with her on her next book. Ken had been Miss Ferber's most recent editor — she had been published by several other publishing houses — expecting he might now become her forever editor and Doubleday her forever publisher. How do you know her? His harsh question demanding. I had an explanation. Corey Ford had introduced us.

Years earlier, Corey had been sued by Miss Ferber, seeking legal damages for a kindless, possibly libelous, remark he'd made in *Vanity Fair*, a reference to her outsized head, having the appearance, he wrote, of a plains buffalo. Citing truth as his defense, should the suit proceed, Corey threatened to bring a live buffalo into the courtroom.

Corey was soon vexed by what he had done and apologized publicly, his *mea culpa* appearing in a John Crosby *Herald Tribune* column. Ferber and Ford kissed and made up and when Corey was in New York, he would sometimes call on her, penance for something he wished never to have done. I was with him on one of his brief visits.

No more than that.

Ken appeared mollified. He gave me her unlisted phone number.

Miss Ferber lived by herself in a street-side, nine-room apartment at 880 Park Avenue. I walked up the avenue for our first meeting. Like Corey, as a writer she was driven. She wrote short stories, she was a playwright, and she had so far written 24 historical novels, among them *So Big* (for which she was awarded a Pulitzer Prize), *Showboat, Cimarron,* and *Saratoga Trunk.* Yet to come, *Giant* and *Ice Palace.*

A small woman, no more than 4'10", she dressed as a grade school teacher might, plainly and with scant appeal, preferring to stand or walk about her writing room as we talked. She lectured me about writing, specifically her writing, referring callously to other women writers. Her one exception, Edith Hamilton, whose book, *The Greek Way,* she gave me as a gift, wrapped in decorative paper and tied with a ribbon.

I asked how she managed her research. To show me, she pulled open drawers of 3X5 file cards, one drawer for each of her published works, with one file drawer empty as if anticipating her next effort.

How much of your research do you use? I asked.

I don't know for sure, she said. After compiling it, I don't refer to it. What's important, sticks with me; what shows itself I then put into the book, every goddamn bit of it.

She paused. And when it's published, she emphasized, I get every goddamn penny I can get for it!

During the 30s and 40s Miss Ferber's accumulated annual income — from royalties and other rights — her secretary told me, made her one of the two highest paid professional women in the United States. The other: actress Barbara Stanwyck.

One Basket, Miss Ferber's third autobiography, was near completion. She didn't need an editor. Though she said she found my comments helpful. She'd call when she needed a break from work. Not more than eight blocks from where she lived, I was easy to reach. She once asked me to drive her to South Dakota. She wanted to see Mount Rushmore.

Ken and I accompanied her and famed attorney Morris Ernst, a co-founder of the American Civil Liberties Union, to a Commencement exercise at Adelphi College where she received an honorary

By Way of Luck

doctorate. She had given her original manuscripts, her files and her extensive library to the college. Ernst made sure she got a hefty tax deduction, as much as she could goddamn get.

Robert Graves. Louise Thomas came back into my life, briefly, inviting me to her home to meet England's poet laureate, a suave Fernando Llamas look-alike. My wife was shaken by the event, by Graves' posturing and his drunkenness, but mostly by John Sargent having cornered her, eliciting her life story and asking, she said later, too many questions. She was soured, by the company, by publishing and publishers and by seeing her husband as one of them.

W. Somerset Maugham. I had written in my senior year at Williston a "paper on a subject of your choosing," a requirement for graduation, my choice, a study of the work of W. Somerset Maugham, his novels, his plays and miscellaneous writings, *Of Human Bondage*, the best known novel, perhaps, of all he had written. Other prominent Maugham novels: *The Razor's Edge, Moon and Sixpence,* and *Cakes and Ale.* I read them all, and more. My study began in my sophomore year. I felt expert on Maugham, the School agreeing and citing me at graduation for my effort.

Ken called me to his office. It was a nothing special call, but as usual I hurried over. Ken sitting at his desk. Opposite him, a tea cup raised daintily to his lips, unmistakably sat W. Somerset Maugham. We talked about the mechanics of writing, a subject, he said, no one had ever asked him about, what paper he wrote on, what pencils and pens he used, where in his home he wrote, how he bundled his manuscripts for delivery to his British agent, when he broke for lunch, and so on. I could tell by his oddly approving smile, a barely noticeable rise at the corner of his right lip, that he was satisfied by or meeting. Or was it by my youth?

Bobby Jones. Doubleday had acquired the publishing rights to golf prodigy Bobby Jones' book, *Golf is My Game*, to be published as written, no editorial work needed. Ken asked that I make the presentation at our up-coming sales conference. What could I say about the book? It was about golf. I called Jones at his law firm in Atlanta, reaching him on my third try and asking him for a quote.

Tell your salesmen, Jones said, not to take the game seriously. It should be fun. That's the way I played it.

Considered one of the great athletes of his time, alongside Babe Ruth and Jack Dempsey, playing for fun I thought overly modest. From his book, I learned he was a practicing lawyer who played golf little more than three or four months of the year. Yet, as an amateur, he won 13 of the 31 major championships he entered, placing in the top ten 27 times. A record unmatched since.

When I made my presentation to the salesmen, Doug Black wandered into the meeting room to listen how I handled my duties.

Charles Van Doren. In the late 50s television quiz shows had become big business, attracting record audiences and creating its own stars, among them psychologist Joyce Brothers for her unflinching, quick answers on *$64,000 Question* and, on *Twenty-One*, Columbia University professor and author Charles Van Doren who, after obvious somber thought, seemed to whisk his answers out of the air. Building on her popularity, Brothers went on to a respectable career as a writer and frequent commentator on morning television. Van Doren's career was steeped in ignominy, revelations of cheating — his answers rehearsed. Chased by the tabloids and pushed out of Columbia, he soon vanished from the popular media, only to emerge some months later at Doubleday ensconced in a guest office adjoining mine. He had been given refuge by Columbia trustee Doug Black to write and to contemplate his future endeavors.

For weeks Van Doren came and went in self-imposed silence, as though by his stillness he might go unnoticed, to be invisible his wish. But that was not to be. One evening, working late, on some shallow pretext I cornered him in his office. Admitting to the distress he had suffered, he told me it was unending, one woman in particular following him around whenever he appeared in his Greenwich Village neighborhood and shouting at him, "I know who you are."

Eventually tiring of her tirades, he confronted her. Just who do you think I am? According to Van Doren, she replied, "You're Alger Hiss."

(Hiss, a one-time State Department official and involved in the

By Way of Luck

founding of the United Nations was accused in 1948 of being a Soviet spy and jailed in 1950 for committing perjury at his trial. The case, involving the House Un-American Activities Committee and Hiss's accuser, *Time* Magazine editor and correspondent, Whitaker Chambers, made first page, headline copy for endless months.)

Van Doren said he was confounded, and a little bit amused. "I assure you," he told the woman. "I am not Alger Hiss."

Apparently satisfied by his attention, the woman disappeared.

S. Ralph Harlow, Ph.D., Doctor of Divinity, an Ordained Minister and Professor of Religion. Professor Harlow preached once a year at Williston, just five miles away from Smith College where he taught, addressing an indifferent student body from a pulpit in a crowded, noisesome chapel, seeing and hearing him difficult. One year, he made an additional visit, a lecture on life in the hereafter and, when we passed on, what we might expect. He told stories of the inexplicable, for effect lowering his voice to a whisper, all of us leaning anxiously forward in our seats, absorbing his entertaining claims, of flickering lights, bells in the attic, paintings disappearing and reappearing, and of a talking horse used as a channel by someone from the "other side." It seemed great fun, until we recognized that Dr. Harlow was serious.

I recalled all this, and wrote Dr. Harlow, by now aging and near retirement. Had he considered writing a book? He had, and sent me a 30-page, hand-scribbled, barely decipherable manuscript. Undeterred, I hired Evan Hill, a free-lance writer living in a nearby Vermont village, to collaborate with Dr. Harlow on the writing of *A Life After Death*. By phone interview alone, I knew Evan could get the story told. He did, and with but a smattering of edit from me Doubleday published the book. It made nobody's best seller list, but it sold extraordinarily well by mail and as a club selection and was a constant seller for years in off-center specialty book shops alongside another Doubleday title, *The Power of Prayer on Plants*.

On publication day, Dr. Harlow came to New York by train to have a celebratory lunch with me. He had a confession to make, he said. The book was out, the publicity taking hold, signs of a reprinting already showing, what could Dr. Harlow possibly have to confess? I was worried, but about nothing I could think of.

I've never told anyone this, Dr. Harlow said, sitting at a restaurant table. Taking my hand, he started to cry. You're the only person I could trust to say this, he went on. I've needed to tell someone. After the birth of our only child, my wife moved into another bedroom. The familiarity we'd had since marriage abruptly disappeared. I've respected our vows, and for more than fifty years I've gone without any physical contact with her or with any other woman. Dr. Harlow stopped. The pain was in his eyes.

There, he said. And changed the subject, within minutes in a cab to Grand Central Station for the return trip home.

Senator Olin D. Johnston. An unusual assignment from Milton Runyon who handed me a still-born biography of South Carolina Senator Olin D. Johnston, Chairman of the Committee on Post Office and Civil Service and an early Southern populist who had defeated Strom Thurmond in a State primary election, the first for both, each vying for the Democratic Party's nomination for the U.S. Senate. The biography had been written by the pastor of Barker's Creek Baptist Church which Johnston had attended since boyhood; it was short on detail and long in its fawning accounts of the Senator's good works; and as it stood, lacking substance and wholly unpublishable.

Runyon's direction was clear. The biography had already been scheduled for publication, a scant six months away at a time when a year or more from approved manuscript to finished book was common. He handed me the manuscript. I don't want a postponement, he said. Then he went back to doing whatever he was doing when I first walked into his office, a sign that he was not to be challenged. By phone and by letter with the pastor and with newspaper accounts I accessed from the "morgue" at the *Herald Tribune*, I put together a plausible though short book, meeting Runyon's requirements and ordering a bottom basement printing of 1500 copies. As a thank you, the Senator invited me to Washington DC for lunch. We ate bean soup, a Senate dining room special. Senator Johnston was easy to like.

By Way of Luck

I tell this story because months after publication I discovered records that showed a print order of 30,000 copies with bulk orders of 4000 each shipped to Time, Inc., to Sears Roebuck, and to Montgomery Ward and lesser amounts to other publishers, all mail order retailers. Yet I couldn't find that the extra number of books had actually been printed. Milton had his ways, I concluded, and decided not to mess up my life by asking questions. The dots were there. I chose not to connect them.

My career at Doubleday was becoming uneven, for which I was most responsible, with an eye for what I wanted to do and ignoring how Ken's editorial group functioned, more the fertile organism and less the crafted, construction company working from blue prints. Good contacts, good ideas and creative intelligence are hard to come by, not easily managed and best left unconfined by structure. Immersed in building a list, keeping score of my successes and pushing for definition, I didn't see that.

With little more than two years of publishing experience, I went so far as to propose a reorganization of the trade book editorial department, suggesting changes that might make the company's output more efficient, and more profitable.

The idea of doing that came to me from a study of best sellers issued by *Publisher's Weekly*, a trade magazine, and spanning the most recent fifty years of the publishing industry. Poring over the statistics and matching them against Doubleday's own publishing output, the imbalance jumped at me. Bestselling novels, which Doubleday was truly good at sourcing, nevertheless come and go — Allen Drury's *Advise and Consent*, as an example — as did bestselling humor books such as Jean Kerr's *Please Don't Eat the Daisies*, and *Rally Round the Flags, Boys* by author/humorist Max Shulman, possibly known best for his fictional invention of Dobie Gillis. All published by Doubleday.

Yet the study clearly demonstrated that memoir, autobiography, biography and history were the solid building blocks of major book publishing houses, titles that could reach markets that more ephemeral trade books could not — schools and libraries, distribution in

English language countries and in translation throughout the world — their subjects more universal in content; and they could remain indefinitely on a publisher's back list.

Editors could seek out subjects for biographers and historians as Ken did with Supreme Court Associate Justice William O. Douglas for *Men to Match My Mountains*. But there was no incentive for them to do it. There was editorial diversity within the division — two editors scouted mystery novels; another editor, Dick Winslow, topical science books; two editors, cookbooks and gardening books; and two editors, Harold Kuebler and Ferris Mack who sourced how-to and sports books and other diverse non-fiction, collectively an eddy of books awhirl, their subjects and content nobly based on personal interest and quality of content with sparse attention to market opportunity.

The Doubleday trade editorial offices seemed more the literary salon, late morning arrivals, long lunches, early departures, brief cases packed for reading on the train home or for the walk up the avenue to a nearby rent controlled apartment, quiet conversation, humorous non-sequiturs, blank stares suggesting inner contemplation, brows importantly wrinkled, long exhales of disappointment and practice, practice, practice in the art of rejection and ignoring the reality of being members of a profit-making corporation and denying there might be a correlation between sales of the books they promoted and their take home pay, working for the art and not for the money. Among the editors, there were exceptions. I got along with them easily.

Sales reports were a novelty, except for those in Doubleday's accounting office where results were posted, by hand in large ledgers that went back more than half a century. Feedback to editors was limited to copies sold and given only when requested. Authors and/ or their agents were better off, receiving reports regularly every six months, with a check for royalties earned, less a reserve for returns.

Most editors resented receiving financial information unasked, seeing it as a management suggestion they take greater responsibility for their editorial decisions, and finding it offensive.

By Way of Luck

My suggestion, a memo offering a plan, went to Ken McCormick, who was surprised to receive it. He had not asked for it. Yet within minutes he was in my office, asking that I escort him to a meeting with John Sargent.

Ken commented not a whit on my memo.

Jim wants something to review with you, he told Sargent, and sat back in his chair, expecting what, I could not predict. Ken had an indifferent look. As I explained my proposal to John, I knew at that moment that my life at Doubleday was about to change. The certainty with which I had so far worked had been exceeded, I could tell. Would my luck prevail?

After the meeting, in imitation of Mary Astor's literal truncations, I had been asking myself, How no title, as editor, associate editor, or just associate? How no raise of significance? How no performance review? How no criticism of my work? How seen by my colleagues? As Ken's pet? Lee's lunch partner? How get exceptional assignments, while others struggled for theirs? Now Sargent reading my recommendation, telling Ken, will get back to you.

Ken calling. In my office, he said, a recurring command. Was I to be fired? John has passed on your memo to Milton Runyon, Ken said. Milton has read it and told John and me to proceed along the lines of your recommendations. I turned giddy. Milton and I have been talking, Ken continued. He thinks you deserve a promotion. The book club division needs a Managing Editor and Milton wants you to take the job. My giddiness ebbed. I sunk into my chair in semi-shock, everything blurring and breathing hard, and as from a distance, hearing Ken say, At twice your salary.

The Doubleday Book Clubs

Doubleday today is but one of many imprints of conglomerate publisher Bertelsmann SE, its headquarters located in Gutersloh, Germany. Once it was wholly American owned and an industry behemoth, its trade publishing division but a small part of it. The company's book club division, a mail order merchant of books and learning materials, was the amazon.com of its day, its sales volume easily matching catalog retailers Sears, Roebuck and Montgomery Ward.

The Division's flagship was the Literary Guild, a book club larger in scope than its competitor, Book-of-the-Month Club, and offering a wider ranging selection of titles.

Its volume leader was the Doubleday Dollar Book Club. Yes, reader, its books, hardcover, newly printed and bound, sold for a dollar, yet produced a gross profit of more than 40% a pop.

Twenty-five additional clubs and learning programs followed, among them the Mystery Guild, the History Book Club, the Know Your America Program, the Know Your Bible Program, Best in Books, the Audubon Nature Program, the Cookbook Guild, and so on, products that zeroed in on specific reading interests, targeted marketing before there was such a term in a pre-zip code era when most U.S. mail order marketers, buoyed by low postage rates, dumped mail into an abyss and crossed their fingers waiting for buyers' responses.

Privately held, Doubleday's book club revenues were not generally known, but in every home with a mailing address and a bookshelf, likely there was a book with a Doubleday imprint.

How the Book Club Division did it is an exercise in production and manufacturing efficiency:

For featured titles, it acquired mail order rights from other publishers, selections they were called, the club's contract including use of the publishers printing plates, smartly skipping the need and expense to set type and produce new plates.

For the printing and binding of the larger volume clubs, Dollar and the Guild, that were shipping 500,000 to 600,000 books a month, it built a manufacturing plant in a Virginia hayfield, with high speed rotary letterpresses utilizing rubber based plates — conversions from metal plates — and a bindery that had made the transition from sewn signatures to glued signatures, thereby eliminating hand stitching. Inexpensive stock, as rough as a paper towel and just as cheap, with rough cut edges and irregularly course, held low-grade inks unevenly and just barely acceptable. Costs were shaved to the

By Way of Luck

lowest fraction, in the aggregate allowing Doubleday to produce hardcover books as cheaply as paperbacks.

For the Dollar club, in 1961, the Virginia plant produced an average size, 5-1/2 by 8-1/2 hardcover book with jacket, its lowest cost as little as 10¢ copy. Add a carton, affixing a mailing label for 7¢ and put in the mail at 4th class rates for 4¢, the cost per copy sold made Milton Runyon smile.

For the programs, sold by subscription and shipped loosely, Doubleday out-sourced art and copy and bought manufacturing from a score of suppliers. It accrued additional savings by its ability to print and ship a specific title to an exact number of customers, with few if any returns. Its methods were in hard-ball contrast to the clubs which offered a choice of titles with purchase commitments of no more than, say, four purchases a year.

All promotional art and copy were produced internally in Garden City. The book club division's was A. Milton Runyon's fiefdom.

For me, how the clubs operated was an eye-opener, a precisely engineered, vertically integrated, tightly managed, turn-on-a-dime enterprise without equal and, except for the Literary Guild, without competition.

But I soon realized the Doubleday Book Club Division didn't need a Managing Editor. In an organization so precisely structured, where would I find a place to work? I had to create the job.

Ed Fitzgerald, hired just weeks earlier to replace retiring Book Club Editor-in-Chief, John Beecroft, would be my boss. Ed had no book publishing experience. He had been editor of *Sport*, a monthly magazine. He had written biographies of New York Yankees catcher Yogi Berra and Yankees radio announcer Mel Allen. He had given up trying to pin down erratic Yankee manager, Billy Martin, for still another biography.

How Ed had been deemed fit for the Book Club assignment, I couldn't have guessed, nor did I care to. For our first lunch together, Ed took me to Yankee Stadium and into the Yankee's locker room where, suited up for an afternoon game, I met the supermen of 1960s baseball, Mickey, Roger, Yogi, Bobby, Moose, Whitey, Tony,

Bob, Elston, Ryne, Ralph, Hank, Johnny and Clete. Ed Fitzgerald was greeted as family.

Ed's Doubleday job was to pick and develop selections for the clubs. My job was to manage the picking and developing, with a staff of eight, located on the Madison Avenue premises, in an open bay, with blank walls and flickering neon lighting. On hard seats, as I was, at the first desk in an end-to-end row of metal desks, sat my readers, all of them John Beecroft's hires, five men and three women, rarely looking up from their galleys and as a group troubled by my arrival and uneasy, their resentments obvious and chilling. My new work space was like a walk-in cooler.

I had one truly editorial task: producing *Best in Books*, a new issue released every other month, a bulked up 320 page tome, a compilation that invariably included one full length book, either fiction or non-fiction, one condensed novel, one poem or collection of pithy sayings and two to four excerpts from other books, as many as I needed to meet the 320 page requirement. With the input of my readers, I could assemble a new *Best in Books* in several days. The assembled pieces were forwarded to Garden City where the finished book emerged.

Ed sat in a separate office, himself reading and assessing readers' recommendations and clipping his finger nails, the sounds of his snip-snipping drifting through his open door and down editorial row noticeably irritating the readers.

What do? I imagined Mary Astor whispering.

I told Ed he needed privacy; he didn't need people looking in. He agreed, thanked me, and closed the door. The air in the open bay warmed.

My second task was to negotiate rights, either for the lease of plates or the acquisition of publishers' over stocks, or both. Simon and Schuster, as an example, had over printed or else under sold a bestselling novel, *The Man in the Gray Flannel Suit* by Sloan Wilson, and wanted to dump 8000 excess copies. I gave them 10¢ cents a copy for the inventory, a royalty of 5% for each book Doubleday sold, got the plates tossed in, and featured the book in an upcom-

By Way of Luck

ing Guild promotion where it eventually sold 40,000 copies more or less at $3.95 each. I wanted to think I knew what I was doing, but I didn't. Admittedly, I was making it up as I went along and only coincidentally pushing the right buttons.

My experience with the Outdoor Bibles told me I could manage the details of publishing inexpensively, and I did, angering publishers who had been getting better deals, they said, and complaining that Doubleday was throwing its weight around. They had but one other realizable option, the remainder dealers who paid even less and charged the publishers freight and handling costs. The late Tony Schulte, in both editorial and sales at Simon and Schuster, cursed me on the telephone.

At the bar at the Harvard Club, months later, I met author Sloan Wilson, introducing myself as the biggest buyer of *The Man...* He was perplexed; I explained my remark. He thanked me for the "found money" the deal had earned him, and signed for my drink.

I didn't consider what I was doing a publishing job. It was assistant brick layer's work, like wearing overalls, shouldering a hod, climbing a ladder, emptying it, and making the journey all over again. It was repetitive. I read good stuff and when I felt strongly about a potential selection, I could sometimes draw the professional readers together as a way of helping Ed's final decisions. But there was no fun in that. No satisfaction, nothing created from scratch, or from a proposal, or from bringing along a work in progress. Though learning the business side of the clubs had its rewards.

I began spending time at Garden City, Long Island, Doubleday's headquarters, observing and learning how the clubs and programs operated. Finding the promotions director an easy talk, I picked up on the fundamentals, later the nuances, and still later the practice of assembling disparate pieces into a whole. While there was joy in producing a book or mounting a program, for me, selling brought an even greater joy, for it confirmed the publishing decisions made by writers and editors years earlier. Nothing in the creative and production process really happens, I realized, until the sale is made.

A. Milton Runyon

Unless one knew Milton Runyon, intellectually quick, he could be seen as ordinary. He was bland and without wit, dressed in suits sizes too big and rumpled, shuffled rather than walked, kept his secretary close by in an office they shared, with the door ajar, to be knocked on and swung open only by a hoarsely delivered command. "Come," he'd say. He had none of the charisma expected of a leader.

The club division's accounting books were freely available to me, the arithmetic of what was bought, what was published, what was sold, what the results showed, title by title, in dollars and percentages, infinitely detailed, as if Scrooge himself were the overseer.

I made a bothersome discovery. The clubs, apart from books acquired from other publishers, created books internally as premiums for joining and as bonuses for staying as "members." Runyon had set up two former Doubleday editors, Mel Evans and George DeKay, in a company of their own, Mel Evans & Company, to package — a production term — premium and bonus books. Theirs was an effort Runyon had hired me to do.

Casual research revealed that royalties paid out for many of the premium and bonus books went to Milton Runyon and his secretary whose names usually appeared on title pages as Editors. Surprised, sure, yet there was nothing secretive about it, no phony names or closed corporation subbing for live people. Odd, yes. An incentive program approved by the board or by Milton's boss, Doug Black, probably. But somehow indiscreet. In no publishing house I knew of, did trade editors get to share in royalties unless, as authors of an original book they were, well, authors, not publishing executives. How was it that employees got as a reward what writers earned to get? I was troubled by what I had learned, a practice that vexed me, to the day I write this.

Seeing I was at loose ends editorially, and hearing Ed's hinting complaint that I might be circumventing his authority — an excuse contrived to bring in my replacement, a former *Sport Magazine* colleague — Milton had a plan for me.

By Way of Luck

He was pleased I had grasped the mail order business. Create new clubs, he suggested, work with Mel and George on new books. He gave me a separate office and secretary, Elizabeth Dempster, and a free hand.

I inserted myself into a project just getting underway, *The Cookbook Guild*, seeing it as a winner and taking a role in its management, working through the titles to be licensed, the promotional materials to be developed, the budgets to be spent, and the advertising to be bought, through an agency, as it turned out, headed by a former Doubleday ad manager. Runyon kept his chums close.

As with all new Doubleday mail order projects, a test was constructed, results analyzed and projections made, and the decisions decided before further action was taken. The test, magazine ads and mailings to known book buyers, women exclusively, as much as they could be identified in the Book Club's data base, was expected to enlist as many as 25,000 members, a minimum threshold for a roll-out.

Within the three months following mailings and ads, the promotional effort brought in nearly 250,000 members, ten times what had been sought, a rate of response no Doubleday club or program had ever come close to. To quote a Doubleday manager with an ear for excitement: "We gotta monster here!"

No one person sought credit. Everyone on the project had worked diligently. Everyone cheered the results. I was simply wowed by how quickly the market opened to us, with little speculation, without the need to maintain big inventories, and without the middlemen, wholesalers, retailers and remainder dealers, a pure from-our-home-to-your-home endeavor, no stores to be shopped, and satisfaction guaranteed, with all books available at discounts from publishers' retail pricing. Had a Yankee stadium vendor tossed me a hot dog for a dime, I could not have been more astonished.

Clouds were gathering. I didn't see them. One disastrous event turned the sky solid gray. Runyon had a project in his hip pocket, a Doubleday atlas, a compilation of existing materials. It would be a mainstay as an enrollment bonus. Manage it, he said, and gave me the details. Map maker Hammond World Atlas Corporation would supply the maps and handle the printing. *Holiday* magazine would supply previously published articles and photography, a stunning scrapbook of people and places shot the world over by *Holiday* cameramen. Mel Evans & Company would produce interstitial text, largely lead-ins and captions, construct the paste-ups and the layouts, select the photography to be included, and turn over the pieces to Hammond for printing. I was to bear the responsibility of making sure that everything came together.

Milton had given me a word of caution. No snakes, he said.

Huh?

Reviewing the photographic selection with George DeKay, I understood what Milton meant. George had chosen from the *Holiday* collection thirty stunning photographs, each to run full page, one of them of a snake, a Yellow Rat Snake. It was sunning itself on a slab of gray stone, its body a languid flow of esses, poisonous, yet its poise benign, girded by rings in colorations of rust and corn yellow, browns in varying blends of earthy soils and deep greens, its beauty elegant and memorable. It has a permanent place in my mind's eye.

"Kill it," I told George. He was not surprised. Milton had given him the same instruction he had given me. No snakes. Milton assumed, George told me, that snakes are feared, especially by women. A photograph of a snake in the Doubleday Atlas would result in a high level of returns, too many in Milton's calculus to take the risk.

George insisted it be kept in. The layouts are complete, he said. The snake has an entire page to itself, and there are no other photographs of comparable quality to choose from as a replacement. George was adamant. And nonsensical, I thought. I looked through *Holiday* tear sheets and pulled a photograph Slim Aarons had shot overlooking the harbor in Nice. I was familiar with it. Aarons told me he had waited a week for the right light to take the shot. George demurred. Artistically, he was right. Practically, it was of no consequence that he was. Use the Aaron shot, I instructed him.

George shipped the photographs and the final layouts to Hammond and from there to press for a first printing of 40,000 copies. I

By Way of Luck

had not signed off on the final assembly.

Milton received the first copy. His secretary called me, to come see the Atlas, she said. Runyon had it open on his desk, to the page featuring the Yellow Rat Snake.

The reason I'm not firing you, Runyon said, Hammond's eating the costs of the entire printing. They bound the wrong maps. He never looked up from the photograph. We'll go back to press, he said, at Hammond's cost, but with the right maps and without the goddamn snake. Now get back to work, he said emphatically, and get rid of the fucking snake.

There was nothing I could say. George and Mel were Runyon's former associates and longtime editorial contractors, and their work for him would continue. There was good history among them. Obediently, I sat with George and the layouts, saw the Yellow Rat Snake removed and the Aarons photograph substituted. The Atlas was reprinted and served for years as an attractive bonus for club readers. But in Runyon's eyes, I was no longer credible. I was angry, at myself, that I had not demanded a look at the final layouts, that George had betrayed me — and, by extension, Milton Runyon — and I was the luckless goat.

The Clubs were rapidly expanding. Runyon elevated a longtime senior employee, Jack Cassidy, as Division General Manager, assuming many of Milton's responsibilities as a way of absorbing some of his growing work load. Jack had been in charge of warehousing, shipping and handling, a "keep-your-eye-on-the-pennies" guy, rolled shirt sleeves, a haircut every other week roustabout who took shit from no one. He was my new boss.

Jack was buck-sergeant brass. He was not a teacher; he was a pusher. He assumed everyone understood their jobs. Employees learned from one another. His approvals were conveyed by a nod. Disapprovals, a pause and a frown, how he communicated, then he'd spin on a heel and walk firmly away.

But Jack was persistent, a disciplined second tier guy who'd learned to manage up, ingratiating himself with one boss after another, from the mail room to the senior-most position in Garden City. With his promotion, he now reported to Milton Runyon. From there, he had no farther to go.

Perhaps his experience managing hourly employees, laborers in a small Long Island town who needed their jobs and feared losing them, would continue to sustain him. But how would Jack handle a creative work force that now included artists and copy writers, admen and editors, and coming to work every day in a suit and tie? I was among the first to find out.

Jack approached me cautiously, asking questions, what I did, how I did it, nodding as we talked, with no evidence that he was managing down, his behavior that of one fraternity brother to another. I could not perceive from him how Runyon or Ed Fitzgerald might have positioned me, what evaluations of me they may have given Jack.

Less than a month later, following phone conversations I had with Jack Cassidy, the firing I expected might happen, did happen.

Jack and I had been talking about adding new clubs, like your Cook Book Guild, he said. A money maker. He knew I hadn't started it, but he credited me with "booting it home," his language. He was attempting to be friendly.

At lunch, at the Drake, a Friday afternoon, Jack said he wanted a club devoted to reading for men. He was pushing me into an alley.

What kind of reading? I asked.

You decide, he said.

I don't get it.

What's to get? Call it *Reading for Men*.

Deliberately, I pointed out that the clubs address specific reader interests, naming long running clubs *Mystery Guild* and *Garden Guild* as examples, though smaller were simpler to start and easier to stop if expected results weren't achieved, and doubly more profitable than giant, general interest clubs such as the Literary Guild and the Dollar Book Club. Men are half the population, I went on. That's not a specific audience. That's a statistic.

I offered an alternative. Let's take a look at what members of the

By Way of Luck

general clubs are buying, by subject. Possibly we can glean an idea or two for one or more new clubs.

Instead, Jack called for the check. You don't respect my ideas, he said, speaking in gruff tones and ending the conversation.

We left the Drake Hotel dining room and headed to our separate offices, I around the corner to 575 Madison Avenue just steps away and Jack by chauffeured car to Garden City. Shortly before 5 PM, Bob Barnes asked me to come to his office. Bob was the company's bench player, adept at several positions, that afternoon subbing for Louise Thomas who, he said, was unavailable.

Bob handed me an envelope. He was curt; there was no small talk. Two weeks, he said. Get your personal belongings together. He walked me to the elevator and told me not to come back. As the elevator doors closed he threw me a good luck salute.

Louise was waiting in the lobby, and for still another time that day I was in the Drake Hotel, at the bar, in my hand the drink I'd refused at lunch and having a consoling companion to talk to. What next to do? What next to tell my wife?

I had acquired skills. Skills unknown had surfaced. The certainty thing, going about my job stiffly resolute was a liability. Could I manage it? I'd find out.

I had a bridge to carry me to the next job, if I needed one. Joe Marks, among his many enterprises, ran a syndication. He'd buy serial rights from various publishers, topical books most often, have them broken up in short pieces and sell them to newspapers to run serially, usually in five or six consecutive weekdays in installments. I was already one of his serializers, a task I could do on a weekend and earn $200 to $500 an assignment. I found the work fairly easy. I could do it with scissors, a pot of paste and a red pencil.

The first installment would run 1200 words, then the next three or four installments 1000 words each, the final installment, no more than 800 words. History and biography took less time than, say, chronologies or memoirs, and novels the more interesting, one in particular, *Marnie*, a psycho thriller, I recall, eventually made into a movie. The plot was tight, the room given me to explain it confining.

To get it done, I combined three characters into one and wrote a fresh, pivotal line for another. The author, Winston Graham, wrote Joe a satisfied note.

Was I an editorial candidate for the Reader's Digest Condensed Book Club? Following an article accepted by the *Digest*, I had met founder and editor-in-chief DeWitt Wallace and several of his editors in their offices in Pleasantville, New York. Not an option. Digest editors were given little latitude. Mr. Wallace had a hand on every word, in every issue.

Something would turn up, Louise assured me.

My wife was equally sanguine, although she expressed it differently than had Louise. I was surprised you lasted that long, she said, with that bunch of butterflies.

We drank deep dish juniper berry pies and went to bed groggy.

Corey was distressed by the news. We'd kept our working relationship together, two books for Doubleday, *The Day Nothing Happened*, a spoof on all the Day...books, *The Day Lincoln Was Shot, Day of Infamy, The Day Pearl Harbor Was Bombed*, and so on. A comic compendium, cartoons and text, commissioned by IBM, The IBM Guide to Thinking we created together, and lending him my support on two books, *A Peculiar Service*, the story of George Washington's Spies, and *Come North With Me*, Norwegian Explorer Bernt Balchen's autobiographical accounting of his polar expeditions as chief pilot on Admiral Richard Byrd's historic flight over the North Pole, a first.

Corey wanted to help. I wanted his help. I missed the partnering, however imbalanced it was, the give and take, ideas and articles emerging from the old Underwood, the self-structured life and, except for an editor's Yes or No, independent of authority and moving toward destinations of our own design. But it was not to be. By now I was a father and a husband, with three daughters — Corey's god children — and a mortgaged house in Riverside, CT.

The following Monday morning, elevenish, Ken McCormick reached me at home. He gave me a number. Howard Cady has an

By Way of Luck

open spot for you, he said. He's expecting your call.

Howard Cady, once at Doubleday and once a competitor for Ken's editorial job, was the editor-in-chief of Holt, Rinehart and Winston's trade division and one of the more gifted editors in book publishing. He was a bird dog. He sniffed out best sellers where no one thought to look. He managed writers easily, his humor coaxing, and could smoothly suggest deep edits without stirring the mud.

I met Howard the following day at his Madison Avenue office.

4
Holt, Rinehart & Winston

Since its founding in 1866 by German immigrants, American publisher Holt, Rinehart and Winston has passed through so many iterations, mergers and reorganizations, expansions and contractions, its 20th century leadership in constant flow, that today it is merely an imprint of publishing giant MacMillan & Company, scarcely visible and of shrunken importance.

At the time I met Howard Cady, in 1962, Holt was a mainstream publisher of trade books, text books and magazines, *Field and Stream* its headliner. It was too big to be considered a boutique publisher, but it operated like one, offering a limited publishing list, with both promising new writers and authors renowned. It was owned then by Texas oil man Clint Murchison and managed by Holt's President, Alfred Edwards, who'd risen through the company's ranks, from bottom to top, a stern and uncompromising man. Murchison and Edwards, operating like partners, posed a hierarchy that would have scared away most editors. But not Howard Cady, a flinty Vermonter who had learned his trade the hard way, known for taking positions of certainty regardless of the professional risk. I saw him more as brother than as boss.

Howard walked me around the offices, a glass partitioned assemblage of modular cubicles with but two windows on Madison

By Way of Luck

Avenue. One in Howard's office and the other in Al Edward's. The building had been built by the Zeckendorf's, father and son, to be leased as show rooms, wall space a premium. Their idea had foundered, Howard explained, and windowless space went cheap.

First meetings usually start with introductory chit-chat, what's going on in your life, what brought you to New York, and such. But not with Howard. Uncapping coffee in paper cups, he said, Pick yourself an empty office, we'll pay you $750 a month and see how it goes, start when you want. Before I could respond, he took my hand and led me out of his office. Come on, he said, Al wants to say hello.

I had been remiss not to have remembered an earlier meeting with Edwards when visiting *Field and Stream*. Editor Hugh Grey had published my articles and my photographs. I was family. My hiring was a near shoo-in. The next morning I moved into my cubby.

Howard put a half dozen manuscripts on my desk, assuming I knew what to do with them. I'd be backing him up as I had Ken McCormick and Lee Barker and sourcing new projects.

Al Edwards, always in executive dress, crisply pressed and starched, looking more the banker than the publisher, gave me an assignment. Navy Captain Edward "Ned" Beach, author of a truly commendable novel, *Run Silent, Run Deep*, and a Rickover protégé, had just taken a nuclear powered submarine, the Triton, around the world submerged — staying that way throughout the entire voyage a way of publicly demonstrating the capabilities of the Navy's new breed of submarines. His article about the journey would soon be published by *National Geographic* magazine. Ned was working on expanding it into a book. Would I work with Beach? Al asked.

Of course, I said.

Recalling Ed Stephens' novel *Blow Negative*, I thought editing two general interest submarine books a record of sorts. With Beach, I was already half way home. He liked that I had served, my Pentagon tour impressing him and easing our working relationship. What shall we call the book, he asked. I suggested we use the *National Geographic* description: *The Voyage of the Triton*, with the sub-title, *Around the World Submerged*.

Of course, he said.

Thereafter, he delivered manuscript in chunks, accepted my edits, and seemed buoyed by our collaboration, telling Al Edwards I was a "good pick."

I fit in speedily at Holt, making my rounds with the various departments, and establishing a helpful, on the Q.T. relationship with a vice-president, head of sales for the trade division. Jack, his full name he told me never to reveal, had sales histories at his fingertips, the numbers a telling record of how the company had fared since he was hired. The increases were steady and, by title, showing where the strengths lay.

Later, the numbers would be a revelation of a different sort.

Howard was in and out of my office two, three, sometimes four times a day. He was feasting on me. Read this, write that, handing me a phone number, make the call, he's expecting to hear from you, damn this is fun, oh, and one other thing, ask Al for his dead file, meaning contracts with authors who'd accepted advances on royalties but had yet to deliver a manuscript, mistakes Howard was wont to say.

Al gave me the file, happily. It showed initiative, he said, and he liked that.

Leafing through the manila file folders, the mistakes were apparent but in the aggregate not critical nor unusual among publishers, each book by itself an investment, each contract a risk. One name burst upon me: Richard Tregaskis. He was a methodical chronicler of World War II, his experience solely in the Pacific theater, a war correspondent pictured in worn GI boots and wearing gear marked by a shredded shirt tail, finding his stories close to booming artillery and flying shrapnel, and author of *Guadalcanal Diary*, a #1 best-selling journal that told of the foot soldiers' war on the ground as sharply realistic as had Bob Scott's book, *God Is My Co-Pilot*, told the story of one pilot's war in the air. Why was Dick in the file, a no show with a $5000 advance?

Al Edwards gave me the OK to track him down.

Dick Tregaskis was embarrassed by my call. I was not. How can

By Way of Luck

I help you? I asked. He'd spent the advance, decided the book he and Holt had agreed to wasn't worth much more than a magazine article and, after a time, forgot about it. I'm out of ideas, he said.

I've got one for you, I said. How about a reprise? The Vietnam War was an everyday headline, the news heavily politicized, President Lyndon Johnson's positions shifting, General Westmoreland assessing the war's progress by body counts and Secretary of Defense Robert McNamara reciting his original postulates with lessening conviction. Reconstruct your former self, I told Dick. Go to Viet Nam and write a report the American people can believe: *Vietnam Diary* by Richard Tregaskis, author of *Guadalcanal Diary*.

He was silent. But for a moment. I could hear him thinking. Good thoughts, I hoped. The logistics are tough, he said. Getting there and back, plus two months in-country, at least, I haven't the dough to cover it. Besides, I'm not "the hop-skippity-jump" guy I used to be.

If we can fix all of that, I said, will you do the book?

Yes.

Start working out, I said. I'll get back to you.

Howard was the first to shake his head. You put a pretty big promise on the table. Can you do it? Even if you can, Al won't go for it. It's a risky deal. You sound like me when I was your age, his comment an off-handed offer of support. Let's talk to Al.

Al said, Absolutely not. By the time we get the book out, the war will be over.

I countered. Unacknowledged, we've been there three maybe five years. Acknowledged, a little more than two years. We'll be lucky if we're out of there in five years, plenty of time for Dick to write and publish the book, its popular acceptance perhaps contributing to the war's end. This was me, again, making it up as I went along, the certainty thing. Counting on luck.

What about costs?

We give Dick another $5000. And I'll put the touch on Pentagon friends. Perhaps they'll pick up the logistics.

Al shaking his head, a bit bewildered I thought, by what he saw as the complexity of it all. This was not a matter of reading a proposal or a manuscript and deciding whether or not to pursue and publish.

Howard nodding approval. His love of imaginative, high risk stuff compelling.

Find out first what the Pentagon can do, Al suggested. Then we can decide whether we've got a plan.

Howard now smiling, a first step, one foot in the door.

Careful, Jim, thinking how to phrase my rebuttal.

That may be a problem, I said finally. Think of what the Pentagon folks will have to do to evaluate my request. Manpower hours in the hundreds. How to handle transportation? What credentials will be required? Whose responsibility? Here in the United States, on the way, on the ground in Viet Nam? Tregaskis is a civilian. Is there State Department involvement? And so on.

Al, if my military contacts agree with the concept, we can't put them to all that work if, in the end, we tell them Holt and Tregaskis are not together on this. Al, is it the five thousand dollars?

It was a cruel challenge and I wished at once I could take it back.

For just one moment, the longtime Holt employee and executive had to stop thinking like a CEO and think, instead, like one of the kids on the block. He nodded an okay. Go ahead with it, he said, agreeing to something he patently didn't want to agree to, as if he were tossing one our way.

Summary: I called Jim Sunderman, by then a Lieutenant Colonel, still in the Public Information Office of the Secretary of the U.S. Air Force. We'd stayed in touch during my reserve assignments. Hearing from me was not unusual. With his support, Ferris Mack and I had published several excellent aviation books for Doubleday. He had replaced Major Tim Dunn. Jim understood the book business. He had facilitated the publication of over 50 books on Air Force subjects. He liked the idea. He had one reservation. Tregaskis is an Army guy. You're asking the Air Force to do the work, he said, while the Army will get the credit.

By Way of Luck

Stop thinking like a twerp, I said. Tregaskis will cover the war, not just a slice of it. What Sunderman said next surprised me. I'll put it together, all of it. Have Tregaskis call me, he said, and I'll take it from there. Jim's long time stint in the Pentagon had given him a deserved power base.

A year later, the Viet Nam war on-going, *Viet Nam Diary* by Richard Tregaskis was published by Holt and like *Guadalcanal*, it sped to the top of the *New York Times* non-fiction best seller list, Richard was that good.

Al Edwards, with Howard's prompting, asked me to be editor of J. Edgar Hoover's next book, *A Study of Communism*.

All along, since leaving the Pentagon, I had kept in touch with many of the people I'd met in Washington, some military, some Congressional, but mostly people in the press, journalists, writers and editors. The decade of the 60s was unfolding, revealing our country's ineptitudes and imbalances, Viet Nam forcing social divides, an uncommon mixture of WW II veterans and baby boomers in common discontent, evidence of cataclysmic change everywhere in the newspapers and news magazines, *Time, Newsweek, The Saturday Evening Post, Look, Life, The Washington Post, The New York Times* and most major city newspapers picking up the beat and raising questions, about ethics, about solidarity, about responsibility, and the biggest question of all, about our role as a country, with a drumbeat we had never before experienced, television, news instantly reported, words and pictures instantly produced and bringing reality to wherever we lived. For the first time in our nation's history, we had nowhere to hide.

Don Schanche called me from *Life* magazine's K Street office. He was driving to New York and wanted to meet. Don had written the *Life* article on Lt. Colonel David Simons' 1957 record balloon ascent to 109,000 feet, 19 miles above Albuquerque, New Mexico. Together, editor and writer, with Don's notes we produced an expanded version for a book, *Man High*. Doubleday published it in 1961. Now, a year later, Don had another story he wanted to discuss.

Don Schanche was a writer and reporter, a journalist. He had covered the Korean conflict for United Press, a credentialed war correspondent. The story he was about to tell me was big, he said.

Captain Francis Gary Powers, pilot of a U-2 "spy" plane, was shot down and captured by the Russians almost two years earlier. The incident led to the cancellation of President Eisenhower's much anticipated meeting with Nikita Khrushchev. Powers was about to be released. His story would attract international attention. Don felt we could use our Washington contacts to engineer a meeting with Powers and judge best how to publish his story. Don and *Life* would have the magazine rights and write the articles. Holt would get the book publishing rights and I would edit and produce the book.

Between Time, Inc., and Holt we thought we could find sufficient support to make a serious, substantial offer for the publishing rights. But newspaper reports on Powers were suggesting he was at fault for having been shot down and captured. Some writers even ventured that his crash was deliberate, that he had been paid by the Russians to defect. Others charged that he should have swallowed a poison pill, non-existent it turned out, to save the United States from embarrassment.

I laid out the proposition to Howard and Al. There was no hesitation on their part. If it was good enough for *Life*, it was good enough for Holt. But the up-front number had to be agreed. Reluctantly, and only after several tense meetings, both *Life* and Holt gave us a reasonable budget.

We got an OK from the CIA to meet with Powers. Don would handle the initial interview. He was an experienced interviewer. Understandably, going one-on-one would make it easier to gain Powers' confidence. Don's two-hour session with Powers was very emotional, he said, and very revealing. Gary was not a complicated man. He was an airplane driver. He did exactly what he was supposed to do. He was misled into believing that the Russians were incapable of downing him from high altitude. Unarmed, he was attacked by Mig-16s, his plane critically damaged. He had activated a self-destruct

By Way of Luck

mechanism while still airborne, as he had been instructed to do, but it had malfunctioned. Had it not, he and the U-2 would have been blown up together. He survived a crash landing and nearly two years of intensive interrogation. He was glad to be back home. The detail of his narrative was compelling. He was authentic.

Joining me in the hotel lobby where the interview took place, Don reported, "Powers is a fucking hero."

We may have learned more that day from Gary and his doomed flight than the CIA had from its investigation. Chagrinned, possibly, or just everyday bureaucratic, the CIA embargoed the yet-to-be-told story, shutting us out. Years passed. Don and I were long gone from *Life* and Holt when the embargo was lifted and Gary was given permission to talk about his experience. By then the story's value had faded. A few publishers were willing to pick it up, but Gary, characteristically honest, said no. He had told his story to *Life* and Holt and although there had never been a signed contract, it was still theirs to publish. Bits and pieces eventually came out, a book appeared with Gary as a co-author, but he was never fairly treated.

Don's biggest assignment was the series on the Mercury Astronauts he wrote for *Life*, some episodes under his by-line, others under the by-lines of the astronauts themselves or their wives. Cover after cover, week after week, with staff support, Don did the research and ran the interviews. The articles he wrote alone. Still not in his fifties, Don was aged by it. I could see the lines deepening in his face.

According to Holt's corporate roster there was a vice-president in charge of the trade publishing division, sandwiched between Howard Cady and Al Edwards: Bill Buckley. The son of a notable New Jersey printer, he grew up a printing salesman, in time migrating to publishing and to Holt and instructed by Al to develop "important relationships." Bill dressed like Al, slicked his hair as Al did and could be seen more often at the best local restaurants or one of his clubs than in his office. He lived at 400 Park Avenue, a chic address from which he could walk to work. He was deft at recalling names and faces. Months later, Bill and I would be a team, but not at Holt.

The J. Edgar Hoover project was a befuddlement. Al said here was no contract; there was a handshake agreement. I couldn't see the manuscript. It was in the hands of a book designer. Young men dressed commonly in dark, off the rack suits, white shirts and black ties, from a distant office on a lower floor, came and went, protecting a large black briefcase as they passed, avatars on a spiritual mission.

Hoover's book was listed on the production schedule, my name next to it as editor. The initial print order was in bold type: 500,000 copies. The publication date but six weeks away.

What's going on? I sought out Jack the sales manager. Behind closed doors and drawn shades, his voice a whisper, he had a suspicion. I put in a print order of 25,000 copies, he said, pretty big. There's no way we can move a half million copies. We'd swamp every bookstore and department store in the country. I don't think the country has an appetite for another Hoover book — there had been four of them so far — we'll be overwhelmed by returns. Lowering his voice still further, he said, You understand what I'm saying?

Recalling my experience with Senator Johnston's autobiography, I told Jack I understood. He was suggesting what I had anticipated, that money from big supporters, like Murchison, were flowing to Hoover conveniently laundered as royalties from non-existent books.

Jack was expectant. Well? he said.

So? I answered. I had already decided to be not interested, his speculation too wild to be true.

Yet during the 90s and after, I was reminded of Jack's story by news reports of celebrity politicians whose books had first printings of two million copies, and more. Even in our enlarged economy, I had to ask myself, where did all those copies go?

Schanche was calling again. He had left Washington and left his job at *Life*. He had joined *The Saturday Evening Post* in New York. I want you to come work for me, he said.

I was a *Post* loyalist. The checks I'd received for two articles covered my college tuition for my senior year. At Dartmouth's Baker

By Way of Luck

Library I had spent countless hours in a cubicle high in the stacks reading its uninterrupted collection of back *Post* issues. I knew its fiction. I knew its writers, its photographers, its cartoonists and cover artists.

On leaving the Pentagon, Ben Hibbs, the magazine's long time editor, had offered me a job in the Washington office at $10,000 a year. His son Steve and I had become friends, first at Dartmouth and later when I'd gotten him an assignment at Cape Canaveral in the USAF PIO office there, reporting to Lt. Colonel "Shorty" Powers, the voice of the Mercury astronauts.

Ben's editors were supportive; I knew most of them, old school gentlemen. The magazine's history dated from Benjamin Franklin. It was a venerable institution and by my writings I had become part of it.

A sad story was developing. Television was overtaking general interest magazines as a primary advertising medium. Attempts at retaining magazine advertisers were failing; ad pages were shrinking. The *Post* was particularly vulnerable. Owning forests and paper mills in Maine and Canada, giant presses in South Philadelphia and running its own trucks and railroad cars to distribute its magazines, Curtis Publishing, the *Post's* owner, was totally and vertically integrated. A drop in a single advertising page could be painfully felt all the way from an editor at Sixth and Walnut in Philadelphia to a forester harvesting pine in the far off northern woodlands of Quebec. Like a house of cards, its collapse seemed inevitable.

Don Schanche and *Life* magazine associate, Clay Blair, Jr., whom I'd worked with in Washington, were planning the rescue of Curtis Publishing and the *Post*. With their tour at *Life* magazine behind them, they had found fresh capital from Perfect Film, Inc., a venture capital firm, and its owner, Marty Ackerman, to sustain them. Robert Sherrod, a historian and *Life* alumnus, would be Editor-in-Chief; Clay would be Editorial Director; and Don, Executive Editor. They had each put down payments on new homes, Don in Mamaroneck and Clay in Greenwich, told to me as a way of making their personal commitments obvious.

Meeting them in a suite at New York's Berkshire Hotel, they asked me to join them. Curtis's entire editorial staff would be located in New York, the *Post, Ladies Home Journal, Jack and Jill, American Home,* and *Holiday.* I would be the *Post's* Fiction and Book Editor, replacing two editors in Philadelphia who had angrily rejected the offer to make the move. I knew them both. The transition would be uncomfortable. Negotiations for space at 666 Fifth Avenue were already underway. Until then, temporary space would be available a few blocks south. They put an acceptable offer on the table.

I was torn.

In but a few months I had become valuable at Holt. But it was not a place to stay, as comfortable as it was, yet knowing I would in time be dulled by it. The *Post* job, with the tumult to come, a publishing company in upheaval, and at age 29 my central involvement in it attractive, I could not say no.

Howard understood. Al gave me my final pay check. Grateful for the work I'd done, he said, with an added bonus, a nice touch.

Was a move wise? I was not fearful of the risk, to be part of the rubble should Curtis collapse, nor chary about leaving books for magazines. Nor about the work. But what would it tell me about me, the youngster in the front row of his grandfather's theater in St. Johnsbury, Vermont, still wondering, twenty years later, when would he emerge from dark and into light?

I came from competent and industrious families, bending willingly to the labor of their lives, the farms they had run, the theaters they had built, the restaurants they'd owned and managed, rarely if ever seeking help or borrowing from others, never afraid except for the welfare of one another, aunts and uncles, cousins and siblings, their heritage the foothills of Macedonia's Pindus Mountains, from war ravaged small towns, Vovousa and Samarina, émigrés fleeing from the burning and the shooting, the looting and the raping, and finding in America the freedom to be themselves, and the safety. I was the child of many mothers and fathers, born American and lucky.

I was baptized in a Greek Orthodox Church. In Thessalonika

By Way of Luck

I had worshipped at the tomb of St. James, my namesake. I spoke our ancient language. I was godfather to children of my relatives, picnicked in summers with families from my parents' hometowns in Greece, to this day still seeing and talking to my cousin, Rita Zoukee Mehos, now in her eighties, my name for her, Tula, her name for me, Jimma. When we are together we speak with hugs, we suffer the warmth.

My name is an Anglicized version of Pisperikos, my father's surname, changed by a judge when he was naturalized in 1925. My mother's surname, Tegu, was left untouched. So who am I, Jim Perkins?

Prepped for five years at Williston Academy, schooled by Dartmouth College, tutored by a skilled and open-hearted writer, Corey Ford, thrust into the highest levels of the United States Air Force, and an editor at two renowned publishing companies, where do I go from here? Are there echelons to surmount, discoveries to be made, conquests to seek?

I decided while assessing the virtues of becoming a magazine editor that I serve myself best as a mechanic for hire, my tools a notebook, a typewriter, a keyboard, and like my forebears, never afraid, never expecting help from others, and never in doubt, the certainty thing, and like Corey, comfortable in my own structure, a good decision I thought then in 1962 and with one exception — which I write about later — I have stuck with it since.

I accepted the offer from Don and Clay.

5

Ben Franklin's Disappearing Legacy

The expansive lobby of Curtis's Philadelphia headquarters at Sixth and Walnut featured a fresco designed by neo-classical artist Maxfield Parrish and executed by Tiffany. Facing the entrance and mounted at the farthest end of a rotunda-like space, it spanned an area 50 feet across and 28 feet high. It framed a modest reception desk and seating area; for visitors it was an ornamental fantasy that spoke of beauty and serenity.

Saturday Evening Post covers sported Norman Rockwell's endearing and memorable paintings, each a romantic depiction of family and home, of heroic, small town people, and of an idealized life in a wonderland called America. He had become America's artist soon approaching when soon no magazine would buy his work.

By the 1960s, the company like its art was of a time long ago passed and clinging to an exaggeration of its idyllic self. Its relevance shrunk, its fortunes waned, its trucks, its railroad cars and its paper mills idling, and its editors functioning more like curators than the creative intellects they were expected to be.

Worse, in one desperate move, when inevitability could no longer be ignored, the company borrowed heavily to replace its printing presses with new presses that within eighteen months, because of changes in printing technology, fell into obsolescence.

By Way of Luck

Curtis had ignored opportunity, whether by acquisition, by divestiture or by internal growth. It had, in fact, rejected a proposition from ABC, the American Broadcasting Company, to acquire a majority stake in its new network. ABC was taking on competitors CBS and NBC and needed the visibility the *Post* could give it. Leonard Goldenson, ABC's founder, was willing to share control. The cost of the merger was but a few pieces of paper. There was but one brief meeting.

The investors at Perfect Film had been promised a turn around, and they pressed for action. The burden fell on two men: Joe Culligan, formerly president of the NBC Radio Network and an acknowledged advertising sales genius, and Clay Blair, Jr., a famed magazine writer and editor who had swiftly become a stalwart in Henry Luce's *Time* magazine empire.

Blair was a bull of a man with renegade zeal, and bullish, with a keen sense of story, of what might turn good narrative into great narrative. He was most celebrated among his colleagues for having rescued the career of the brashly outspoken, spit-in-your-face and about-to-be-fired Admiral Hyman Rickover, the irascible engineer in charge of developing the first atomic-powered submarines.

Congressmen and fellow officers had tired of Rickover's abusiveness toward Armed Forces Committee members, his unmet promises and the excuses that went with them. They wanted him retired, fired or both.

(Still another brush for me with Admiral Rickover and the nuclear submarine story: First Ed Stephens, then Ned Beach, now Clay Blair, Jr., and still later with the account of the U.S.S. Nautilus, my narrative is not to be interpreted as a special interest. It was mere coincidence.)

Clay Blair, Jr.

A former naval officer, having served aboard the submarine Guardfish during World War II, and a staunch Rickover advocate, Clay sought the personal approval of Henry Luce, the magazine's co-founder and Editor-in-Chief, to write a *Time* cover story supporting Rickover. Clay was prepared for the meeting with Luce. He told me he had already written a draft of the story. Using it as he would notes, he made a forceful, factual argument in support of Rickover and his atomic-powered project. Convinced, and without seeking other counsel, Luce gave Clay the green light.

The cover story was featured in *Time's* very next issue. Henry Luce and his weekly magazine, more so than big city daily newspapers, were arguably the country's principal movers and shakers of national news, influential and with political clout. Rickover's detractors on the Hill and at the Pentagon backed off. Rickover had survived his critics.

Rickover, however, wasn't about to give up his caustic ways. He insisted on a final snub. As earlier reported, he ordered Navy Captain Edward "Ned" Beach, one of his closest officers, to take the U.S.S. Triton around the world as a public demonstration of an atomic powered submarine's capabilities. He needed no authority but his own to OK what was clearly a stunt.

Staying close to Rickover, Blair learned of still another underwater spectacle. The newest long-distance Polaris class submarine, the Nautilus, commanded by Captain William Anderson, was already underway, its mission, by way of the Bering Straits and under the ice cap, to surface at the geographic North Pole.

Blair flew to Scotland where the Nautilus was to dock upon its return and met with Anderson. Together, in ten days, virtually nonstop, building on the ship's log, they wrote a book length account of the trip, a journalistic feat unquestionably as prodigious as the voyage itself.

Ben Hibbs, the longtime *Post* editor, told me what happened next. His words here as best recalled: Clay flew back to Philadelphia on an overnight flight, exhausted, came into my office, put the manuscript on my desk, plopped into a leather chair and while talking the story, fell asleep. It was nearly comical. Blair was awakened by his own snoring. He'd go on talking, fall asleep, snore, wake up, talk and again fall asleep. And on it went until Clay grew deaf to his own snores.

By Way of Luck

While Hibbs' staffers were editing a shortened version book for the next issue of the *Post*, Blair spent what remained of the day snoring in the leather chair in Ben's office.

My admiration for Clay began when he was still with *Life* and I was serving in the Pentagon. We were thrown together in 1957 in what was for me a project and for him a story. A U.S. Air Force single engine T-33 jet trainer, flown by Lt. David Steeves, on a nighttime ferrying flight to an Air Force maintenance depot, had disappeared over the wild and heavily forested terrain of the Sierra Nevada Mountains in northern California. Fifty-four days later, after search parties, airborne and on foot, had given up finding him or any sign of wreckage, miraculously Lt. Steeves, unaided, bearded, and surprisingly fit, walked onto a highway, hailed a passing automobile and got a lift into the nearest town.

What had happened? Steeves' claimed there'd been an explosion in the cockpit. His instruments had shorted. In the dark, disoriented, with no idea how long he could stay airborne and over a thinly populated area with few towns in range of his out-of-control aircraft, he made the decision to bail out.

Except for the beard, he appeared barely distressed, said the good Samaritan who'd picked up Steeves, as though he had just tired of a long walk and thumbed the ride. His story had an odor. Assumptions surfaced, including one that Steeves had faked the crash, that he had delivered the T-33 to Mexican buyers for resale to Fidel Castro, and returned secretly to the Sierras as an end piece to his plot. Far-fetched? Yes. Likely? Who could tell?

Steeves was summoned to the Pentagon; there, facts had to be ascertained. Clay and *Life* wanted Steeves' story as well. No one was buying it; yet no one could disprove it, admissions by Steeves adding to the doubt. He was in debt. He had a failing marriage. He drank. And he gambled. In the aggregate, defining someone in desperation and needing money.

I was assigned to handle Steeves throughout his stay in Washington, including through the interviews by military staffers and by Clay Blair, Jr.

Unable to disprove Steeves' accounting, the Air Force made a muddled decision: Steeves was transferred to a non-flying job and eventually released by the Air Force.

I felt he should have been assigned to Stead Air Force Base, home of the Air Force's survival school located, coincidentally, in the Sierras. His merit as a survivor would be proven there, or not.

Clay was conflicted. A champion of rugged individualism, once aligning himself with deep sea treasure divers operating in treacherous waters, he felt Steeves capable of surviving a parachute drop into the wilderness and making it to safety. But he wasn't sufficiently convinced by Steeves' story to take it to his editors. Finally, he gave up on it, a hard decision for he wanted desperately to believe Steeves and to write what he saw as the ultimate story of man versus nature.

Joe Culligan

Joe Culligan was of a different stripe. He'd been severely wounded and lost an eye during World War II at Bastogne, during the Battle of the Bulge. A handsome man, when he donned a black patch to cover the emptiness and the scars, glamour swept over him. He dressed simply, dark suit, white shirt, plain tie, his looks compelling. His polished appearance was mimicked in ads by shirt-maker Van Heusen. The patch sold a lot of shirts. Whether Joe could manage a complex company in distress was to be proven.

Joe had been President of the NBC radio network — a subsidiary of RCA, some same-generation readers may recall. He was a salesman who sold advertising, a lot of it, anecdotal evidence investors concluded, that he was the right guy for the Curtis turn around. Bob McNeal, the longtime president of Curtis resigned, and Joe took over.

Joe's first move was destructive. He recruited three highly placed RCA executives — one a woman named Gloria whose hire, quite possibly, made her one of the earliest, high ranking women executives of a publicly held corporation — and put them in charge of the

By Way of Luck

company's operations hub in Philadelphia. Joe set up his office in the New York City editorial quarters.

Until the not-very-far-off off day of Curtis's eventual dissolution, the polarity crippled the company, contradictory decisions the norm, shouting telephone conversations, heated and loudly vulgar, tearing at the employees and shrinking morale to a bottomless low.

For those of us in New York, Joe was the good guy. For those in Philadelphia, Joe was the bad guy. The editors sided with Joe the good guy. But the Philadelphia bad guys held all the assets and they were smarter at what they were doing.

Clay's mostly new staff was comprised of magazine publishing's biggest names: foremost, Robert Sherrod, from *Life*, the new Editor-in-Chief and Bill Emerson, from *Newsweek*, where he'd been Managing Editor. Otto Friedrich from *Time*; Gerald Astor from *Sports Illustrated*; David Brown from *The New Yorker*; and Don Gold from *Playboy*. Clay's new editorial entourage, largely from very visible weeklies and with big, promotable reputations, had a common flaw unnoticed: he'd put together a crowd of Type A personalities, me included.

I avoided the on-going politics and the gossip that went with it. I settled into my office in hurry-up mode. I wanted a quick out-of-the-box win, an editorial scoop. The *Post* needed it. Also, I wanted my magazine colleagues to know, being a book guy, where a book editor fit into the mix.

During my time at Holt, I gave up scouring titles scheduled for publication as I had at the Literary Guild, assessing possible club selections. I called Ed Fitzgerald, looking for help. What's hot? I asked. *The Sand Pebbles* by Richard McKenna, he said. We just lost book club rights in a bidding war with Book-of-the-Month. We ran out of money before they did. Movie rights are in negotiation, he told me.

Accepting Ed's judgment, I sought exclusive magazine serial rights. McKenna's agent had yet to consider serialization. He sent me galleys. Ed was right. Hot. *Sand Pebbles* was a beautifully crafted first novel of romance and adventure, its hero a navy seaman, in China, aboard a U.S. gunboat likened to the Panay, on the Yangtze River during the Opium Wars, colorfully told, for readers, a page turner, for movie goers, it would fill seats.

I broke into a meeting in Bob Sherrod's office, excused myself for the interruption, and got his approval to buy the rights I wanted.

Up to $10,000, Bob said. No more. It was the biggest single editorial expenditure he had ever personally authorized. We'd publish in two parts, of 10,000 and 8,000 words. *Sand Pebbles* would dominate two consecutive issues. We got the rights. For $10,000. A few days after we had a signed contact, the movie rights went for $300,000, a price that made our acquisition look good, for our board, our investors and for our advertisers.

Two copy editors who'd moved to New York took on the task of condensing the 250,000 word novel. I was appalled by their work. They had treated it as they might an old *Post* pot boiler, shrinking to almost nothing the drama, the conflicts, the liaisons and the historical recounting of the U.S. Navy's gun patrols on the Yangtze in favor of bedtime reading for aging spinsters. McKenna's vigor as a writer was quashed.

I knew the novel intimately. I reconstructed the first five pages of the condensed version and with the copy editors' first five pages, took them to Sherrod's office and put them blind on his desk, explaining why I was there and what I wanted. Take your pick, I said. He was pissed by my temerity.

His lips pursed, he read only the first page of each version. That was all he needed, he said, and told me, "Get out!"

By myself, I condensed the two-parter, to the word count agreed, and forever angered the two copy editors.

Highly publicized, when the issues appeared, at an editorial meeting I got nice nods from my colleagues. But the more satisfying comment came from author Richard McKenna. At lunch, at the Algonquin Hotel, his first visit to that historic literary site pleasing him, Dick asked, How did you manage to put the 250,000 words I'd written into 18,000 words for the *Post*...and telling the whole story?

By Way of Luck

If I'd known how to do that, he said, I could have saved writing the extra 232,000 words. He shook his head in mock disbelief and ordered us another scotch.

Saul Alinsky, Helen Gurley Brown and Bob from Ohio

Bob from Ohio was a freelance newsman hired by the *Post* as a contributing writer after surfacing and writing a story on block busting in Chicago's south side. Real estate speculators, the worst kind of scoundrels, had descended on Hyde Park, a prosperous, all-white community, its residents a mix of Jewish and mostly Christian families, knocking on doors and telling families a fictitious tale of houses on nearby streets being bought by blacks. Their message: real estate values are plummeting; the value of your house is dropping fast; in weeks if not days it may be worthless; and you'd be smart to sell now, offering owners ridiculously low prices and fast closings. Residents panicked, selling their homes for mere fractions of their actual worth and moving to newly emerging suburbs north and west of the city, coincidentally developed by many of the same speculators.

Encouraged by the exodus and able to afford substantial houses at lowered costs, blacks, in no way precipitating the sell-off, were indeed moving in. The real estate agents' fictions became fact. Their profits from the flip scandalously high.

Bob from Ohio saw the story not as news but as an affront to the community, to both whites and blacks, and with the full support of *Post* editors he wrote it angrily and with passion. Sourced and published by the *Post*, it was the best news story the re-made magazine ran during its attempts to become a timely journal.

Around the editorial offices, Bob from Ohio was not easily accommodated by his news seeking peers. To them, he was a quirk. He chased underdogs. He thought not as a journalist but as a reporter of social issues, news not a factor in the stories he chose to write. Most of his proposals were ignored.

Why he sought me out, I cannot recall, just as I cannot recall nor retrieve Bob's last name. But he showed up in my office, sat down, and talked about a man he had met in Chicago. His name was Saul Alinsky. And would I have lunch with him when he came to New York — as it turned out, after I'd agreed, *just* to have lunch with me. And with Bob.

It was 1964. Alinsky was not known then as he is remembered today, some fifty years later, Barack Obama's political emergence surfacing their earlier relationship. At lunch, he was a steely presence, plainly suited, jaw set, wanting to be heard and rejecting questions that Bob and I raised. He had a message he wanted Bob to write and the *Post* to publish: the United States would be engulfed by a revolution, coming from within, the poor and the oppressed rising and overturning the upper classes.

Alinsky saw himself as the leader of that revolution. His explanations of how he would accomplish it were provocative, though impractical, his prediction of the political chaos to come, a threat, I saw, unconnected to reasonable suppositions. After the revolution, I asked him, then what? More revolution, he answered. During my school boy vocabulary studies I had learned the meaning of the word demagogue. I had now come face to face with one. Though distanced, we parted amicably.

Bob was beaming. I was beset. The story was no story. Alinsky was a walking, talking political tract and while his message might be of interest to like-minded people, it would be of no interest to the larger audience the *Post* served. Perhaps my decision was a reflection of my immigrant heritage, my New England prep, college and military education, or maybe I just didn't like the guy, but I did not see Alinsky as any more than a rabble-rousing, self-serving Messiah who would in time disappoint his adherents. Bob backed away, his disbelief in me obvious.

Helen Gurley Brown, by the time she died, was a proven revolutionary who changed irrevocably her part of the world. I was introduced to her by Bernie Geis, her publisher, who built his company's reputation for audacity on Helen's book, *Sex and the Single Girl*. We

By Way of Luck

met late one week-day morning at the Benjamin Franklin Hotel in Philadelphia, too late for breakfast and too early for lunch. We had coffee and toast. She was visibly surprising, a girl just launching a sexual revolution, flat chested and scrawny, with legs like pipe cleaners and a face too serious to be flattering.

She, like Alinsky, wanted the *Post* to publish a story about her. I countered. Write the story, I said. I saw her by-line as far more attractive to a reader. She was of another mind. She wanted the story for its promotional value. We argued a pleasant argument. She saying, No. I also saying, No. Bernie telling me after, No hard feelings.

Helen was a true woman, to herself, to her friends and to her readers. She built *Cosmopolitan* magazine from its time of struggle to an international powerhouse, its surging circulation revenues coming not from subscription, but from newsstand sales, each copy representing a deliberate, unforced effort by a reader paying cash and carrying home a copy in her hand or in a bag.

Her contact with readers was personal and honest, something she'd learned how to do in part from Hugh Hefner who she saw as a counterpart. On taking the *Cosmo* job, she had, in fact, spent a day with him at his mansion office in Chicago, taking notes as they talked, Hefner already learning as Helen would, how an editor could best communicate with a reader. (I heard of this meeting from both Helen and Hefner.)

For the gains women made, from the 60s through the 90s, in business, in the professions, in the arts and at home, no woman writer-editor of her time deserves greater credit, not Germaine Greer, not Kate Millett, not Betty Friedan and not the editors and writers of Ms. Magazine. Through *Cosmo*, Helen had the greater reach and the more personal message. Authentic, she lived the life she preached.

(One of our family's closest friends was Helen's # two, as her executive editor and loyal confidante for 27 years, Roberta Ashley, whom my wife and I knew as Bobbi Hansen.)

During the 80s, at lunch with Helen and a couple of Hearst

biggies, I reminded her of our Philadelphia meeting. We had toast, she said, at the Ben Franklin. She paused, momentarily. You were right, she said. I should have written the story. The biggies were impressed by her admission. Hearst editors didn't make mistakes.

After no more than six months with the *Post* I concluded I was in the wrong place. Clay's new editors were journalists. They saw news as redemptive content. Fiction and derivative book content they saw as promotable but of little journalistic value. I stuck to my trade. I ran a short story by John O'Hara. I excerpted a stand-alone tale from John Updike's novel, *The Centaur*. I condensed Eric Ambler's thriller, *The Light of Day*, also published as *Topkapi*. I condensed *Love, Let Me Not Hunger*, a Paul Gallico, yet to be released novel.

(Gallico, I had met personally on several occasions, a productive writer of popular fiction, his best known works, *The Snow Goose, The Poseidon Adventure, The Small Miracle* and *Mrs. 'Arris Goes to Paris*. Well read through the 50s and 60s, his reputation did not last beyond the 70s. He was a newspaperman, his critic's complained.)

I received approving nods from Sherrod and Blair but I doubt whether they'd read what I'd brought to the *Post*. I was necessary but irrelevant.

Blair and Sherrod, meanwhile, were focusing more and more on major news events: Cuba — the missile crisis and the Bay of Pigs debacle — and Viet Nam — General William Westmoreland and Madame Nhu, president of South Viet Nam, as examples — god knows incredibly important historical events but a wrenching departure from reader and advertiser expectations. They were attempting to compete editorially against *Time* and *Newsweek*, cutting closing time from six weeks to six days while squeezing an editorial staff of ten to do the work of a hundred and simultaneously building circulation to a level where its readership could compete against television's growing audiences. The turnaround had become a centrifuge, spinning in ever tightening circles. Curtis was dizzying.

Some Curtis components were seen as profitable. But they were

By Way of Luck

not. It was illusory. They were divisions doing business with other divisions and recording empty gains. The company, in its entirety, was at the mercy of shrinking ad pages and flagging subscription revenues. When Clay and Don joined Curtis, the behemoth was already in an early stage of collapse.

Solutions were wounding, knife stabbing attempts by manic managers chasing the next plausible idea, and the next and the next. Joe Culligan chose the *Post's* Publisher, John Veronis, to be Executive Publisher of all Curtis magazines, their publishers reporting to him, and becoming Clay's equal. John ran meetings, promoted his brother Peter as a # two, and together they lunched with advertising agency media buyers.

Clay fired *Holiday's* revered editor, Ted Patrick, replacing him with Don Schanche. Clay asked me to become editor of *American Home* magazine. I said no. Clay closed it. Both *American Home* and *Holiday* were profitable, but barely, burdened by needless overheads assigned them by accountants in Philadelphia.

Joe hired a problem solver, Ray Brousseau, a Fagan look-alike, his garb invariably all in black, his technique, asking questions that were unanswerable. He turned down a request I asked of him. His response: "I'm not sure what I'm supposed to do around here, but I know that's not it."

Clay assumed greater authorities, acting the visionary, dealing with creditors, investors and the company's dwindling finances, pulling Joe Culligan along as his consenting adult and turning over editorial directorship to his Managing editor, Dave Thomas, whom he had much earlier hired away from *Life*.

Bob Sherrod became redundant, still at his desk and attempting to maintain his dignity. For the management strength Clay sought, he reached out to a friend and publisher of one of his first books, *Atomic Submarine* and *Admiral Rickover*, naming him vice-president of the corporation and Director of Special Projects: Bill Buckley, formerly of Holt, Rinehart and Winston Suddenly, the Bill Buckley I had rarely seen at Holt, was in my world.

Bill would head Special Projects, an assignment with two loosely defined but essential responsibilities: one, to lower the noise in the editorial group and give it a sense of cohesiveness; and two, to fish about for assets that could be turned into cash, an example, Clay suggested, by publishing or licensing previously published magazine materials.

Bill needed staff and asked me to transfer from the magazine to work with him. This time, I said yes, for the outlook at the *Post* was dim and I thought Bill and I, working together, we just might participate productively in the survival of the Curtis Publishing Company. It was naïve of me to think so, but the idea was cloaked in valor and I succumbed to it. Don Gold took over my job.

What I learned about Bill Buckley, from a diary entry

Bill found glory in his name: William E. Buckley. That's William with an E. Not an F. Not the author of *Man and God at Yale* and not the intellectual founding editor of *The National Review*, but simply a former book publishing executive.

Bill dwelt handsomely on the confusion of names. Whenever the question of E. versus F. arose, he would admit to the E., but somehow leave the questioner, well, questioning whether Bill was or wasn't who he admitted to not being. It was a practiced deception. He'd don the cloak of the famous personality to attract the admiration of those who did not know that Bill was but 5' 7" and William F. stood 6'3".

Not a tall man, neither was Bill particularly distinguished in his appearance. Natty, yes, but he looked the catalog model, as if groomed in two dimensions. He spoke in ambiguous sentences made up of cautious words and punctuated by finger jabs, scowls and accusatory looks, a practiced manner that could unsettle his subordinates. Yet he had a style valued among corporate executives. He could trigger a disarming smile when it suited him, dialing its warmth up or down as needed, and his memory was dazzling, able easily to recall not only the names of his male associates, but those of their wives and children, and some birth dates as well.

He also had guile. He could side step responsibility with the deft-

By Way of Luck

ness of a torero, look threateningly askance at a critic, or wander importantly from a meeting when an issue he chose not to engage in might surface. Or show up deliberately late as a way of avoiding uncomfortable items at the top of an agenda. I wondered at first whether he was as calculated as his behavior appeared, or was he just petty. I soon found out.

"James!" It was how Bill called me from his office next door. We were located temporarily at 666 Fifth Avenue and later at 641 East 54th Street, in the middle of Manhattan where in 1962 Curtis had once again moved its editorial and advertising departments.

"James!"

I entered Bill's office. He was sitting at his desk, a document in his hand. An expense report, I could see. Mine. "Explain something to me," Bill said. "On your report, you listed $7.10 for a train ticket to Philadelphia." I nodded.

"I happen to know," he said, "the fare is $7.00." He appeared utterly satisfied with what he was about to say. "You owe the company ten cents!" he exclaimed.

Was he kidding? I stood silent for a moment or two until I realized he was serious. So I recalled for him a meeting we had on the day of the trip. "It ran long," I said. "I didn't have time to buy a ticket at the window. I bought it on the train." I managed my anger. "The conductor charged me the dime."

Bill gave me a querulous look, contemplating a response. "OK this time," he said finally. "Don't let it happen again."

I had my answer. Petty.

I tell you this archly trivial recollection for it coincided with a change in our relationship. Bill had become increasingly stymied by the task he had taken on. How could he, in a company on the verge of bankruptcy, have sufficient credibility to conduct what he saw as an auction of *Post* editorial assets and, at the same time, manage a pick-up squad of magazine editors and writers who saw themselves as not needing management? Bill was as good as shipwrecked, far from land, and hoping to be rescued.

Although not formally given the assignment, I assumed the nearly abandoned task of surfacing properties that could be put to a productive purpose.

Coincidental with the shift in responsibilities, I got a glimpse of just how bad business had gotten. Curtis's Chairman of the Board, in a call from his secretary, requested that I join him for a private meeting in Philadelphia. The word "private" was emphasized. He's seeking advice, she said. I said, sure, okay, deferring to rank and curious to learn what "private" was all about.

The Chairman and two friends, all three stiffly suited and old-world mannerly, owned a modest book publishing company in Harrisburg, Pennsylvania, I learned at the meeting. They wanted me to run it.

"On behalf of Curtis?" I asked.

"No," came their reply. "Leave Curtis and come work for us."

I was stunned. Was the company's Chairman on a raid? How many other key employees had been solicited by insiders with "private" interests? How long had this been going on? My throat dried. I rasped, "Isn't that a conflict?"

"I also have an executive recruiting company," the Chairman said, as if that made everything right. I got up, said I'd consider it. And excused myself.

What then should I do? Tell Bill, talk to Clay? Stir the mud? Nothing good could come of saying anything, so I said nothing.

There were no further calls from the Chairman's office.

The Purple Moose

With my assumed responsibility, I was unknowingly put on a trail that led to an unexpected encounter with a purple moose.

The route it took began when Bill Buckley side-stepped Les Schwartz, a publisher of professional educational materials and a talker who pestered Bill endlessly with fanciful publishing propositions. Instead of escorting Les to an elevator, Bill led him to my office and walked away.

By Way of Luck

He had a friend, Les said, Irv Kligfield, a printer with a contract from the Audubon Society to produce an anthology made up of published articles from the Society's magazine. Kligfield assumed he could make a distribution deal with a recognized publisher, and get an advance against projected earnings. But Kligfield had been turned down, Les admitted, by every publisher in town and was desperate because Irv had made hefty financial commitments to Audubon.

So what did I think? Les asked.

Saying No to Les might have been easy. He was comical in his appearance, in his early sixties I guessed, his face drawn and pale. At perhaps six two, angular and anxious, he seemed the sad clown. I could have been dismissive. Instead, I thought, was it possible that Les was the right guy, come at the right time and to the right place?

I had to consider the coincidence of his abrupt arrival and my equally abrupt new assignment. A suspicion that the fates were at work? Possibly. I was curious. Was this part of a movie plot? Just as the heroine, tied to the rails, is about to be run over by a train, Les Schwartz comes to her rescue? Was I about to luck out?

Beginning in the late 50s and into the early 60s publishing multi-volume works had become fashionable, and profitable. Jerry Hardy, a former vice-president and advertising director at Doubleday, had joined Time, Inc., bringing with him Doubleday's experience in "continuity" publishing, selling books in series or through clubs, such as the Literary Guild. Hardy applied what he'd learned at Doubleday, launching one Time-Life Library after another and building its book division into a substantial contributor to Time, Inc.'s profitability.

Independent publisher, John Stevenson, his company Greystone Press, published single subject books exclusively in series, on gardening, on pets, on decorating, on cooking, twenty volumes each, delivered in continuity, a volume every four weeks or so, and all sold by mail. I tested one of John's series with a controlled mailing to *Post* readers. The responses were encouraging. John begged for the subscription list. Simply renting Curtis' mailing lists to John was not an option to be taken.

Given Les's story and the current successes in continuity publishing, I had a thought. An anthology of aged articles arranged in a single volume had little merit. But what if Kligfield, with visible support from the Curtis Publishing Company, could reconstruct his contract with Audubon and use its editorial resources to create a multi-volume, A to Z, nature encyclopedia? I asked Les to introduce me to Irv Kligfield. Les was thrilled. It was all he wanted. A simple favor turned burden he'd carried for months was lifted. His eyes shone. He left my office happy.

Kligfield was now mine to convince of the change we might work out together. Having often been in press rooms, learning about plate making, color separations, binding processes, and so on, what happens to manuscripts after signed off by an editor, I shared a common language with printers and looked forward to my first meeting with Mr. Kligfield.

Irv was a dwarfish, composed man of about fifty, articulate, universally knowledgeable, kind in his manner, possibly over polite, engaging, and affable. But, as I soon discovered, Irv was not a printer.

Irv was a classical violinist.

But I was undeterred, for reasons I cannot now explain, a hunch perhaps. (Was Irv the girl on the rails to be rescued?) I took the proposition to Bill.

Bill Buckley said he liked the concept, but it might take too much of his time, it would cost money that Curtis did not have and might represent too big a risk, but in any event corporate would have to be involved, and so on. He was scared, understandably. He was consumed by other things. He dished me off to Alan Hartnick, an attorney representing the investors.

By now Curtis was firmly in the hands of Perfect Film, looking for a turnaround, tackling the decisions to be made, what assets to sell, what to keep, how their investment was to be spent, who to hire, and who to fire. The law firm representing them was Shea, Clemenko and Gould, known widely for founding partner Bill Shea's success in getting major league approval for the return of National

By Way of Luck

League team to New York after the Giants and the Dodgers moved to California. As his reward, the Mets new home in Flushing Meadow Park in Queens was named Shea Stadium.

Alan Hartnick, not long out of the Harvard Law School, was the law firm's on-the-ground eyes and ears at Curtis and my contemporary. We bonded almost immediately and developed a friendship that lasted for years after. He liked my proposition and seemed not afraid to say that, or to say, Let's see how we can get this done. Give me some time, he said. He disappeared for several days.

Meanwhile I had been assigned an office on "executive" row, one of five spaces fronting on Fifth Avenue. I didn't deserve the location, but the office was available and after closing time moved into it. At 8:30 AM the following morning, I learned why the space was empty. A building employee nonchalantly walked into my new office carrying a folded flag, opened the window on to the street, a sharp wind blowing pages off my desk, and hoisted it on an angular pole that stretched over the sidewalk below. At 5 PM that afternoon, he appeared again, opened the window, and while I held loose papers from flying about he took down the flag and left. Because of the intrusion, legitimate corporate executives shunned the space. I had no problem with that, for soon Old Glory would be my implausible benefactor.

My adjacent neighbor was Jim Fuchs, just hired by Joe Culligan. Jim, a Yale graduate, had competed in the 1948 and 1952 Olympics. A shot putter, he had won the bronze medal in each competition. At one time he held a slew of world records in the event. In the same years, Bob Mathias won gold medals in the decathlon. Mathias showed up at our offices from time to time, he and Fuchs close friends and hanging together. They'd often lunch at the "21" club a block away where they were known, customers and staff applauding their entrance. They were proud men.

Joe Culligan had the corner office not more than 30 feet away. I was in good company. Things began to happen.

Marvin Cantor, a Wall Streeter, joined the company, on loan from Perfect Film. His assignment: raise cash. He had a divestiture in mind. Seeing me sitting on corporate row and assuming I was part of the hierarchy, he asked for my help. Marvin was quiet, he was pleasant, a thoughtful analyst, and someone who could quickly be seen as a friend, approving of me, listening to my advice and acting on it. Curtis owned 47½% of paper back publisher Bantam Books. Reprint and children's book publisher Grosset and Dunlap also owned 47½%. (The remaining 5% was owned by Bantam's founder Sidney Kramer. If Curtis and Grosset were ever in disagreement, Sidney had the swing vote.) Marvin said let's sell our 47½%.

You know books, Marvin said. What's Bantam worth? My answer would have to wait. I had current financial statements from Bantam, by way of Curtis. But how would they translate into an evaluation buyer and seller could agree to? I identified six publicly held publishing companies, looked up their price/earnings ratios, picked a mid-point and took it to Marvin. $5,000,000, I said. Marvin made the deal directly with Grosset. For Curtis's 47½% he got $2,500,000. Cash.

(Left out of the deal, and no longer having a swing vote, Sidney threatened to sue both parties. Marvin told Grosset that Sydney was their problem, not Curtis's. Years later, when Sydney and I were part of another organization, he talked bitterly by how the sale had gone down.)

The Curtis Circulation Company was constructing a massive promotional mailing to boost circulation for both the *Post* and the *Ladies' Home Journal*. My informal dossier, in a word or two, depicted me as a direct response veteran, the Literary Guild experience my qualification. Could I assist them? They were wrestling with the copy strategy. Too sweet, I told them, too soft. Direct mail, I said, has to be direct, though subtly so. I rewrote brochure copy. The response to the mailing ran 25% higher than they'd forecast. Any number of variables could have been the cause, weather, time of year, what was happening in the stock market, and so on, but I chose not to offer the explanations, instead accepting their thanks and a drink or two at dinner.

Unknowingly and luckily, my perceived value to Curtis, along

By Way of Luck

with the flag over Fifth Avenue, had been hoisted.

The Philadelphia office called, the Curtis's executive vice president on the line. A merger candidate had surfaced, Rust Craft Greeting Cards, owned by Pittsburgh's Berkman family and run by its two brothers. Meet me in Pittsburgh, the EVP said. We'll talk there. My flight was delayed by weather, the wait on the tarmac interminable. When I finally arrived, the meeting had been concluded, the EVP just leaving and saying, why'd you even bother to come?

The Berkman brothers were courteous and reprised the meeting. Nothing went further with Rust Craft. But I had acquired a distaste for the EVP and the Philadelphia group. Both there and in New York, the company I had once known as a writer seemed taken over by aliens.

Alan Hartnick came back into the picture. He'd asked how much a test of the Audubon project might cost. I told him. I can get that money, he said. Let's negotiate a contract with Kligfield and call on the Audubon Society, he advised. If we can get the rights and permissions in exchange for a modest royalty, we just might make it work. Alan had vision, always thinking beyond the practical and assuming the possible. I saw that we shared the "certainty" thing.

The deal came together, the contracts signed on terms of our making, helped along by an Audubon Society editor who'd had a role in the USAF Conservation project. We would have his full cooperation, access to the Society's voluminous files and a license for the use of the Audubon name.

Irv Kligfield bought me and Alan lunch, offered a toast and burst into cheerful tears. I thought him a bit overly expressive until he told us he'd already invested in the project, even without knowing how the negotiations might turn out. He'd gambled, my concert violinist, and bought a Hell scanner from a German manufacturer, a first in a string of new technologies that would slash the costs of color separations and printing. He had writers and researchers standing by, space rented in a 5th Avenue loft, and manufacturing quotes that enabled him to forecast his costs and how we might work together financially. He had a simple formula. He would produce the books, to my specifications and with my approval. He would charge $1.00 per copy, all inclusive, in whatever quantities we might need, thereby taking the bigger risk upon himself.

Alan and I were neither dumbfounded nor in awe. We were struck more by his audacity, this violinist, or was it by his artlessness, we weren't sure.

We concluded he took the risk as a way of showing us his commitment. It was unnecessary, yet because to his way of thinking — plucking the right strings, as it were — it was the expected thing for him to do. He went further. He would begin the editorial work immediately. He would not wait for test results, he had that much confidence. Speechless, I got up from my seat and walked to the other side of the table where he sat and kissed the top of his head.

Bill Buckley was shaken. His indifference had not stalled the Kligfield/Audubon project. We had the contracts; Alan found us money for the test; and we had a way of keeping Bill in our camp. We would list him among the credits as Publisher.

But Bill was helpful. He suggested I work with The Richard Benson Agency to develop the mailing materials.

Dick Benson was a constant in the mail order advertising business, all other like agencies measuring themselves against him, their executives wondering how an obese, arthritically crippled, nearsighted, broken-toothed, sarcastically mouthed and occasionally foul smelling ad man was so consistently successful. Dick was also a scolder who ridiculed clients, challenged their convictions and would walk out of their meetings, as if in disdain, snorting and wiping his nose as he went. Perhaps he succeeded because he delivered more and better than other agencies might, sometimes investing personally in his client's projects, a rarity. Or at other times, good times, insisting on it.

He showed me rough layouts. There was the moose, a mature male, its horns spread broadly like butterfly wings, featured big on the page, angled toward the sky, its jaws agape, ostensibly baying in search of a female. Right away, I liked the moose, its appeal to the eye and totally appropriate as a frontis piece. The rest of the promotional material was rough, but close to what I was looking for, commenting on the direction the copy was to take and, most importantly, how the offer was to be positioned, and leaving the rest for Dick to manage. Within a couple of weeks we had finished art and copy ready to go to press.

A New Technology Emerges

Meantime, I had a growing concern. Among the roughly 12,000,000 active names and addresses in Curtis's subscription files, because of cross promotion among its magazines there had to be duplicates. Perhaps as many as 30% of the company's magazine subscribers, my guess, would receive two or more simultaneously delivered mailings, a waste, I saw, and adding to the expense of the promotion. Seeking a solution, I took the seven dollar train to Philadelphia to meet with Bill Charlton whose city-block-sized mail processing department managed the files, keeping them up to date and printing the mailing labels.

Coincidentally, an entirely new file management technology was bumping along: the conversion of subscriber data — from two-inch by one-inch, metal Speed-O-Mat plates, one per subscriber — to magnetic tape, a change required by the U.S. Postal Service as part of its introduction of the Zip Code. On tape, in addition to names and addresses, all kinds of pertinent information could be added to a subscriber's record and, as data storage technology emerged, limitlessly in fact. The conversion would take time to implement, in some cases years. The change-over was seen by the mail order industry as an added, unnecessary expense. Plates had done the job easily and inexpensively for decades. The change-over would be expensive and, the moaning went, how tape might be managed was not yet proven. Charlton had no such qualms. He had a view of the future.

Once we've completed the conversion, Bill Charlton told me, we can cut our operating expenses in half, and we can more accurately manage our data in a more timely way. He had already sourced and purchased the machines to do the job. They were called computers.

Charlton was an unbounded man, physically and intellectually vigorous, and an eager thinker. When I posed the question, how do we eliminate duplication? he responded truthfully. I don't know. We're working on it, he said.

He summoned his number two, Jules Cocozza. I sat with them while they took the remaining steps toward drafting a solution. Bill called it the Match Code, a methodology that could identify each individual subscriber or customer in such a way as to be unique. Running subscribers to the *Post* against those to Ladies Home Journal, the duplicates would be matched, immediately recognized and easily edited. They had figured out what soon became a widely adopted file management technique, first by mail order merchants and later by all data base managers. Bill's Match Code preceded the Bar Code by several years,

The subscription lists to be sourced for the promotion of *The Audubon Nature Encyclopedia* would be the first use of Bill's Match Code.

There was a not-to-be-missed schedule for the promotion, mailing dates and times always critical depending on time of year, by month, by week, and often by day or, as often, by weather. The test would comprise 10,000 names from each of five unduplicated magazine files. All promotional materials but one had been printed and were stacked on skids by the insertion machines in Bill's production center. The one missing: the brochure that featured the moose.

Because of delays at Benson's, it would be printed the night before the mailing was to be made. At two o'clock the following morning, I got a call from the print shop. It was located in Lower Manhattan.

Jim, the foreman said, We've got a problem. Can you come down?

At the print shop, just coming off press, I immediately saw the freshly printed sheets featuring the moose. The moose was purple.

From film, the plate makers were unable to reproduce the mottled colors of an adult moose's tawny coat. Every adjustment had been tried, in the inks, in the blankets and in the paper stock.

By Way of Luck

Too, the plate makers had gone through three sets of plates. The moose was, still, unmistakably purple.

The owner of the print shop arrived, coat, shirt and tie and pajama bottoms. He shouted above the methodical whack-whacking of his letter presses, issuing commands, I assumed, for his press operators began scurrying about in fever. In a few minutes, he said to me, we'll have this straightened out.

The minutes passed. The moose was still purple.

In my hands, the sheets felt treacherous; there was a deceit at work. I had no workable options. The art could be reshot, but that would take a day, perhaps two. The plates could once again be remade, by some other printer, perhaps. There was no assurance that either solution would change anything, I would have missed two, three, even more weeks testing alternatives with no confidence that any one of them would work.

Let's go with the purple moose, I said. Crank it up. The certainty thing again.

The sheets came spilling out at a speedy pace. Before heading home, I saw one, then ten, then a hundred purple moose as each sheet fell on top of another, the odd if not bizarre color glaringly obvious. Within ten hours, the sheets would be folded and trimmed and delivered that same day to Philadelphia where, by afternoon, the insertion machines would begin their whizzing labors. And by day's end, the stuffed envelopes would be sorted and bagged and on their way to a Philadelphia bulk mail center.

Early that morning I put a sample on Bill Buckley's desk.

"James!" Bill's face was as red as the moose was purple. He stood furious behind his desk. "Please tell me this is a joke."

"It's no joke," I said. I told him of the 2 AM call and what we'd done to make the corrections and why we'd proceeded.

Bill's response was astonishing. He could have fired me. He might have thought to call the post office and stop the mailing, or whatever portions of the mailing that had yet to be made. But he didn't.

Visibly, he cooled, the change in his manner astonishing. "Make sure you get it right the next time," he said.

Seeing my mouth drop, he slid open a desk drawer and pulled out a sheet of paper. "Take a look," he said.

In scrunchy hand writing was a long list of names, big names, corporate names, American Telephone, Westinghouse, General Electric, New York Telephone, the Chemical Corn Exchange Bank — lots of banks — and name by name the amount of stock he owned in each.

"You know what this is, James? Bill asked. "It's fuck-you money. Why I don't get too upset about things I can't do anything about, you know, like staying awake nights worrying about what you're doing." He shoved the paper back in the drawer and banged it closed. "Make this thing work," he said.

The test mailing easily proved the validity of Irv Kligfield's confidence, by a wide margin, news of its success rippling through the New York and Philadelphia offices. For me the news was old news and fast behind me. I was in a quandary. How would we get the $300,000 cash needed to roll out the program?

Up and down the hall from my office, there were meetings going on, men in suits moving about and eventually convening in Joe Culligan's corner suite. I hunched at my desk, at busy work, should anyone look in. My phone rang. It was Joe, thirty steps away. Usually, being summoned, I'd hear from his secretary. Joe was sitting at his desk; the suits standing behind him, Hartnick, Fuchs and Cantor. We've been talking to the Bank of Boston, Joe said. The guys there expressed interest in funding the Audubon thing. Can you put together a presentation in the next day or two?

With what I heard, an encouraging option, I could have put together a presentation in the next hour or two. Yes, I said.

A meeting in Boston was set for the following week, with Serge Semenenko, a financial celebrity, an independent broker-dealer connected to several banks, not all at once, but by project or by convenience. Currently he was lodged at Bank of Boston, Curtis's primary lender.

By Way of Luck

Semenenko was a Russian émigré, with a parsnip nose, hair lacquered and swept past his ears to the nape of his neck and wearing a Bill Buckley styled suit, though snappier and richer. He dated wealthy dowagers, actresses and society belles, a way of gaining attentive coverage from the social and financial columnists of major eastern newspapers.

Semenenko was no doubt an innovative banker, succeeding where competitors couldn't, and among the early few who popularized investment banking. He had just completed a refinancing of Warner Bros, overcoming the obstructive brothers Warner who threatened corporate suicide rather than submit to his terms.

Without Semenenko's money, likely today there would be no such named motion picture studio.

Semenenko was a star. I would be meeting him. Who else would be joining me for the New York to Boston train ride? The suits looked at one another, heads lowering and hands tugging self-consciously at their neckties. Just you, Joe said. We think you can handle it.

I understood the strategy. If Semenenko turned us down, I would be the piñata to take the hit. If I succeeded in gaining a commitment from Semenenko's bank, the suits would get the credit.

So what? I asked myself. I was already the hairy ape helping fire the furnaces of a floundering ship. Could a rejection from Semenenko be any worse?

The Bank of Boston Meeting

Semenenko appeared at ease with himself, sitting alone in a cavernous, old money, mahogany walled office, offering me tea and asking about the ride from New York. He was calming. He suggested I put my brief case on the floor. Two suits entered the room, introduced themselves and sat down. We're here to talk, he said. Tell us about yourself.

I told him the bits and pieces. He told me about his bits and pieces, the suits having their turn at bits and pieces, too.

There was a similarity to this meeting, much like the session Corey and I had had in General White's Pentagon office, at first affable, then a project to be evaluated, and with me taking on a new responsibility. I could sense a shift coming from Semenenko's friendliness, but from what direction?

Curtis's balance sheet could not support further loans, one of the suits said. The Bank of Boston would not take on additional risk. The promise of money began to drift. Semenenko said he liked what I had to say, affirmed humorously my decision to proceed with the test regardless of how purple the moose, but wanted some original thinking from me. I reached for my brief case. Semenenko shook a finger. "I don't do business with brief cases," he said.

Without my notes, the presentation I'd prepared turned differently: more direct, less detail and more passion. We've only spent $15,000, I said, and we've got evidence *The Audubon Nature Encyclopedia* could be worth hundreds of thousands. (Hard numbers would be remembered. I skirted them, fearful of being held to them.) All we have of substance, I went on, are just pieces of paper, a contract with Audubon, a contract with Kligfield, a promotional package featuring a purple moose and the test results. They're not even itemized on Curtis's balance sheets.

If you can't advance the money because of Curtis's credit, I said, put up the money against the projected return, I said, the idea coming to me at that very moment. Believe me, I was winging it.

It's like publishing a book, I went on, from an idea to a finished novel or non-fiction book, a history or a biography, it's a creative decision, an editor taking a risk and making a book happen. Publishing is a risk business.

Facing Semenenko boldly, I said, And not terribly different from the business you're in. My brief argument was finished. I was heated, the sweat sliding from under my arms, past my ribs and into the waist band of my trousers.

Are you suggesting we collateralize the project? said one of the suits. An off-balance sheet loan? What a creative idea.

I didn't know about loans. Nor had I encountered the word "collateral" before, a banking term, something like a mortgage, like the one I'd taken out to buy the house in Greenwich. My understanding of finance that thin.

By Way of Luck

Yet, I sensed the suit had given me a direction I could not have taken by myself. Yes, I said. Collateralize the pieces of paper.

I left the numbers on Semenenko's desk and took the train back to New York. The money asked was approved, both by the Bank of Boston and by The Curtis Publishing Company, by its Philadelphia version as well as by its New York City version, the Audubon contract and the promotional materials serving as collateral.

When Joe gave me the news, a sweet delirium enveloped me, shutting down sight and sound, and leaving me with no recollection of what I might have heard or said, Joe pumping my hand and finding my way back to my office, alone and sitting in my chair, and muttering to myself, You lucky son-of-a-bitch.

Irv Kligfield, by then, had completed the editorial and pictorial work, including color separations, for volumes 1 and 2, had made a sweet-heart deal with a Queensborough lithographer whose primary business was printing record sleeves, and had Harry Wolf, a Manhattan book binder, standing by to bind, box and ship finished books. Irv was about to make a lot of money, so was Curtis and so was the Bank of Boston.

Bill Buckley was complimentary, neither approving nor disapproving what had so far occurred. His manner hinted at something important.

"What about the purple moose?" he said.

"What about it?"

"Before the mailings can go, you've got to fix it." He was ashamed, he said. "There is no such thing as a purple moose." He readied to invoke scripture.

I interrupted. "Every fix we tried, we came up short."

"Then find some other wild animal."

"Can't," I said, asserting an authority newly earned. The test results are reliable. Any change we make would have to be tested. Not in the budget and a delay we cannot afford. "The purple moose has taken us this far," I said conclusively. "We're letting it take us all the way."

Bill was visibly dismayed. I left his office knowing intuitively he'd open the drawer where he kept his listed stocks and find comfort there. He wrote a contesting memo to Joe Culligan. Bill didn't follow up on it and neither did Joe.

We launched a series of major mailings to subscribers of the *Post*, of *Ladies' Home Journal* and *Jack and Jill* and tested mail order respondents from other list owners. In three years the purple moose sold nearly 90,000 volumes of *The Audubon Nature Encyclopedia*, and thereafter it continued to sell actively until its market was worn.

Efforts were made to replace the purple moose, perhaps to reinvigorate the promotion as results tapered off, but they failed.

By then I was no longer with Curtis.

6

Two Uncles

How are decisions influenced? By advice, by experience, by gut feeling, by imitating what seems admirable in others, how they've lived their lives, made their way, stimulating and providing direction and purpose. For me it came from two of my many uncles.

My Uncle Peter — an ophthalmologist with a practice in midtown Manhattan and married to my mother's older sister, Marion — introduced me to golf, first playing together at a public course abutting the Clearview Expressway in Queens and later sponsoring me as a member of the Westchester Country Club in Rye, New York. By his friends and fellow players, I was nick-named the "gorilla." With ease, I could hit a ball 190 yards with a 4-iron, consistently square, and with a driver, perhaps 240 yards, but rarely on a line. Nearly always, seeking the rush that came from hitting a well-placed drive, I chose to gamble on the longer hit.

Peter cautioned me. He said there were two ways to play the game: one, advance the ball and stay out of trouble; and two, hit the ball as hard as you can and "make do" when the ball flew into impenetrable rough, lodged in a tree or, worse, landed out of bounds or flopped into a hazard, resulting in penalties that add to the score of a game that champions low scores.

He was cautious, my Uncle Peter, a surgeon whose work was fixing eyeballs and eyelids, whether burnt, crossed, torn, smashed, disconnected or in one manner or another just weren't working. He cut and he stitched and during evenings before early morning surgeries, he practiced cutting and stitching. Once, before dinner, I watched him at his preparatory routine. In a corner of his bedroom he sat in an over-stuffed chair with a pillow on his lap, its casing a light colored fabric, perhaps of silk, linen, cotton, or a synthetic — of different weaves and different thicknesses — and on these varied surfaces he laid out different blades, different needles, different threads, some newly designed, some faithful old tools. Like a cobbler punching leather, a farrier shaping a horse's shoe or a sommelier un-corking a grand wine, he practiced as a tradesman might, cutting and stitching until he knew, in the morning, when entering the operating room he would be at his surgical best. My aunt Marion, who ran his office on 140 East 54th Street, was in charge of maintaining their household supply of pillow cases.

I learned from Peter, as much by what he did as by what he said, be cautious, be professional, and be dedicated to what you do. He was a Spartan, literally, born in Sparta, Greece, an austere man and wise. I wished to be like him but I couldn't. Married into our family, he and I were differently constructed, I more like my Uncle Steve.

Uncle Steve was the youngest of the Tegu family, my mother's side, and given a traditional yet odd combination of names: Tegu Steven Tegu, the one being the father of the other. To me, he was Uncle Tegu.

Uncle Tegu played the guitar, sang songs, flew airplanes, boxed in college, the University of Virginia, was adored by women, had a wood-working shop making wing spars for early aviation pioneer Bellanca, drank wine out of a leather Bota, established a restaurant, the Spanish Villa, gave me my first flying lessons in a Piper J-3, had an ear for languages, lived in Greece, Mexico, Spain, Germany, France and Puerto Rico, as well as the United States, was a CIA agent, earned a Ph.D. at the University of Madrid, was a professor

By Way of Luck

at Rhode Island College, linguistics his specialty, at Providence's City Council meetings represented the non-English speaking Latin community, and when he died the *Providence Journal* featured his obituary, with a full color portrait, on Page One. He was married to the first girl I ever fell in love with. Her name is Catherine. She is from Vouvosa, Greece, my mother's home town. I stood as best man when she and Uncle Tegu, then thirty-eight, wed. She was twenty-one. I was seventeen. Today, she lives alone, a widow, has five adult children and still lives in Providence, a short walk from where her husband taught. When I visit her or we talk on the telephone, we talk as youngsters. I think sometimes I may be emotionally in her grasp.

7

A Farewell

What I had pulled off at Curtis was satisfying, a high wire act with no safety net. Looking back on it, it was, perhaps, the only successful act in the publishing division. But the commitment, the long hours, the commute into the city from Riverside Station in Connecticut, the return ride usually in a bar car, separated me emotionally from my family, my children and my wife. Going unnoticed, alcohol had crept into our lives, the relationship we'd had from our college years ago was eroding and one day it crumbled into too many pieces to be brought back together.

We faced divorce. Our families were of little help. My parents, no longer restaurant owners, had built a motel in New Hampshire, a retirement investment, and were distant. My wife's mother had never approved of our marriage. For her daughter a husband of Greek descent was not good enough, an incongruity, for she and her siblings were abandoned by an unknown mother and were raised share-crop poor in rural Illinois by an aunt and uncle. After her husband's early death, at age 52, she was determined to push me aside and move into my home as a live-in grandmother.

Connecticut divorce law at the time favored the wife. She gets the kids, the house, the alimony and the support. The husband leaves town. My attorney, from a distinguished Greenwich law firm,

By Way of Luck

actually told me to forget my children, to find another woman, settle down and have more kids. Was he crazy? No. Before men and women gained equal footing in the family, by Connecticut law mothers got it all. Possibly, a feminist attorney might have represented me better. I had been divorced from my wife but not from my children. I would not give them up as my lawyer had suggested. I would become important in their lives.

I took a studio apartment at the Gramercy Park hotel in New York across Gramercy Park from my city haunt, the Players Club, just two blocks away from an IRT subway stop that would take me straight up Lexington Avenue to a local stop a half block from my office building. I had rid myself forever from the long commute.

Bill Buckley was sympathetic. While managing Irv Kligfield and our promotion of the *Audubon Encyclopedia* and also at work on the next project and the next, Bill offered me an assistant who'd worked at *McCall's* magazine and had managed its book program. He was Jim Fisher, the former editor of Dartmouth's *Jack-O-Lantern* humor magazine, the coincidence remarkable. Bill was surprised when I said, hire him, this before the interview Bill had scheduled.

I was pleased Jim had come on stage. My divorce had left me groundless. Jim could pick up on what I was doing without much training, a perfect fit for what I needed. I had lost interest in the *Post* and Curtis, hanging out at the Player's, actors Jason Robards and Frank Cover (a familiar face on TV comedy's The Jeffersons) my bar buddies and fellow Ted Williams fans, dating the easy dates and squandering hours in remorse and self-pity. I was a mess and acted like it.

I had stayed in touch with Corey, working on articles with him for the *Post* and *Reader's Digest*, and spent days with him in New York and Hanover talking through the books he was writing. He had been the best man at my wedding and was the godfather of my children. He was as much family as I could have. Until the divorce was settled I chose not to admit what was happening. I kept secret from him my own slough of despair. I was depressed and felt myself the cast-off.

From off camera walks in Joe Marks, as if cued.

I had not seen or talked to Joe since leaving Doubleday. By phone, he suggested we lunch at La Caravelle. Deeply tanned, he appeared fresh from a beach-front hotel at Biarritz, suave and coolly elegant, just as I remembered him and as a youth just like I hoped one day I would be seen.

Sitting down and waiting until we'd ordered from the bar, with no introductory chit-chat, Joe said, How'd you like to work for Hugh Hefner?

Now I am at *Playboy* recalling how I succumbed to either my better or baser instincts to move to Chicago.

8

Magazines...Coming and Going

While long-standing, general-interest magazines — *Liberty, Pageant, Collier's, Life, Look* and the *Post*, all now gone — were losing subscribers, consumer publications with articles relating to identifiable audiences were speedily gaining new readers, among them *Good Housekeeping, Sunset, Southern Living, Sports Illustrated, Cosmo* and relative newcomer, *Playboy*, whose newsstand sales in the mid-1960s were increasing at the rate of 50,000 to 100,000 copies per month. *Playboy*, its circulation once peaking at a one-month high of 7.2 million copies, was clearly the phenomenon of the pack.

But *Playboy* had a problem, its pages devoid of homey, everyday content, instead featuring triple-page spreads of unclad young women with the "girl next door" look and highlighting by-lined articles by publisher Hugh Hefner that touted sex between consenting adults as acceptable recreation.

While throwing open exotic doors for young male readers, a generally conservative 1960s nation was alarmed by what it saw as pornography. Women's breasts were never so openly bared. Was Hefner a pornographer? Was he to be condemned? Banned? Shut down? Reviled? Admired? Thanked? Blessed? None of these questions asked then matter today. Because now, 60 years later, *Playboy* is still with us and Hugh Hefner is still its owner, publisher and editor-in-chief. While *Playboy* continues under attack by still another generation of censorious dick-heads, and another, and another, Hefner has nonetheless prevailed, as have both his philosophical and legal positions on openness and individual freedom.

Rarely in social or economic societies does anyone ever emerge after six strife-filled decades as a clear, stand-alone winner. Of anything. Hefner has. He has not changed. The world he occupies has changed and Hefner had much to do with it.

Though I was intrigued by Joe Marks' question, I had little interest in leaving New York and even less interest in moving to Chicago. Joe turned pest, nibbling at me with phone calls and messages of intrigue. At least give *Playboy* a look, he said. I relented to the offer of a "look."

A.C. Spectorsky, *Playboy's* editor in chief, and I met in his East Ohio Street office, the magazine's home base before Hefner acquired the Palmolive Building on Michigan Avenue. Utterly urbane, "Augie' or "Spec", by any measure, after Herb Mays, then editor of *McCall's*, was the best magazine editor in the business. A scholar and a writer, his social thesis *The Exurbanites*, a book that defined for the first time a population shift away from central cities, attracted both professional and general acclaim, as did his books M*an Into Beast, The Book of the Sky* and *The Book of the Sea*.

Born in Paris of eastern European parents, he had the mien of a Russian prince (which he could well have been); he was haughty without displaying haughtiness, correct without being stiffly so, and showed a witty side that gained him sincerity. Moreover, he attracted writers of note to the magazine's pages: sci-fi writer Ray Bradbury, novelist Norman Mailer, historian Arthur Schlesinger and story teller Vladimir Nabokov, as examples, a fondness for *Playboy* growing among them and providing the magazine with a depth of content for male readers unmatched since the 1930 heydays of Arnold Gingrich's *Esquire* magazine. Augie — A.C. standing for August Comte — added a necessary legitimacy to the magazine,

By Way of Luck

countering critics' claims of flagrant indecencies and outright smut. He was a noble man.

We talked through the afternoon of my arrival and through the evening. I returned to New York the next morning, but not before Augie told me of a hurdle that lay ahead. If I accepted an offer that would be forthcoming, Augie said, it would not be confirmed until I took a two-day psychological exam. My competence as a testee, or lack of it, would either affirm the offer or it would be withdrawn. Intriguing, I thought. My inner self was tickled by the novelty of it.

Was there room for negotiation? I gave it a try. Without replying to the offer, I would take the test, leaving me open thereafter either to accept or reject it. There was an additional consideration: Whether I was acceptable or not, either way, I would be given a look at the results submitted by the interviewing psychologist.

"Unusual," Augie said. "Every senior employee at *Playboy* has taken the test, including Hef. Only he knows the results."

I held firm. After a trio of phone calls, Augie told me Hefner agreed to my proposal. Just this one time, Augie said, implying it would never happen again, or was he saying I would be denied a second look?

A week later, walking into the psychologist's westside New York office was like finding myself in the Dartmouth Deke house, immediately comfortable and accepting. For four hours on each of two consecutive days we talked, I wrote answers to written questions, from pictures I described what I saw, offered interpretations, challenged the interviewer at every soft opening and was soon immersed in a one-on-one bull session that could have been held in a college dorm. Plainly, the interviewer liked me, his interest revealed by his behavior, and I liked him, as if after eight hours, head-to-head, we had become lifetime friends. Had luck brought us together?

Don Gold was on the phone. "It's all over *Playboy*," he said, having heard from one of his friends still at the magazine. "A secret everybody knows about. You've gotten the highest evaluation ever issued by the consulting psychologist. Everybody is wondering who the hell you are."

Approbation, how sweet it can be, especially coming by way of a disinterested third party with no stake in the game. I was buoyed by the recognition, making me feel good about myself at a time I was having doubts. The U.S. Air Force had given me a medal, Doubleday gave me the heave-ho, and Curtis had offered me nothing for what I considered Herculean efforts. I had made choices, not necessarily good ones, now I had a possibly better choice to make.

Was there a cinematographer filming all of this? Was Augie the walk-on or was I? What script was I reading from? Make-up? Where's make-up? I don't go on without make-up.

Augie acceded to everything I asked for, succumbing even to the excesses. I would be Director of *Playboy* Press, a unit Hef had set up to produce and publish one-shot magazines, paperbacks and books derived from published materials as well as original books I might produce or acquire. Augie added one benefit suggested by Hef that I could not have thought of. I could come and go at the *Playboy* Mansion. At any time. At any hour.

I was hooked. And, oddly, about to work for a man I hadn't met. Even odder, I was to learn, a man whose personal approval of just about everything was a rigid requirement, the decisions to be made face-to-face, directions to be given in lengthy, archly specific, non-debatable memoranda.

Marilyn Grabowski, *Playboy's* assistant photo editor, rapped on the door of my suite at Chicago's Churchill Hotel on State Street the morning I arrived by overnight train, the 20th century Limited, from Grand Central Station. "I just wanted to be the first to welcome you," she said. She brought cream cheese and bagels from an Oak Street deli, laughing away her assumption that all New Yorkers were Jewish. I called up for coffee, and asked Marilyn what she did at *Playboy*.

She worked for Vince Tajiri, *Playboy's* vice-president and photo editor, she said. My nose is too big, she went on, it's a Polack nose, I

By Way of Luck

couldn't avoid it, you know, born with it, and my legs are too skinny, I'm in charge of managing the photo shoots, the set ups, and then reviewing the takes with Vince and doing a preliminary cut with Hef, mostly running back and forth between the office and the House, I'm sorry I'm not dressed better, I worked late last night or was it early this morning, you're really going to get along here, I can tell, and sometimes Hef has Bobbi call us over so Hef can see what he may have missed or we forgot to bring, and I'm...are you listening, I'm not, so nod your head...or something, you're staring at me, am I wrong to come here, say no and I'll stay.

I said, No, and we talked till noon. Marilyn succeeded Vince and worked for Hef for almost 40 years. She died shortly after retiring.

Marilyn was the first of the many Hefner loyalists I met, worked with and came to admire, professionals all, a team in full submission of their skills and experience to a prodigious and sometimes punishing boss, Hugh Hefner:

Art Paul, Art Director and designer of the logotype and the Bunny colophon. A man with charm and an eye for the unusual, a collector of art and friends, found freshness from artists who may never have been found by anyone else.

Vince Tajiri, Photography Director, on location, in a studio, his full-time staff always on assignment, 35mm shots by the thousands, light boxes always on, Vince selecting, electing, thinking, what would Hef want, the flesh tones, the ingénue look, the perfection, dammit, there is no perfection.

John Mastro, Production director. Ink on his fingers, a patient man, willing to stand by for long hours while Hef looped through press sheets and made changes, and more changes, John nervously eying his watch and counting the dollars lost as Hef held printing presses on standby.

Bob Preuss, Executive Vice-President, Circulation director and Business Manager. Pivotal guy, solid inner disciplines, with glue hot enough to keep together the oddly assembled pieces of the corporate structure.

Jack Kessie, Managing editor. Keeping the growing editorial

department focused. Balanchine.

Vic Lownes. Hef's alter ego, savvy, a bully, a risk taker, cruel, offensive, competitive, always pushing, making things happen, the ultimate, irresponsible playboy that Hef could not be.

Promotion Director, Nelson Futch. Nervous, working late and long to overcome minimal talents, fearful of Lownes greater promotional abilities.

Dick Rosenzweig, Hef's assistant. Yes, yes and yes, get it done, move it along, hold at bay the dozen or more direct reports while Hef slept or played *paterfamilias* to the young flesh that coursed in and out of the House.

Executive Vice-President Eldon Sellers, the originator of the *Playboy* title, an early fund raiser for Hefner, a co-founder of the magazine who took charge of protecting the company's copyright and trademarks not only in the United States but in an additional 127 countries. For years after, still my closest friend. An admirable man.

And Howard Lederer, Executive Vice-President, Advertising Sales, housed in New York City, near the money, he once quipped. Spent his longest hours confirming for advertisers *Playboy's* spectacular circulation gains and explaining the purchasing power of the magazine's readers. Colorless, dreary, necessary.

And, of course, Augie Spectorsky.

How stark the contrast with Curtis and the *Post*.

Meeting most all of them within a few days was like parachuting in to a family outing, taking an offered beer and joining in on the joking and the carousing. *Playboy* the company had become big time but was still run with the quiet familiarity of a small business, with Hefner the family head.

By the time of my arrival, Hef had moved out of the East Ohio Street offices and into the House, the State Street mansion Hef had bought and remodeled into his home, his office, rooms for his retinue, and with top and bottom floor apartments for visiting firemen and, eventually, local *Playboy* bunnies and auditioning models for centerfold shoots. The mansion before it became the Mansion was referred to as the House.

By Way of Luck

I was given Hef's old office at East Ohio Street until the *Playboy* Press offices were readied. It was the beginning of two satisfying years.

Observations

Hef rarely subscribed to his apparent pleasures. He owned expensive automobiles that other people drove. He owned a DC-9 jet airplane used largely as a stage, with bunnies posing on the airport tarmac, he and his retinue of *Playboy* Playmates off on a jaunt to a distant island paradise. The House kitchen and food lockers were packed with good booze and aged steaks, kept for guests. Hef drank Pepsi Cola, ate cheeseburgers, had closets hanging deep with tailored clothing yet chose to live and work in pajamas. Nor did he ever allow himself to fall in love with any of the dramatic beauties he attracted, my surmise. His marriages were likely driven either by guilt or embarrassment, it seemed to me, and not by intimacy or affection. I think he kept count.

His pleasure was *Playboy*. Every issue, every page, every photograph, every text block, he editorially caressed and made his own before releasing it to the printer and distributor. All rumor aside, the kinky sex and the drugs, except for caffeine and an occasional deadline-induced stay-awake bennie, none of it valid, Hef was a sober work horse, committed to self-imposed deadlines, sometimes working 20, 30, 40 or more straight hours, slurping one sugared caffeinated Pepsi after another, and to a standard rarely seen in popular magazine publishing. He was embedded in *Playboy*. Not an issue since the magazine's origins in 1953, however minute the detail, has been released without Hef's hands on-approval. Today, 60 years later, readers are still getting the real thing.

Hef was also committed to promoting readership and to an exotic and openly accessible way of life. He wanted to be envied and emulated. He wanted to be physically seen as a way of adding vitality to ink-filled pages. He wanted to be positioned publicly as a patron of the good life, to be imitated by young men who couldn't figure it out for themselves. He wanted his readers to covet the company of the girls they saw in his centerfolds. He urged readers to reach out socially, to become popular, glamorous, witty and urbane and by reading his magazine they could achieve all that and more. He sought then to embody his audience. And he still does.

Hef didn't expect his employees to match his long hours of work. He expected them to do their jobs and be available when he wanted them, sometimes in the middle of the night, on weekends, or on holidays. Dozens would be awaiting his call. His demands were few. Be competent and be where I want you to be. For that commitment he paid his people well and the benefits were, well, beneficial.

Not long after joining the company, I could visualize Hef's unconventional organization chart. Picture, if you will, a figure 8 aligned horizontally. Hef sat where the loops cross, at the center point. As many as fifteen or more of his direct reports expecting his attention sat amidst the loops. Now, animate the 8, flowing as would a stream, staffers coming and going as he first summoned them and then sent them away, an organism of a kind, breathing in, and breathing out, that faithfully shaped one bestselling issue after another.

I relate all this up-front — though it represents what I learned about Hefner close up over two years — as a way of setting a scene, defining the man I would work for before relating my experiences working for him and providing the reader a perspective of *Playboy* as I saw it.

My early days at East Ohio Street I spent introducing myself to everyone I could find available for a chat. My first stop was at the office of *Playboy's* Personnel Director, Augie's wife, Theo, a fashionable woman who seemed out of place, her dress and manner more that of an up-style haute couturier than of a mid-level manager in a hot men's magazine publishing company. She was crisp. She handed me the psychologist's report. Read it here, she said.

I sped through it quickly, the report embarrassing. My cheeks flushed, I could feel the blood rushing to my face. Can I send my

By Way of Luck

mother a copy? I joked. Theo thought me serious. I backed away trying to explain myself. Mother would have loved it. The report was material for an elegant obituary when I might need one. There was a closing line to the report. A warning: Jim needs to have space for his energy and his ideas. Without it, the psychologist concluded, Jim may leave *Playboy* within two years.

Two editors, staff from the magazine, had been transferred to work with me. They were dead weight from Augie's editorial department. I saw the transfer as an early move to minimize my status. I fired them both and told them to meet with Bob Preuss for severance. Augie called immediately. Hef says thanks. He wanted me to get rid of those guys months ago.

I had attracted attention. Through Bobbi Arnstein, Hef's secretary, Augie set up my first meeting with Hef. Augie would accompany me. Three weeks had passed since my arrival.

From a block or so away, the House appeared an ancient mausoleum sitting amidst a row of somber uber rich early 1900s State Street Parkway dwellings. But as Augie and I turned into the front walk, the columns set forward and flanking the gated front door appeared welcoming, as would hands held open in a thanks-for-coming gesture. An architectural device? Or was I imaging a warm reception? We were promptly buzzed in.

Hef's office was on the second floor of the House. A door opened onto a reception area where Bobbi was stationed; beyond her desk and through the door to a well-lighted room, there was a round, blonde wood conference table where Hef could review layouts and press sheets; and to the side, a circular stair case that led to his bedroom suite below, and a refrigerator serving as cold storage for Hef's Pepsi supply. The meeting was solely social. And awkward.

Hef was in pajamas. I had on a shirt and tie, as did Augie. Both Hef and I fumbled about for opening remarks. What can you say upon greeting a celebrity editor without sounding trite or patronizing? Nice place? Love the magazine? Tell him I'm settling in, meeting the people? Seconds went by in silence. Hef broke the ice, barely.

How's your office, he said. It's your old office, I said. More silence followed, as if we had both met on Mars and were wrestling with the same canister of oxygen.

Hef seemed to be fishing for something. Augie interrupted. Hef, he said, wants to know whether you're getting laid. Hefner smiled an assenting smile.

I said, Yes. Hef relaxed, as did I, our conversation broadened, Hef telling me what he expected me to do, confirming what Augie had already explained to me from the start. He asked that I build an agenda for our next meeting. His closing remark as he descended the circular stairs to his bedroom lair: "By the way," he said. "Here, the girls get first dibs on the guys."

Dick Snyder, briefly at Doubleday, was an early call. The Press needed a distribution partner. Two *Playboy* projects were already in progress — *Playboy's Party Jokes*, a paperback, and *The Best of Playboy*, a one-shot magazine. Dick had become Simon and Schuster's Executive Vice President and Sales Director for both the trade division and its paperback subsidiary, Pocket Books. His organization seemed an easy fit. But Dick was immediately troubled by my proposal.

Hef had made clear to me that *Playboy* would be in charge of all paperback design, in fact would spec paper and cover stock and deliver camera ready layouts to Simon and Schuster and before going to press would have final approval of first press sheets. And would set the pricing. The terms would also apply as well to *Playboy's* hardcover books.

No way, Snyder said, seeing the added expense as a hurdle, his authority compromised. Two of his key sales people argued against him. I said nothing. Just listened. The sales people were eager, seeing how a relationship with *Playboy* could boost Pocket Book's sales across the board, leveraging rack jobbers and wholesalers and opening up new retail locations. Theirs was a compelling argument. We would price the paperbacks at 75 cents, this at a time when the average paperback cover price was less than 50 cents. Too rich for a paperback, Dick said.

By Way of Luck

Even I felt the pricing a bit rich and had argued it with Hef. He prevailed, of course, his manner stoic. It was the first hint I saw of his marketing genius. He understood his readers: they would willingly pay a premium for a *Playboy* paperback. And he was right.

Dick gave in, we agreed on terms, and *Playboy's Party Jokes* went to press, one printing after another, every one of them sell-outs. To my knowledge an unparalleled paperback publishing event.

The one-shot magazine distribution contract went to *Playboy's* magazine distributor, Independent News Corp. The very first one-shot published sold 2.5 million copies at $1.95 a copy in less than a month. More copies were printed. Another half million and another and another.

With the publication of *Party Jokes* and *The Best of Playboy*, my new enterprise, in less than six months, had made a no-nonsense, cash-in-the-bank profit of over $3,000,000. Business manager Bob Preuss showed me the numbers. For me it was an astounding revelation. Coming from Doubleday and Curtis, companies that would have cheered an annual profit — all titles, all issues — of a lesser amount was to me incomprehensible. I was stunned. For days I wandered, transported by the news.

Historically, publishers of general interest magazines and books built profitability over one or more generations, succumbing to the ebb and flow of the economy, and most always putting themselves at risk, managing their finances, their time and their resources, while building their editorial positions. Instant successes are rare.

Hefner had started *Playboy* with less than $10,000, all of it borrowed from friends. That it featured a sensation, a nude photograph of Marilyn Monroe, helped. His magazine, from its very first issue, was overnight profitable.

Yet behind all the explosive nudity and newness of its editorial content, though, lay the slow-to-be-told story of the company's immediate financial success. Another magazine launched by Time, Inc. within a few months of *Playboy's* inauguration, *Sports Illustrated*, its audience nearly 90% male, did not turn profitable for 15 years. Its long term struggle to gain financial break-even brought about by a single annual publishing event, borrowed willfully from *Playboy*: *Sport's Illustrated's* Swim Suit issue, featuring more nudity and provocative photography than *Playboy* had ever shown in its beginning years.

Eldon Sellers' Stunning Legacy

Eldon Sellers was Hef's first investor. They'd met in a Chicago apartment house where they and their wives lived across the hall from each other, played board games, ordered pizzas in and drank Pepsi Cola. It was the early 50s. When Hef was close to giving up on a magazine he was starting, Eldon gave Hef $4000, money borrowed from a girlfriend. Grateful, Hef gave him a chunk of company stock. Another $6000 dribbled in from various friends, former college classmates, neighbors and family, enough for Hef to finish the camera ready layouts...and no more.

There was no money left for a first printing. Hef asked the printer for credit. The printer was unwilling to take a risk on a young man's start up. He wanted proof of credit or to be paid up-front in cash.

The printer applied for a Dun & Bradstreet credit report. By a remarkable coincidence, or was it luck, his request was assigned to a D&B staffer who had just completed one investigation and was next in line for another: Eldon Sellers, who issued a modestly favorable report. The printer extended Hefner the credit he'd asked for. How true this story, I hereby confirm, just as I did before writing this paragraph. But when asked by strangers, usually when Eldon and I paired off on dates, dinners and various dalliances, he smiled a Mona Lisa smile.

When the first issue was about go to press it was titled *Stag Party*. Not *Playboy*. Lawyers for *Stag* magazine fired a shot across Hefner's bow, a polite request to cease and desist using *Stag* in its title. The threat of a lawsuit loomed. Hef didn't have the resources to challenge *Stag*. The first printing was stalled.

Eldon told Hef, don't fight *Stag*, you'll lose. Change the name,

By Way of Luck

he advised, and as an alternative offered up *Playboy!* Editorial changes were made and plates cut to accommodate the change, and *Playboy* went to press.

Consider the odds of happening what I've written about in the last few paragraphs. Hefner meets a guy in his apartment building. With their wives they play board games together. Hefner says he's starting a magazine and needs money. The guy gives him roughly half the money he's asking for. Hefner needs credit. The guy works for D&B; he's assigned to respond to a request for a credit report on Hefner. A potentially rival magazine, *Stag*, threatens suit. The guy, the same guy he met in his apartment house, the same guy who loans him money, the same guy who issues the credit report, says change the name and offers up *Playboy!* A Las Vegas odds maker couldn't have predicted a luckier scenario. What a parlay!

Hef, now living in LA and Eldon, retired and at home in Napa Valley, are still friends, close enough to remember each other's birthdays, Hef now 87, Eldon 92. By the time I got to *Playboy*, both had been divorced and were unmarried.

How Eldon and I bonded, I cannot recall, but we somehow sought each other out and became pals. Eldon had been a B-24 pilot during WW II; I was still flying, leasing aircraft from a fixed base operator at Midway Airport. Eldon became my co-pilot. We hung out together, at local clubs that featured performers we wanted to hear, at restaurants new on the scene, on golf courses and resorts we could fly to, and joining up on occasion with other local pilots for fly-in's. And we introduced each other to girls we'd met and double-dated together.

One such introduction had lasting consequences. I resisted the tempting possibilities that *Playboy* offered, the willing and generous girls who might join me on a night out. I was and still am a private person, and found uncomfortable dating in a workplace where tales told at morning coffee hard-lined the events of the night before. In time, I met a young woman from Iowa, a graduate of Drake University in Des Moines and a recently hired copy writer at Chicago's Leo Burnett Agency. Her name was Maggie. She had a friend who'd just earned a Master's Degree at Northwestern University in Evanston. Her name was Nancy. They were attractive ladies, smart and determined to build careers.

I dated Maggie and introduced Eldon to Nancy; they began dating. Eldon and I had a life outside of *Playboy* and took some grief for it. Augie said I'd drifted into the land of no-no's. Jack Kessie, whenever we might pass in a hallway, simply shook his head in disbelief. He had tried unsuccessfully to match me up with some of his favorite Playmates.

Two years later, Eldon and Nancy were married as were Maggie and I. Eldon was my best man; I was Eldon's. Maggie and Nancy stood up for each other. Along the way we played bridge, took vacations, ate at each other's apartments, and hunted constantly for adventures we could experience as a foursome — golf, theater, concerts, good restaurants and airplane trips.

Meantime, *Playboy* Press was doing what Hef expected it to do. But I felt under-used. Each step in my progress required Hef's OK. He couldn't let go. I explained Hef's MO, his *modus operandi*, at lunch one day at the Tavern Club with Mortimer Adler, the Editor in Chief of *Encyclopedia Britannica*. How does anything get done? Mortimer asked. It gets done, I said, when Hef decides it gets done, often at the most unexpected times.

As if on cue, the Club *maître d'* came to our table. A telephone call, Mr. Perkins. It was Dick Rosenzweig. My name, traveling the loop of the figure 8, had arrived at the intersection. I was next up. Hef's ready for you, Dick said. I excused myself. Mort said he understood but thought Hef's management style unconventional. He'd call to suggest a new date, he said.

I had four hours with Hef. We got a lot done, but I had no idea how to get on his schedule should I again need his OK. Nor was it clear when an OK might be necessary. Augie told me not to worry. Hef will call you.

Managing Editor Jack Kessie and I became close as well. Jack was all style. His editorial focus was assigning staff and commis-

By Way of Luck

sioning free-lance writers to produce the service articles that spoke of manner and means, fashion and demeanor, and advice that could coax a young reader into a world of glamor and self-confidence. Jack saw himself as the model to be imitated.

As Managing Editor, his job was to plan each issue, manage assignments and pull together all editorial materials into a cohesive whole which Augie would then review with Hef for a final OK. Hef, meantime, was focused on all things graphic: primarily layouts, art and photography, and finally, editorial copy in which he had a personal interest, such as the *Playboy* Philosophy Series, and to a lesser extent the content of the regular features, from Party Jokes to Letters to the Editor. Jack was not usually present for the final run to publication. His work had already been done, and he had turned to the next issue and the next, thinking and working ahead to as many as six future issues.

Jack's wife, Carol, was editor of the Letters to the Editor column. At dinner together at a local bistro, Jack wrinkled his nose at my suggestion for a wine. Too sweet, he scolded. Jim, he went on, if you cherish respect, you must know your wines. Jack became my wine advisor. I took him hunting on two occasions at a Wisconsin Shooting Preserve. He knew his guns and was adept at handling them. In his apartment he kept a .357 Magnum revolver, a high velocity cannon he took some pride in owning. He told me it could be fired at an automobile from the front end and the bullet would come out the back end. Other than the satisfaction of having a gun at hand should he ever need one, I had no idea why he would ever need one. But one day he did.

I built staff. Augie encouraged me to fill out a manning chart he and Hef had penciled on a yellow-lined paper pad. The chart overlooked one element: a time factor. Whatever schedule I might build and the time line I might set to publish, it would be idled by the indefinite wait between decisions. *Playboy* Press was making one million after another, but the surge it provided the company's cash flow was met with indifference. *Playboy* Press wasn't building anything; we were simply wringing what was left out of past issues and scrounging among the unpublished inventory for materials we could responsibly add.

Yet, while his work patterns were frustrating, Hef was a good boss. He was direct, explained his concerns, made clear what he wanted, tolerated argument and had no reluctance to teach. But there were no jokes to be laughed at unless Hef told them.

Don Myrus joined me coming from New York City. Don was a writer and an editor, and good at both. He'd been among the first to spot the talent and musical persuasiveness of Bob Dylan's poetry and wrote the first-to-be-published Dylan biography. Don was professional and diligent. He had just come off a start-up, a hard cover magazine, *American Gun*, that under his guidance was beautifully edited and produced, but published for an audience difficult to reach. Gun owners buy guns, Don finally concluded ruefully, but rarely buy books about guns. The magazine had closed after three issues.

Within months of Don's arrival, Augie snatched him from me and put him to work editing and rewriting a Hefner biography that had been abandoned by an earlier biographer. At *Playboy*, Don was seen as a piece that fit Hefner's needs. Hef and the magazine came first.

I hired Peter Lacey, another New Yorker, coincidentally with a sister who worked at the Mansion. Also within months Hefner scooped him up, assigning him an office in the Mansion where he could edit and manage Hefner's scrapbooks. I was dulled by Peter's transfer, but Peter was excited. Without much ado, he had found himself in the middle of Hefner's head, that is, amidst a collection of truly personal records that recorded most of Hefner's life, often in minute detail and graphically replete. Peter had currency, stories to tell and an audience anxious to listen.

I hired a youngster not long out of college, Gary Cole. He was conscripted by the photography department to work with Marilyn.

I was good at recruiting people Hef found valuable. But unable to hang on to them.

While Hefner talked of expansion, he had difficulty devoting his

By Way of Luck

time and energy to something other than *Playboy* magazine. His inattention showed when he started SBI, *Show Business Illustrated*, a monthly that covered the entertainment business. Almost simultaneously, Huntington Hartford published *Show Magazine*, its editor, Bob Wool, a Dartmouth classmate. It was similarly positioned.

According to Augie Spectorsky, Hef appeared uncomfortable taking on a direct competitor, each of them having to compete for similar space on the newsstands. He also had difficulty articulating a strategy for what would become a competitive fight. He soon gave up trying. SBI lasted a mere eight issues.

Not long after, discouraged by general indifference to *Show*, Hartford pulled the plug on it. Hef might have outlasted Hartford, but clearly it was not an option for him, fearful, I believe, that it might drain resources away from *Playboy* magazine.

Other *Playboy* failures classified as "suspended operations" followed: the resorts at Great Gorge in New Jersey and Lake Geneva, Illinois; the *Playboy* Clubs, for a while highly popular and profitable, but unmanageable; the London gambling casinos, shut down for "legal" reasons; the TV specials, starring Hefner, expensively produced, with all-star performances, yet dimmed by Hefner's insistence on appearing as Host. A Johnny Carson he was not. Appearing most often in a smoking jacket or a stiff-fitting tuxedo, a pipe in hand and attempting to be congenial, he seemed the antithesis of what *Playboy* was all about. There was no fun and no sex.

I got the feeling that Hef wasn't having any fun either, that he wasn't the playboy featured in *Playboy* the magazine. One of his rituals was to preside at one of the more solemn occasions of the week: the Sunday movie at the Mansion, a screening of a newly released film. Staffers and invitees would begin gathering in the Great Hall around 4:30 PM. A banquet sized buffet was set up in front of the fireplace: there was food and drink aplenty. Hung from a longer wall, a screen was rolled up, ready to be unfurled. Directly in front was a puffy couch, seating for Hef and his girlfriend of the moment. Others would find cushioned seats behind. Sometimes at 5 PM, more often at a later time, Hefner would stroll into the

Great Hall, wave indifferently and plop onto the couch, holding his girlfriend around the waist with one hand, holding an open Pepsi in the other. The lights would dim and the show would begin. At the end of the showing Hef might wave hello. He tried to be social, but he appeared distracted. Perhaps his mind was on unfinished work, either in his office or his bedroom. He'd find some way to slip unnoticed from the room. Seldom did he stay long.

What struck me most about the Sunday gatherings, it was non-discriminatory. Age up, age down, white, black, Hispanic, boy, girl, straight or gay, corporate exec, mail room gopher. There was but one obvious exclusion: I saw no flat chested women.

Apparently, I could not — within what I might consider a reasonable time — build the enterprise that Augie and Hef had talked about, not if I had to wait in the wings for Hef's fetching call. So I began looking for other ways to achieve the growth I assumed was Hef's goal, of building a bigger publishing enterprise. I had come to know the owner of Popular Library, Ned Pines. His company was based in New York City and after Bantam Books, New American Library, Dell and Pocket Books it was the fifth largest paperback publisher in the United States. Ned was struggling. Fifth place didn't allow him what he needed most. He had good titles. He was a good publisher. But he didn't have the muscle to get front and center rack space. And he couldn't afford to acquire and promote the blockbuster books that would get it for him. Though he was Popular's founder, he had no illusions regarding its promise. He and I had a meeting at his apartment at the Stanhope Hotel on Fifth Avenue. Ned was a willing seller.

Back in Chicago, I sat with Bob Preuss and cautiously told him about Ned, about Popular Library, and the possibility of *Playboy* as a buyer. Just fishing, I said, unwilling to be seen as assuming an authority I clearly did not have. Bob could not have cared less. He saw immediately how an acquisition could work. Popular would become a wholly-owned *Playboy* subsidiary. Popular would have the exclusive license to publish *Playboy's* paperback and hard cover

By Way of Luck

books, and its one-shot magazines. The publishing lists would be merged and *Playboy's* magazine distributor, Independent News Corporation, also the distributor of *Mad Magazine*, would become, except for the hard cover books, the *Popular/Playboy* distributor. In time, if not right away, the Popular name would be dropped.

Though it would have to give up its relationship with New American Library, Independent supported the proposition strongly. Among wholesalers and jobbers, as distributor of the two best-selling, national point-of-sale magazines, *Playboy* and *Mad*, Independent would become the largest player in magazine distribution, and dominant.

Bob thought the proposition commendable. It could not have come at a better time, he said. It would give *Playboy* Enterprises the leverage it needed to establish a substantial and diversified publishing platform while reducing the risk of its dependence on a single publication. Further, Bob said, Popular Library, merged with *Playboy* Press, would add extraordinary value to an IPO then being considered by *Playboy*.

I'll take it to Hef, Bob said.

Bob had earned his position. Hef had confidence in him as Executive Vice-President and Business Manager, as the company's CFO and as head of distribution. I was the new guy on the block and didn't carry enough weight. Bob would have to make the sale.

Bob returned from the Mansion discouraged. Hef said no, he reported. Was it the price? I felt we could buy Popular library for $2,000,000 cheap. Was it the acquisition of a company that stood number five in a competitive business? Was it Popular Library's back list?

None of the above, Bob said. Hef didn't like the idea. "All it would prove," Hef had told him, "is that *Playboy* could buy its way into a business." He'd rather build the company internally than pay for its growth.

Bob's argument went nowhere. It would be financially safer and faster, he told Hef, to acquire a going business than taking on the risk of building one.

Hef still said no. There was no room for appeal.

Bob Preuss was depressed by Hef's decision. Sitting in his office, he confessed to having higher hopes for the company he had helped build. Further, arguing in favor of acquiring Popular, Hef had intimated that Bob was being disloyal. Bob shook his head in disbelief. "Can you believe? he said.

I could.

Similarly depressed, I had to conclude that Hef was more interested in show biz than publishing, SBI, The *Playboy* Clubs, *Playboy* television, *Playboy After Dark* and, later on, yet to come, *Playboy's* cable channels, all evidence of that. Clearly, he saw himself more as a celebrity performer and less as a publisher. He was then, and still is, the featured act in on-going TV appearances, now at age 87 a sweet old man still playing the lothario.

Did I have a future at *Playboy*, one that met my needs? I liked *Playboy*, just being there, doing a job at an acceptable level, being well-paid in a company with a strong cash flow and no debt, engaging with interesting people, and if I kept my place in Hef's figure eight organization chart, I could have a relaxed, no sweat, long run with the company. That I'd gotten a 15% raise after nine months of employment — with apologies from Augie that he had hoped I'd get more — confirmed my perceived value.

Moreover, I liked the people, they appeared to like me, and I was having fun. After prep school, college, the US Air Force and a confusing go at book publishing, followed by the failure of the *Post* — and having my marriage break apart — I had been under constant pressure. At *Playboy* there was little pressure. Stress, yes. A meeting with Hef could be stressful even if we were just sitting at a poker game in his office. And not knowing how and when Hef might appear or disappear could be stressful, too. But the pressure wasn't there.

The mood throughout the company was up-beat. Editors, production people, promotion managers seemed always to have good things to say to one another; the economic burden that depresses most folks just didn't exist at *Playboy*, not then, and not until the

By Way of Luck

competition from *Playboy* look-alikes began and Hefner showed himself as more the imitator than the competitor, giving in to panic and going gross. But that was a long way off.

One evening, having a late night drink at the Mansion and chatting with a few of the residents, Jodie, Hef's butler, told me there were several men at the front door wanting to say hello to Hef. Norman Mailer was among them.

I asked Jodie to find out where Hef was and meantime, I said, let Mailer in. I wanted to meet him and I thought Hef might wish to as well.

Accompanying Mailer, in Chicago for the annual meeting of the American Library Association, and also at the front door, were ALA guest speakers and authors John Cheever, Ralph Ellison and David Halberstam. The four were among the most publicly acclaimed writers of the 1960s. Halberstam had won a Pulitzer Prize for his reporting on the Viet Nam War. Mailer was best known then for *The Naked and the Dead*, a World War II novel that won the National Book Award; he would later win another for *Armies of the Night*. Cheever's New England novel, *The Wapshot Chronicles*, had won a National Book Award as well. And Ellison, author of *The Invisible Man*, was also a National Book Award winner. I made sure they all had a drink before finding out whether Hef was either awake, working or sleeping. He would want to meet them, so I thought.

Jodie said Hef was working and couldn't be interrupted. Our guests were four of the best working writers in the United States and if Hef were available, not meeting with them would be seen as a snub, however late the hour. I demurred. Jodie disappeared. In minutes, Hef emerged in pajamas and dressing robe.

How would Hef would handle them, I wondered? Had he read their writings, any of them? I doubted it. Could he be his usual urbane self in discussion with these masters of literature? Yes.

Hef was put swiftly on the spot. The four writers pumped him as might a questioning presidential press corps. They wanted to find out, in picky detail, what it was like being Hugh Hefner, asking about the magazine, about Bunnies and centerfolds, probing for the nitty gritty, and prompting Hef to talk about his "*Playboy* Philosophy" articles. Hef's questions were ignored. He was the greater star. Late night finally caught up with them and I walked them to the door while Hef went back to work.

(The night Norman Mailer won the National Book Award for *Armies of the Night,* he took me and my wife Maggie, his publisher Sidney Kramer and his wife Esther, and his mother and father to dinner.)

The following day I got a call from Dick Rosenzweig, Hef's assistant. Hef says thanks for letting Mailer and his friends into the house.

My children were living with their mother in Vermont. For visits I'd either go there or bring them to Chicago. On one such visit, on a rainy day that scratched a promised afternoon at the Oak Street beach, I took them to the Mansion for a swim in Hef's indoor pool, known to most *Playboy* readers for its grotto, a room below the pool's water line with a bench and a thick slab of glass through which observers could watch swimmers frolicking underwater. It was the middle of the week during daylight hours. We had the pool to ourselves. But not for long.

Hef came by to say hello. Told by Dick Rosenzweig that I was in the pool with three "babes," he was noticeably surprised the girls were 6, 8 and 10 years old and my daughters. Yet, he was affable, and asked the kids one or two friendly father/child questions before returning to his quarters, saying in an aside to me, "They're probably the only virgins who ever swam in this pool."

There are but three Hefner long-time, almost from the beginning, loyalists still with *Playboy*: Vic Lownes, Dick Rosenzweig and Hef's brother Keith. Vic was unquestionably the bigger personality, a promoter, able easily to ingratiate himself with others, and a formidable presence. My observation: he invented and played the public Hugh Hefner while the private Hugh Hefner did all the work. Vic conceived and drove the build-out of the *Playboy* Clubs, the resorts

By Way of Luck

and the British casinos. He was magnetic. People at all social and business levels were drawn to him. There wasn't a closed doorway he couldn't open without being welcomed.

I spent a week with him in his Park Lane town house in London, there to re-establish relationships with International publishers whom I'd done business with at Doubleday and to evaluate possible distribution partners for the UK and the larger international English speaking market. On my arrival, Vic handed me a schedule of appointments. He'd booked time for us with every major publisher in the city!

(Hef appeared baffled by what Vic and I had done. Again, I was confronted by his insistence that all things Playboy had to be developed internally. That seeking outside relationships as adjunct to our primary business was somehow forbidden. But...*Playboy* was his company. I respected that.)

On a side trip to Frankfurt where the annual International Book Fair was in progress, Vic joined me. It would be a new experience for a man who fed on new experiences. Within minutes after entering the exhibition Hall, word sped through the giant display area that a vice-president of *Playboy* was in attendance. Vic was soon surrounded by a score of foreign editors and publishers turned curiosity seekers. How could that happen? He hadn't sent out an advance press release. He just showed up. Vic, I was convinced, was the sorcerer's apprentice.

An example: On one early evening after we'd returned to London, he asked, "Anything you'd like to do?"

Weary, I said, "No."

He said, "Let's just hang out and see what happens."

By 10 o'clock, the house was swarming with young people, mostly lithesome girls all wanting a piece of Vic. From a nearby restaurant where he was known, food and drink arrived as if heaven sent — obviously this was not an unusual event. By 3 AM, when the boy-girl ratio had evened out, and the magic had waned, I went upstairs to bed wondering how the party had come about. What began as an uneventful evening had turned riotous.

The next morning, Vic shook me awake. Someone had told him I'd taken two girls up the stairs with me and he was anxious to find out how it went. I told him it hadn't happened. But he refused to believe me. Were I to tell him today that I had slept alone that night, he'd still have me going up those stairs for a threesome. For Vic, it was an event to be celebrated.

Vic asked me to give up Chicago and work with him in London. He'd square it away with Hef and Augie, he said. He painted a glowing picture of the action: the casinos, the girls, the international clientele, the girls, the expansion onto the continent, the girls, the country estate he was buying...and the girls. He was so far a one-man show, he said, and needed a sidekick. He couldn't accept that I was serious about publishing; it was what I did, I told him. Serious comes second, Vic said. Play comes first.

After I got done in London what I'd come to do, I went back to Chicago. Giving Augie an anecdotal report of the trip, he told me Vic had been playing me. Vic was no longer with *Playboy,* he said. There had been a falling out between him and Hef. Vic was a cast-off. Hef had fired him. (Later there would be a falling back together again.) Vic settled in London. Operating under the guise of a *Playboy* executive (he had the business cards, the stationery, a check book and his name on the magazine's masthead), he started the first *Playboy* London casino, opening up bank accounts and borrowing the money to do it as though actually part of *Playboy* which, Augie assured me, he was not.

Hef had made an ineffective, half-hearted attempt to stop him. But half a heart was not enough. Though angered by Vic's assumptive play, Hef apparently couldn't say no to Vic. Vic was trading on a Hefner weakness: Hef dearly admired Victor Lownes.

Vic asked me to work with him just to irritate Hefner, Augie said. Stealing the new guy with the great promise would be seen by *Playboy* people as a coup in Vic's on-going face-offs with Hef. After a couple of months, after Vic had run his last victory lap, Augie said, he'd have fired you.

Augie added, Don't take it personally.

By Way of Luck

Learning all that, how could I not feel the innocent?

Meantime, with the demise of so many iconic magazines, as a defensive move major publishers, Hearst, Conde Nast, Bertelsmann, Meredith, Time, Inc., and the Los Angeles Times' parent company, Times Mirror, among them, had begun to acquire and consolidate their various publishing enterprises, managing change and at the same time diversifying their holdings. Keeping track of the jostling and the repositioning and astonished at how fast it was happening, I questioned whether there was a larger trend afoot, what could it mean for *Playboy* and for me?

Further, I asked myself, should I ignore the changes taking place in New York and elsewhere and, also defensively, hunker down in Chicago with a good job, obviously appreciated and with the possibility of a long run? Or? Or what? Or make a change.

The questions I was asking of myself would unexpectedly be answered.

Fade to black

John Budlong called me. He had been for a decade the president of McGraw Hill's trade publishing division and had within the last two years become President of paperback publisher New American Library following its acquisition by Times Mirror. He would be in Chicago in a few days and wanted to talk about the possibility of acquiring future rights to one or more *Playboy* paperbacks. We were happy with Simon and Schuster, I told him, but he thought it might be useful for us to talk, whether or not anything came of it. He brought two of his colleagues; we chatted in my new office in the remodeled Palmolive Building, now the *Playboy* Building. John thought the office spectacular, on a corner overlooking Michigan Avenue on one side, on Lake Michigan on the other. He didn't stay long.

But in the short time he was there, I heard said more than once that the Times Mirror Company was investing hugely in books and magazines, their strategy, diversification to reduce their dependency on newspapers. Among their properties: *The Los Angeles Times, Newsday, The Denver Post,* the *Houston Post* and the *Dallas Times Herald*. Altogether Times Mirror's newspapers were delivering over 60% of the company revenues and a far greater percentage of the profits, a precarious balance TM sought to correct.

Quite coincidentally, within a week of Budlong's return to New York, Ed Ernest, the editor in chief of Grosset and Dunlap, called. I'd met "Ernie", as he was known in the trade, during Curtis's negotiations for the sale of its share of Bantam Books. We'd had lunch at the Lotus Club on East 66th Street, an affable get together, and until his call I had not heard from him since. He said he had recommended me to the Times Mirror Company. The company was establishing a presence in New York City. One of Ernie's former colleagues would be running it and needed a number two.

How did they come to you, I asked, finding the back-to-back phone calls confusing and wondering how two Times Mirror encounters, first Budlong, then Ernie, had come about, just as I was contemplating a change.

Ernie didn't know who Budlong was. Ernie's contact was Martin Levin, once Grosset's Senior Vice President and Sales Director, now Times Mirror's new guy in New York with the management responsibilities for seven book publishing subsidiaries. You'll be hearing from Martin, he said.

Seven publishing subsidiaries! A return to New York. And being part of perhaps the largest publishing conglomerate in the United States. It could not be coincidence. It had to be luck.

Reprise

Dick Rosenzweig, a graduate of Northwestern University and an assistant to Hef while I was there, emerged decades later and after the retirement of Hef's daughter, Christie, as the rock around which all things *Playboy* today cling like moss. He did what Hef wanted done, advising but never questioning, interacting with associates senior to him with respect and poise far beyond his years. As the

By Way of Luck

Hef empire grew, Dick grew with it, taking on an ever wider array of responsibilities and discharging them with skill and diplomacy. He is today the main stay of the company.

Dick is still with Hef, as are Vic and Keith. Eldon Sellers, now 92, lives in the Napa Valley.

Peter Lacey, tiring of editing and producing Hef's scrap books went to work for the *Reader's Digest* in Pleasantville, New York.

Don Myrus returned to New York as Associate Publisher of *Penthouse* magazine. Don said *Penthouse* owner, Bob Guccione was easily the best boss he'd ever had. "He left me alone," Don said, "and paid me a lot of money."

Hefner continued hiring exceptionally well qualified people to head *Playboy* Press. Few of them stayed long.

Playboy, these many years later, and after working there but two years, still has a place in my heart. I was comfortable there. I felt the affection of my colleagues and my Chicago friends. My minor mishaps were ignored. How Hef managed his employees was tolerable. The management structure was simple: there was Hef and everyone else. Seniority did not depend on a traditional organizational chart. Employees were valued for what they did, not where they stood. I enjoyed what I was doing. But I was driven to do something bigger.

Graciously, Augie Spectorsky gave me a lavish going away party, opening afresh a 75 year old hand-me-down cognac and toasting my decision to return to New York. In an aside, he said, "I'm perturbed." Hefner had scolded him for letting me get away, he told me. And had offered a sharp critique of his management style. Augie was visibly upset.

The Long barreled .357 Magnum

In 1981, my friend Jack Kessie put the business end of a .357 Magnum against his hard palate and tapped the hair-trigger. He knew how to do it. The blast blew the top of his head apart and he was instantly and presumed painlessly dead. Jack had long fought the slow onslaught of hepatitis c. The virus known as HVC inexorably won. He'd held it off for several years, ever thinning and drifting deeper into depression, this once vital man plunging into dark places, the pain and the humiliation, mostly the humiliation, making his decision easier. He just did it.

9

Location, Location, Location

Martin Levin was a Grosset & Dunlap lifer, and grateful to have the job. Although Grosset had an exceptional back list of children's books and hard cover reprints, the company was obscure and operated in book publishing's backwater. Owned in the 1960s by three major publishers, Random House, Little Brown and Harper, it was likely to remain that way. Levin, though smart and resourceful, dwelt in anonymity and was also likely to remain that way. Martin was not high on himself nor on his chances of advancing to any higher level as a publishing executive.

The decision by the Times Mirror Company (TM) to have a New York City presence changed all that for Martin Levin and in the years following his recruitment by the Times Mirror, Martin Levin had an influence on how book publishing in America was perceived and valued. In part, because of his ascension to a major publishing position, and with TM's predatory resolve, the book industry began a slow but obvious shift from a closed, secretive New York City social club to a more open, publically conscious business community.

Just days after accepting an offer from Albert V. Casey, Times Mirror's president and CEO, to consolidate and head up the company's book publishing subsidiaries, Martin leaned on his Grosset colleague, Ed Ernest, for advice on personnel. Ed gave him my Chicago number.

I was Martin's first hire, named vice-president to Martin's presidency of the New York operation and thrust suddenly into the dynamics of the publishing business — newspapers and books — at its topmost levels.

Casey, too, was new to Times Mirror, brought in by the company's owners to fix a decade's worth of not so worthy acquisitions, a grab bag of marginally positioned companies either troubled or without discernible upside potential. Among major corporate CEO's, Casey stood as a celebrity. Boston born, his southie's accent faintly audible, with a Harvard MBA and a career in fast ascent, he was indifferent to corporate protocols. If he sought information, I soon learned, he'd by-pass the layers of management beneath him and go directly to a primary source. Most often, he knew the answers to the questions he posed; he sought confirmation, he said, but likely it was a technique to keep a sprawling company from Balkanizing itself. I liked him, his affability genuine, his concerns real. If he had detractors, it was among those who froze in fear when Libby, Al's secretary, came on the phone, her formal voice asking, "Please hold for Mr. Casey."

Martin arranged for us to spend several days at the Times Mirror's Los Angeles offices where in a series of informal meetings I was introduced to the Chandlers, the Times Mirror's principal owners, Norman Chandler, Dorothy Chandler and their son and publisher of the *Los Angeles Times*, Otis Chandler, and to the senior executives of company. The introductions included house counsel Bob Erburu who later became Times Mirror's CEO and still later the Chairman of the Board of the J. Paul Getty Cultural Center.

Times Mirror and its flagship property, the Los Angeles Times, was a formidable company. Located at the intersection of 1st and Spring Streets, its headquarters building in downtown Los Angeles, it owned multiple newspapers and television stations, magazines. news services, printing plants and a world-wide news gathering organization.

In 1967, Casey decided that TM's eastern subsidiaries could not be managed solely from Los Angeles. It had to become more visible in New York City.

By Way of Luck

Martin's hire preceded my hiring by several months. When I joined him, he had already set up offices in the tower of the Banker's Trust building at 280 Park Avenue. Mrs. Chandler had furnished our space, an entire floor, highlighting our conference room with an exceptional Hans Hoffman painting, one of her favorites, she said. As soon as we settled in, a stream of West Coast TM corporate leaders stopped by for visits and a briefing on what we would be doing.

The celebratory dust quickly settled. Martin had come slowly to the demands of the job. TM's east coast publishing companies, managed from a distance, were in financial and operational disarray, without direction and, in three instances, unprofitable. Casey set the priorities: fix them, sell them or shut them down. And he added, if you find a company we should buy, make the case and buy it. Martin's challenge was far greater than managing a simple reorganization as he had expected; he was faced with bringing about a major transformation.

Martin was palpably unsettled by what he had to do. I was not. Though Martin's junior — it was 1967, I was 34, he was 49 — I had the larger experience. Martin was a salesman and a good one, but he hadn't dealt with companies in trouble, as I had at Curtis, nor with the volatility of a surging bestselling magazine, nor the high level politicking that goes on in a major government organization. Martin had grown up in a modest home, had a modest education, had a modest job and had modest expectations. It wasn't a question of smarts — Martin had plenty of that.

He had thought of himself as a one company loyalist and down the line enjoying a satisfactory retirement package. He was quick to catch up, but during those first few months, while we argued our priorities, our office was muddled by uncertainty and the plotting of endless scenarios. Martin sought sureness. We could not proceed, he insisted, if there was the possibility of failure. Yet we had to start somewhere.

The bigger problems lay with paperback publishers New American Library (NAL), in New York, and its British subsidiary, New English Library (NEL), in London, and book publisher World

Publishing Company in Cleveland. Both losing money and without adequate direction. Martin and I collaborated in their re-organization; he took the lead at NAL and NEL and I took the lead at World.

NAL had a new senior management team — recruited almost entirely from McGraw-Hill's trade group and overseen by John Budlong — with the company a little more than two years. The team had a self-destructive strategy: the bigger the royalty advances paid, the greater the opportunity for NAL to acquire reprint rights for the potentially better selling books. It outbid competitors by wide margins. But the best-selling titles were not earning back their advances. The company was imploding.

Meanwhile, NAL was deferring the expense of the income shortfall, in effect, cooking the books. When the evidence surfaced, Martin fired NAL's John Budlong. He immediately replaced him with Sydney Kramer, the same Sydney Kramer who'd once stood astride Curtis and Grosset.

Book publishing in the United States in the 60s was a small industry. Annual sales, 1968, all imprints, all categories, text, technical, medical, children's, trade, fiction, non-fiction, retail, mail order, hard cover, paperback, and all related subsidiary rights, amounted in the aggregate to $4.4 billion, a *Publisher's Weekly* conclusion and substantially less than the same-year sales of the Lockheed Aircraft Company. Further, the industry's growth rate was historically slow. Wall Street analysts predicted it would continue that way. The Times Mirror's expectations appeared unrealistic.

The publishing of books was seen then as a gentlemen's endeavor, with the comings and goings of high level players managed quietly and without fuss. Few book publishers were publically incorporated. Deals were made among them by an "old boys" group. Ivy leaguers and men from substantial families sat at the heads of most boards, belonged to the same social clubs and played golf together on Westchester courses and on the distant reaches of Long Island. The1960s were a throwback to the 1930s. Budlong's firing marked a change,

Now comes a new scenario: A publicly held Los Angeles, California, newspaper company buys a few independently owned, marginally

By Way of Luck

profitable though highly visible eastern book publishers. The LA company is headed by a little known CEO, Albert V. Casey, with no publishing background, his feet concrete deep in the financial community. Casey is unsatisfied with the Eastern publishers seeming indifference to profitability and financial growth, maintaining the status quo apparently satisfactory, yet to TM an unacceptable business strategy.

Casey hires a salesman, Martin Levin, Jewish and from a minor league company to straighten out the TM subsidiaries. Levin then hires as a number two from *Playboy*, a skin magazine, a former editor fired by Doubleday. Further, Levin augments his staff by hiring two financial types from his own side of the street, Herb Schnall and Ed Ruzinski, from *Parents Magazine*, their only publishing experience. Then as one of Levin's first moves he fires one of the "old boys," John Budlong. New York publishers were amused. I could hear the chuckling and the patronizing commentary.

If the East Coast people were to meet Casey's goals, the labors that lay ahead could be brutal.

I don't believe Martin had ever before fired a senior executive. He agonized the firing before and after letting John go. I felt badly for Martin, and John, too. The mismanagement of NAL had gone on long before either of them had become involved with the company. Within a few weeks, John was re-employed, but Martin was left to figuring out NAL's much needed fix.

I welcomed Sydney's appointment. But I was not sensitive to the antipathy that lay between him and Martin. Sydney blamed Martin, among other Grosset executives, for being left out of the deal in the sale of Curtis's ownership of Bantam Books to Grosset. Yet Martin hired him to lead NAL, to me a confusing move but not at all confusing to Sydney. He sought the job and convinced Martin to hire him. Sydney immediately put up a wall between himself and Martin. Martin had put the right guy in the right job but now couldn't talk to him. I became the interlocutor.

Sydney, in his quiet and steadfast way, eventually fixed NAL, largely by ignoring Martin.

World was a bit more complicated. The company was a publisher of general trade books, dictionaries and Bibles. Its biggest seller was the renowned *New World Dictionary*; its biggest asset lexicographer David Guralnik and his querying team of editors and researchers who kept the dictionary up-to-date.

World also had a printing plant and a bindery.

World was showing a profit, but it was eating cash, calling regularly on TM for infusions, millions at a time, and demonstrating that the cash was needed for the growth TM demanded. The profit was unreal; like its books, it was being manufactured.

Both the printing plant and the publishing division reported to World's president. His incentive plan was rich, a combination of TM stock and cash. Over the short term, the payoff could be easily maximized. Print orders were placed unrealistically high. The printing division would print and sell its output to the publishing division; by controlling both the cost of printing and the amount of the sale, the division was assuredly profitable. The publishing division simply warehoused the unsold books and never wrote them off. Their potential losses, hence, were never realized. The warehouse was a morgue, books still on skids shrink-wrapped, piled high and forgotten. Yet they appeared on the corporate balance sheet as valued assets. Inevitably, World's strategy could lead to financial disaster.

Further, the company was rife with nepotism, most employees having close relatives in the company. That a sales manager's assistant was his son and his secretary a niece, it was not surprising that his wife was a supervisor in the bindery managing her sister and one of her sister's children. On the day before Thanksgiving when traditionally employees were given a free turkey, six gobblers were carried home by one family. The ties, one family to another, created an immovable block to management, stronger than any union and challenging to the owners.

Martin, still fretting the decision he'd made canning Budlong, nonetheless bit hard and fired the president of World. Immediately I was shuttling between New York and Cleveland. After wrestling with several options, we split the company in two, transferring its trade editorial operation — keeping the dictionary and bible edito-

By Way of Luck

rial in Cleveland — to New York City where Martin could keep an eye on it and transferring two editors from NAL to run it.

The two editors, Ed Kuhn, a Dartmouth alum, and Bob Gutwillig, had promoted NAL's strategy of offering heavy, unrealistic advances. Their move to World, I counseled Martin, was equally unrealistic. They would simply continue doing at World what they had been doing at NAL. Our opposing views led to a nasty argument. Martin, a religious man, believed in redemption. I did not.

Kuhn and Gutwillig lasted little more than a year at World, leaving finally to take on a new job and a new company: *Playboy*. They would, from offices high in New York City, work for Hugh Hefner and run *Playboy* Press.

(Who's the director here? Can't he see that such a coincidence is an unbelievable twist in the plot line?)

Neither they nor *Playboy* sought my advice. I would have told Kuhn and Gutwillig that sitting in Hef's Mansion, not 20 feet from Hef's office, I had trouble getting on his calendar; that from New York, it would be impossible. I would have told *Playboy* that Kuhn and Gutwillig were arbitrary, big spenders and fundamentally unmanageable. Fact bore out the comments I might have made.

With Martin's approval I hired a qualified manager I'd known previously to manage World's printing operation. In time, the manager gathered several investors and bought the plant and the real estate. Times Mirror financed the deal. And when the printing company was later sold, TM recovered its investment and showed a profit from the sale.

Along the way, Martin suggested I might want to move to Cleveland and take the job myself. What? Martin's suggestion was incomprehensible.

I shared my concern with Sydney who was not surprised. Martin has a history of abandoning people who get too close, he told me. Martin, he went on, actually pushed his eldest son out of their home. The son moved to Peru. Their estrangement had gone on for years.

Yet Martin could occasionally show some class, though it showed only in small gestures. Mary Hemingway and Jack Hemingway,

Ernest Hemingway's widow and son, called for an appointment. Contracts for the elder Hemingway's books published by Charles Scribner and Son were about to expire. Confidentially, Mary and Jack were planning to auction the rights, but TM, given acceptable compensation, could have first refusal. Martin was polite, thanked them for considering TM and said he'd be in touch. They left.

With little hesitation, Martin dialed Scribner's. Waiting for "Charlie" to pick up, Martin whispered, "This is the right thing to do." As Martin suspected, Charlie had no inkling of a Hemingway auction. Charlie had talked neither to Mary nor Jack and he was — sitting six feet away from the phone I could hear his voice — loudly pissed off.

Charlie settled the matter with Mary and Jack. Charlie told them that trade practice granted Scribner renewal rights, a weak if non-existent negotiating position, and gave them a modest advance on future royalties which they accepted. Charlie sent Martin a bottle of scotch and a nice note thanking him for an "above and beyond" act of friendship.

Yet Martin's civilities were limited. One late afternoon, screen writer and novelist — also a Dartmouth alum — Budd Schulberg, *What Makes Sammy Run*, and *The Harder They Fall*, and novelist Elia Kazan who directed Schulberg's screen play, *On the Waterfront*, stopped in, accepting an invitation from one of my sales managers, the circumstances too complex to relate. I'd asked Martin to join us for a drink and perhaps dinner. His refusal was a slouch and a shake of his head. "Not my kind of guys," he said.

I understood why. Kazan and Schulberg had been caught up in the 1954 McCarthy hearings, in their testimony revealing names of suspected communists working in the film industry. In a reprisal of sorts, the industry turned its back on Schulberg and Kazan, publicly blacklisting them and informally but constructively banning them from further work in Hollywood. In the political turmoil of the McCarthy investigations, there were only losers including, eventually, McCarthy himself. Ever the liberal, Martin saw Schulberg and Kazan not for their artistry but as turncoats to be shunned.

By Way of Luck

Schulberg and Kazan were creative people, naïve perhaps, or just dumb. Their political positions scarred them. I thought Martin had overreacted. I respected his political principles, but I did not think then, nor do I now, that artistic expression should be held to a political standard. Once the censor, where does it stop? I still feel that way.

Martin missed several hours of authentic dinner conversation, all of it about writing, publishing and the making of movies. The McCarthy hearings were not discussed. By the late 1960s McCarthy had been generally forgotten. Schulberg and Kazan recovered, but not before more than forty years had passed.

Martin and I travelled to London. With NAL's encouragement, New English Library (NEL) had adopted the same big-advance, low-return practice and like NAL had sustained large losses. Martin was snubbed by NEL's chief executive who, in an indignant rage, promptly resigned and flew off to Australia. Martin elevated NEL's sales director Christopher Shaw to the senior management post.

Meanwhile, Martin and I made some needed though minor restructuring at the Harry Abrams Art Book Company in New York; strengthened President Matt Birmingham's position at the Matthew Bender Law Book publishing in Albany; established Times Mirror School and Library Services in Chicago to manage the sale of all Times Mirror imprints to the educational market; set up an international sales organization to serve all TM imprints basing it in London; acquired two medical book publishing companies, C.V. Mosby in St. Louis and Year Book Medical Publishers in Chicago London; and acquired two direct marketing publishers, Southwestern Publishing in Nashville and Fuller and Dees in Montgomery, Alabama.

(Southwestern was sold nine years later for more than ten times TM's original acquisition cost, a hefty profit and all of it pure luck.)

Further, we acquired the Popular Science Publishing Company which included, in addition to *Popular Science* magazine, *Outdoor Life* and the Outdoor Life Book Club, and a general interest book publishing division. The acquisition would become the backbone of TM's newly organized magazine company, Times Mirror Magazines. All this within three years.

From time to time, we'd pull in staffers from Los Angeles who could take on specific assignments, an example, leasing contracts for office space. But the human toll behind what we had done was proving ugly.

Martin's timidity was showing. He checker-boarded people, moving them about, hiring and firing without clear purpose. The problem companies were lop-sided; they had either strong distribution and weak products, or strong products and weak distribution. A balance had to be struck.

Meantime, he was playing push-pull with me. Pushing me toward increasing responsibilities, then pulling me back, and then pushing again: first at World; then as a possible successor to a recalcitrant Harry Abrams who bucked every suggestion Martin made; parking me for a time at NAL, then bringing me back when Sydney took over; and by Al Casey who suggested a move to Los Angeles and taking on a super-editorial responsibility, essentially keeping track of the publishing progress of the non-newspaper subsidiaries and by introducing new products that could improve their profitability. I wanted none of that, but I did have an interest in splitting away from Martin and heading up one or more subsidiaries, either those known or those I might acquire.

The shift in our relationship began with the hiring of Chris Shaw or, as he preferred to be acknowledged, Christopher J. H. M. Shaw, or, for short, just Christopher. Christopher was an Eton graduate and married to one of Great Britain's wealthiest non-royals, with a town house in London, a country estate outside the city, a flat in Paris — and quiet hide-aways in various Mediterranean harbors, fully staffed, all this told me in casual conversation by Christopher.

Christopher had the look and demeanor of a young Winston Churchill, prompting him to act the part, fingering fat Havana cigars he'd bought from Churchill's tobacconist, and being driven to both social and business appointments by a personal, full-time

By Way of Luck

chauffeur in a Jaguar MK four door saloon. Each morning, on his desk, placed by his secretary in a porcelain vase, there would be a fresh cut red carnation. On his arrival she would rush to pin it to his lapel.

Martin Levin from Grosset was easily seduced. Christopher took him by the hand to his personal Jermyn Street tailor, to his shoe maker, to his shirt maker and his tie maker and in a matter of months Martin's wardrobe had shifted from off-the-rack, non-descript suit jackets with two pairs of pants to one-of-a-kind, hand-tailored three-piece worsted woolen suits. There were lunches with prominent British publishers, dinners at fashionable restaurants with local writers and editors, and introductions to the movers and shakers in London's financial community.

Martin bought an expensive house on Long Island Sound in Rye, New York, moving there from a suburban neighborhood in Port Chester. The house had provenance. Its owner was actor and performer Robert Preston just concluding his long run starring in *The Music Man*. Martin was enjoying new comforts. But the job was wearing on him. His therapist seemed not to be making any progress.

Penthouse Surfaces

NEL had a highly profitable asset it was about to lose: its contract for the international distribution rights to *Penthouse* was ending. There was little chance of renewal. Already seen as a potential competitor to *Playboy*, and yet to be distributed in the United States, publisher and founder Bob Guccione was planning a move to New York and establishing his international operations there. He coaxed Christopher: if Times Mirror facilitated the move, a costly one-time expense, by financing and managing it, Guccione would grant NEL a three-year extension of the expiring contract.

Christopher did not wish to be seen unable to make a deal with Guccione, but there was no way Bob's demands could be met without involving TM. When Martin and I arrived in London, Bob and Christopher, except for the crude invectives they were hurling publicly at one another, were at a stand-still in their negotiations. Without the distribution revenues from *Penthouse*, NEL could fold.

Martin asked me to intervene. Find out what help Guccione needs. Smooth things out, he said.

I met Bob and his girlfriend, Kathy Keeton, an exotic dancer from South Africa and later Bob's third wife, at their flat in Knightsbridge. It was a modest dwelling and by no measure showed the roughly $250,000 a month Bob was earning from European, Indian, North African and Australian sales. Bob apologized for the disarray. The fancy digs could wait, he said. He was hoarding his cash for the move.

Bob was colorfully costumed, his dress an open collared silk shirt, an array of gold chains girding his neck, tight trousers with embroidered leggings, stylish gold-buckled Italian-styled leather shoes and, I thought, wearing make-up, just a touch. Kathy was enveloped in Spandex and looking more lustful than a Chicago Bunny. On a Parisian or New York fashion runway the two would be seen as a comical pair, but in the milieu of their London flat they were in their comfort clothing, hard-nosed business people working at their trade.

Kathy and Bob were a team. *Penthouse* was an attempt to duplicate *Playboy*, but it was a shadowy imitation, short of quality and smutty as *Playboy* was not. *Penthouse* was crude. And always would be, its crudeness part of its appeal. Bob shot the photos, drew most of the cartoons, wrote or re-wrote the text, designed and carried the layouts to press every issue, and ran the entire business out of his back pocket. His office was the living room we sat in. Not surprisingly, Bob and Kathy had questions about *Playboy*.

I liked them both, their sincerity obvious and not a show for their visitor. They knew what they were doing and were not embarrassed by it. Their sense of the magazine's commercial appeal was gut driven. They didn't need NEL or the Times Mirror for their move to New York, I would report to Martin, but I wasn't sure they knew that.

Tell Levin and Shaw, Bob said as I was leaving, "I get the move, NEL gets the contract. TM gets no equity in the deal."

By Way of Luck

Bob surely saw my surprise. When had equity been part of the deal? Martin, without telling me, had upped the price. He'd instructed Christopher, in addition to the renewal of the distribution deal, to demand 5% of *Penthouse's* U.S. corporation. Martin had left me hanging stupid.

Back at NEL's offices I asked Christopher to leave me and Martin alone. What the fuck are you up to? I asked. Martin, angered and with but one apparent yet cautious move short of verbally punishing him. He melted into a defensive guise, sorrowfully apologetic, he said. He'd thought to involve me, but feared I would tattle to *Playboy*, somehow screw up the negotiations, and what could he do to make up for his mistake. He actually brought a tear to one eye as if in supplication for sins past. He could not have been more the beggar, an art he had practiced more than once, I could see.

What happened next was even more bizarre. Bob Guccione flew to New York and met with Martin in our Park Avenue offices. Martin did not include Christopher in the meeting, nor did he include me. Bob came and went, waving a hand and smiling as he passed my open office door. He and I had already agreed we would have dinner together that night.

Martin was the man in full, announcing he had negotiated "the beginnings of a deal" with Bob and told me it would work out "to everyone's satisfaction." You will work full-time for *Penthouse*, Martin told me. For at least six months and up to a year, you will handle Bob's transfer from London to New York — offices, printing contracts, and distribution, whatever he needs. Times Mirror will give him a loan and you will have oversight of his company and given a budget you and I agree on. Martin sat back in his chair, his narrow lips drawing into a tight smile.

My immediate reaction — he was talking Christopher's talk. He was crafting a deal that would enhance Christopher's status, a probability, but I couldn't be sure. Or was he kidding? Or had I mistaken his smile? Or was I just being mistrustful?

He was serious. In his mind he had just crossed the goal line and was expecting a stadium roar.

Bob has agreed to that? I asked.

Martin nodded.

"How does TM make money on the deal?

"We're working on that."

Christopher had won him over, with the suits, the celebrity and the suck-up Mayfair dinners and late night parties.

That evening, my wife Maggie and I entertained Bob and Kathy for drinks at our Upper East Side apartment and then walked down Second Avenue to a new restaurant that had earned an early 3-star review. Bob laughed all the way. The way the meeting with Martin went, Bob said, he would give me Perkins in exchange for a 10% interest in *Penthouse* and loan whatever money was needed to set up operations in New York.

Your *Playboy* experience and contacts would be valuable to me, Bob went on, but how does Martin get off offering a trade, like what happens in baseball?

Had I missed something? Martin first wanted me to negotiate with Bob, then left me out of the negotiations. Then he had made a wildly improbable proposition he knew would be tested that very evening. I had told him that Bob and I and wives were meeting for dinner. Did Martin believe nothing would be said?

The interchange among Martin, Christopher, Bob Guccione and me left me triply conflicted. I couldn't serve Martin who was himself conflicted. I couldn't serve Guccione either as an employee, as Bob had at one time suggested, or acting as one. Further, I saw *Penthouse* as rubbish, no more, and I chose not to be associated with it.

Remarkably, none of my colleagues considered that I might not be comfortable giving up Hugh Hefner to a competitor. I bore great respect for Hefner and still had a good many friends at *Playboy*. Though I was fearful my role at TM would be diminished, I turned bad guy. I told Martin I would not subscribe to his bizarre proposition.

Al Casey called me at home. You and I and Martin should sit down together and fix things, he said. I don't believe he had been adequately truthfully briefed on the negotiations. Not a good idea,

By Way of Luck

my immediate reply, and begged off. Further, I had been present at one of Al's peace-keeping missions some months past. There'd been a territorial dispute between Martin and a similarly high-placed colleague based in LA. Al brought them together with me and two visiting TM Senior VP's for dinner in a private dining room at the Sky Club atop the Pan Am building. To talk it out, Al said.

During soup and salad, the discussion went well, but in a flash, after the entrees were set, discord erupted. Someone had said something, I wasn't paying attention, and Martin had leapt across the banquet-sized table, dish and glassware flying, and was physically pummeling another senior VP, Al trying to break them up and eventually dragging the two of them by the collar from the table and retreating to an adjacent private room where they couldn't be heard. The dinner was over.

Three of us remained in the dining room attempting to recall what had been said, why the flare-up had happened. No doubt there were lingering, unspoken differences we were unaware of. We were in shocked confusion.

Corporate in-fighting, I understood, and often participated in. But corporate fist fighting was taking differences a step too far, and beyond anything I might choose to participate in.

Martin had shone his coarser self.

Al returned, alone. He'd sent the two combatants home in separate cars. Things are OK, he said. But they weren't. There'd been a permanent breach and Al had decided to live with it. On taking the TM job, he had hired them both, his loyalty a continuing burden.

A constant in the Times Mirror mix — for me a willing counselor — was its chief financial officer Dennis Stanfill. He had supported my hiring. He was an Annapolis graduate, an Oxford scholar, a Lehman Bros. alumnus, and the elder son of a multi-generational Southern family, formal in his manner and speech. When we got together, usually at dinner when he was in New York, there was no joking. Small talk was not on the menu. He preferred Mama Leone's, explaining his choice by telling me, "My wife is of Italian extraction." His daughter was engaged to a royal, he'd say, a cousin of an Italian Crown Prince. Southern gentry, I assumed, was given to heritage. The marital pairing would appeal to the kinfolk.

In labored circumlocution, Dennis would ask questions and trade for answers. I'd tell him something. He replied with something. A simple "yes" or "no" was unacceptable. Three or four exchanges might take place before we got to something he truly wanted to know about, or I wanted to hear.

Usually, he chose to talk about people I valued or didn't. If my reply clicked with him, he'd click right back. We were practicing a tortuous form of office gossip from which I learned he had been passed over for TM's presidency, had inveighed against Martin's hiring — not of our kind, Dennis clicked — and had angrily condemned TM's diversification strategy. "There's nothing wrong being good at one thing," he said.

Dennis told me my concerns regarding the Guccione proposition were correct.

At our last click fest, he said he'd given both Al Casey and Otis Chandler his letter of resignation. He was joining 20th Century Fox. Pending the approval of its board, which was assured, he would become 20th's President and CEO. And so it happened.

Within two years Dennis bought the Pebble Beach Golf Course and Resort, a diversification move so said a 20th press release. Dennis paid $30 million for the property. Ten years later, Fox sold it for $600 million.

"Nice diversification," I wrote in a cajoling note. His reply was stiff: "They were both entertainment properties," he answered. End of clicks.

I explained my *Penthouse* conflicts to Martin. He thought them foolish, and said so. I thought them appropriate, I told him. Given his secretive and ever changing posture and, worse, his penchant for creating confusion, I had to be short and direct. My words bounced off his back like a duck. I gave him contacts Guccione might need, whether for his use or Christopher's, the key people at Curtis Distribution and the head of Meredith's printing division and advised him

By Way of Luck

of the availability of 4000 square feet in Abrams new offices that Guccione could use as an initial base.

I unhooked myself, totally, knowing I would pay for it.

A deal was finally struck. TM would loan Guccione money to make the move and on *Penthouse's* behalf engage the suppliers required to set itself up in the United States. NEL would, as compensation, get a three year extension of its *Penthouse* distribution contract. No more than that. The original proposition had come full circle.

Martin withdrew a promise to me that I would head the newly organized World Publishing group, just moved from Cleveland to New York. He gave the job to Christopher who had no editorial experience, no management experience and spoke to his staff in muttered syllables, unsure and covert.

I had been punished. It would continue.

As a sop, Martin asked that I set up a lunch. The TM Board would be holding its up-coming quarterly meeting at our 280 Park Avenue office, lunch to follow. I would be invited to the lunch and introduced to the board.

I called Pete Krindler, an owner of '21 and the ever present host. I had met him when Corey and I dined there. Corey and Pete were friends from the 30s, both bird hunters with stories to tell. Corey always got the most desired table, a banquette on the immediate left in the exclusive first floor bar and dining room.

Pete and I met the same afternoon, went over a menu, selected the wines and agreed on the table center pieces. I showed him our guest list. There would be 20 of us: board members (four Chandlers, Norman, Dorothy, Harry and Otis), officers of the company, and me. Plus a last minute addition, Christopher Shaw.

The '21 Club lunch, as might be expected, went smoothly. As the proceedings progressed, Christopher and I were introduced to the board by Al Casey as "the future of the Times Mirror Company." We each stood, grateful for the recognition, thanked Al, and sat down to an audience beaming and nodding their approval.

When the lunch broke up — everyone graciously warm, the wine exceptional, and amid abundant hard pumping handshakes, Martin threw me an approving nod.

When the '21 bill totaling just over $2200 arrived at the office, however, Martin was aghast. You were cheated, he said, his tone scolding. Yet he was wearing a suit that cost easily that much, perhaps more, he had so little understanding of values. Or was it an excuse to beat up on me?

I had been with TM for three tumultuous yet oddly satisfying years. I had learned the flip side of publishing, the business side, reading easily balance sheets and operating statements, evaluating budgets, and negotiating with publishers and distributors on three continents, from Johannesburg to Frankfurt, from London to New York, from Chicago to Tokyo, Hong Kong and Sydney, Australia.

I was still with TM and coupled with an unpredictable Martin Levin, together standing in a drenching cloud burst and awaiting a day of sun and fair weather.

Corey Passes On

In 1969, at age 67 and much too young, Corey Ford died, suffering first a near fatal stroke and two weeks later a life ending heart attack. On hearing of the stroke I rushed to Hanover. He was by himself in his bedroom, clothed, lying on his bed, but for twitches, motionless. He blinked recognition. I sat beside him and took his hand. There could be no answers to questions I might ask. I reminisced, telling him stories of our travels, the people we'd met, the times we shared, the jokes that made us both laugh, the bird dogs we'd hunted with, Cider's son, Tober, an English setter, in the room with us and quiet. Corey fell asleep. I kissed his cheek. The nurses came and he was whisked away.

He passed suddenly. I was not with him. He died alone in a bed in Dick's House, the Dartmouth infirmary. His death was my death, sorrow and guilt engulfing me and for days moving idly as I dealt

By Way of Luck

with grief, Corey so much a part of me, and confused by a loss I never saw coming.

I eschew funerals. I am crippled by them. When a youngster, maybe eight years old, taken by my mother to the wake of a neighbor's daughter who'd crashed through the glass windshield of a 1937 Hudson Terraplane face first, I was pushed to look into the open casket. The local funeral home had not done good work. The girl's face was grotesque. I have stayed away from funerals since.

Dorothy Olding was angered. We were in her apartment. "Where were you? she questioned. "You should have been with me, you selfish bastard!" Her vehemence was real. "I was the widow," she cried. "You were the orphan." Her words were choked by her sobbing. "We were the only family he had."

She held the door open and I left. I never saw her again.

Corey gave his estate to the College, his will directing that it be used to build a club house for the Dartmouth Rugby team. More than 20 years passed before the college, under heavy pressure from rugby alumni, freed up the money to build the Corey Ford Rugby Center. At its dedication, I was a keynote speaker. I began by asking the crowd of over 100 former Dartmouth rugby players, gathered under a large tent on the playing field, "How many here knew Corey personally?" A hundred hands were raised.

"We are family," I said. A hundred voices cheered.

I concluded my remarks in a few minutes, reminding the audience of Corey's generosity and asking, "What do you call a man who has given so much and has asked so little in return?" I paused. "You call him an angel." I sat down. The applause, not for me, but for Corey, of that I was certain, was long and loud, coming as from the sidelines. Had I made up for the services not attended?

How he influenced me, I cannot construct, not totally, but were I to take a guess, it was not pushing me to write, to publish, or to pursue creative goals. He had assessed my talents. It was to be an independent thinker, to be self-reliant, to find my own way and to be, as he was, unafraid. I do not try not to emulate him. But how could I not? I still hold his hand, still talk to him, still tell him stories.

Harry Abrams

Of the book publishers I worked with, I favored Harry Abrams, a charismatic personality, socially gregarious and ultimately generous. As early as the late 1950s, he had a rare grasp of the international marketplace and the opportunities that lay there. He had been Promotion Director of the Book-of-the-Month Club (BOMC) and understood the importance of "bonus" books made freely available with new membership. The more lavish the bonus books, outsized and colorful, the higher the response rate, the longer the tenure of a member and the larger the per-member profit. Art books were an attractive financial asset for BOMC.

In those times, art books were expensive to make. Usually printed in small quantities, reflecting the paucity of the art book market, on linen-infused paper, immaculately bound, and featuring art reproduced in a costly process — four and sometimes five colors separated then matched on press one color at a time — their publication was a high risk endeavor. Few titles were published. Return on investment might stretch out for years.

BOMC wanted more titles and larger printings, yet were unwilling to take on the publishing risk. Dealing with publishers who survived by issuing few titles and printed small editions was nightmarish. BOMC needed better and more dependable sources.

Harry saw an opportunity that would eventually make him the largest and arguably the most profitable art book publisher in the world. With a contract that guaranteed BOMC would over a year buy a specific number of titles in large quantities and at prices well below the current wholesale market, Harry was able to raise sufficient start-up money from friends and business pals to launch Harry N. Abrams Art Book Publishers, Inc.

To fulfill his contract with BOMC, Harry went off-shore. He partnered with Fritz Landshoff, a known and respected Amsterdam publisher, to produce high quality books at low cost by having expensive color separations made in Europe and Asia where skilled engravers could be marshaled at fractional costs. By creating consortiums

By Way of Luck

of four, five or six publishers, one from Spain wanting a Spanish language edition, one from Italy wanting an Italian language edition, and so on, each publisher ordering the smaller quantities their market could sustain in the aggregate would gave Harry and Fritz a sizeable printing that on a per copy basis would be dramatically cheaper. But how get it done?

Their brilliance shone. Harry and Fritz would go on press, printing color only, and ship printed sheets to the consortium participants to imprint text only in their respective languages, to bind locally and to sell in their respective territories. Abrams would issue and publicize the U.S. edition simultaneously with BOMC's adoption of a title, each company benefiting financially from the publicity and the lowered costs of production.

When I joined TM, Harry and Fritz had staff in Amsterdam and Tokyo managing the separation work and buying printing from suppliers in Singapore, Taiwan and Australia as well as from European suppliers. Harry went global when "going global" had yet to be chic.

Harry enjoyed the happy reward of selling his company to TM, but was appalled by TM's demands for growth and profitability. TM insisted that Abrams match the same rate of return — the bottom line — of mass market paperbacks and popular fiction and non-fiction books, quarter by quarter. Art books, Harry insisted, unlike other consumer books whose popularity can come and go in months, have an indefinite life, their subjects having relevance for decades if not longer. The rate of return comes more slowly and not by what Harry sarcastically termed "profits by fiat."

Nor should Abrams be required, Harry complained, to write-down unsold books in the same time frame as paperbacks. Martin pushed Harry hard. Harry pushed back, loudly voicing his frustrations, and ignoring Martin's demanding memoranda.

While at Doubleday, I bought Harry's art books to offer Literary Guild subscribers. He was easy to deal with, quantities open ended and offering to buy back what I might not need.

"I can always sell excess inventory," he said — and at prices available nowhere else. He mentored me as well, based on his BOMC experience, advising me on selections, pricing and, by title, market effectiveness, which books sold by mail, which didn't. He was amused, I believe, by my eagerness to learn how he ran his company. He was the charitable tutor eager to teach.

I understood Harry's business rationale. TM did not. Martin was slow to support Harry, Al Casey urging him to lean on Harry to conform to TM's requirements. I supported Harry and in time Martin did, too. But we were at a standstill, obliged by our employers to take action but in agreement that the Abrams Art Book Publishing Company was a unique business and had to be treated as such.

Surprisingly, as the Abrams versus TM confrontation peaked, Dorothy Chandler sent a memo to Al Casey, copying All Concerned Parties. She wrote that TM's directors regarded Abrams as the "jewel" among TM's many companies, that TM was "proud" to be its owner, was little concerned whether Abrams ever showed a profit and encouraged Harry to act as independently and creatively as he had before becoming part of the TM family. *Tout fini.*

With the memo in hand I bounced into Martin's office, congratulating and thanking him for reaching out to Mrs. Chandler. Martin shook his head. I had nothing to do with it, he said. It was a surprise to Al, too.

Left unanswered, the question we thought should be asked, and didn't. I returned to my office and called Harry. He and Fritz were in their shared office relaxing and toasting each other with a split of Mumm's.

Millard Fuller and Morris Dees

In 1961, two students at the University of Alabama School of Law, Millard Fuller and Morris Dees, started a business on campus that led to careers they could not have foretold. They obtained college records containing student names and home addresses and dates of birth. How they came by them, I do not know; they could have found a print-out in a dumpster. The list fostered an idea. They

By Way of Luck

would, a month or so ahead of an Alabama student's birthday, write letters to parents promising to deliver a freshly baked cake to a student's dorm room on his or her birthday with a greeting card from Mom and Dad. For a fee, of course, that would turn them an ample profit.

Morris and Millard wrote the letters, signing them as fellow students, banked the checks, and hired a local bakery to bake and box the cakes and enclose a card. And recruited students as delivery boys "as a favor" and to sing Happy Birthday as they handed over the cake from Mom and Dad. The business took hold so quickly Morris and Millard had to hire help. They were selling, according to Morris, "a ton of cakes" and learning, as well, how to sell by mail. They graduated modestly rich, and started a direct marketing company, Fuller and Dees, they hoped would become a long term sustaining business.

Morris and Millard stayed together for the next eight years as the principles of Fuller and Dees, finally breaking up, and at different times pursued different aspirations.

Millard founded Habitat for Humanity to build homes for the needy.

Morris founded the Southern Poverty Law Center to defend the poor in the courts of law.

Beginning with the proceeds from the sale of birthday cakes and the business that grew from that, Millard and Morris, from small-town Alabama, law school roommates and business partners, independently from one another, found the financial support to establish two extraordinary social ventures that reached out to the indigent and the homeless. Overcoming incredible odds, they succeeded in making their not-for-profit ventures effective, permanent and unarguably successful. From dirt poor farms in the rural south, with little awareness of the world beyond the cotton fields and the cattle pastures, how did this happen?

After graduation from Law School, Morris and Millard built Fuller and Dees into a sizeable publishing and direct marketing company in Morris's hometown of Montgomery. Their objective: make lots of money. Before they were 30, they were millionaires. Millard, apparently embarrassed by his wealth and claiming he'd had a troubling religious vision, assigned his share of the company to Morris. In 1965 with his wife Linda, Millard moved into the poorest forests of south Georgia, joining a multi-racial community in Americus where they found a purpose to their lives. They traveled to Central America and to South Africa as a way of measuring the implications of what they might do. By then they had founded Habitat for Humanity International as "an ecumenical Christian organization dedicated to eliminating homelessness and substandard housing...."

Habitat, as of this writing, unique in the United States, has constructed over 300,000 homes for the poor.

President Jimmy Carter and his wife Rosalyn became close friends of the Fullers. The Carters joined Habitat as partners and initiated a very visible project in New York City. Carter's prestige drew international publicity to Habitat; for a time, many people mistakenly believed that Carter had founded the organization. Delivering a eulogy at Millard's funeral, Jimmy Carter, called him "one of the most extraordinary people I have ever known. He used his remarkable gifts as an entrepreneur for the benefit of millions of needy people around the world."

Morris Dees history is equally remarkable. What follows are excerpts from an article in the American Bar Association Journal in 2012 on the occasion of the ABA awarding Dees with its highest honor, the ABA medal. Previous recipients include Leon Jaworski, and U.S. Supreme Court Justices Thurgood Marshall and Sandra Day O'Connor:

> Dees was born in 1936. His father was a poor cotton farmer in Mount Meigs, just east of Alabama's state capital of Montgomery. Their house didn't have running water, and the family couldn't always afford the electric bill. But in an environment where racism was rampant, the elder Dees taught his son to treat their African-American neighbors as equals.
>
> Starting in 1980 and continuing for the next three decades, the Southern Poverty Law Center, which Dees co-founded in

By Way of Luck

1971, filed a series of historic and highly successful civil lawsuits seeking to hold various chapters of the Ku Klux Klan and other white supremacist organizations responsible for the wrongdoings of their members. And he's got the death threats to prove it — at least two dozen by his count.

In 1984, for instance, Dees filed Donald v. United Klans of America in federal district court on behalf of the mother of Michael Donald a young black man who had been lynched by two Klansmen three years earlier in Mobile. The jury's verdict: $7 million. The judge awarded the plaintiff the deed to the United Klan headquarters building.

In one of the most recent cases, the SPLC won a $2.5 million judgment against the Imperial Klans of America and its imperial wizard, Ron Edwards, for the brutal beating of a Latino teenager at a Kentucky county fair in 2006. The Kentucky Supreme Court upheld the verdict in March.

Morris Dees is known as the lawyer who bankrupted the Ku Klux Klan and effectively put them out of business, but he's accomplished so much more. Morris has dedicated his life to public service," says H. Thomas Wells Jr, a shareholder at Maynard Cooper & Gale in Birmingham who served as ABA president in 2008-09.

Morris told me that only once did he truly understand what he had accomplished: it was the night the Ku Klux Klan mounted and set fire to a cross on his front lawn. By then, Morris said, he knew he could win his cases against them.

Morris also offered me a perspective. Racial inequality, he said, is undoubtedly a major social problem, largely because it is visible. But the larger, underlying issue is "rich-poor: lifting people out of poverty will help solve racial strife." The Southern Poverty Law Center is his commitment to that issue.

My introduction to Morris and to his relationship with Millard Fuller began on a low note. In late 1969 Fuller and Dees was running out of cash and facing the possibility of bankruptcy. Morris had invested heavily in an ambitious publishing project, the multi-volume *Encyclopedia of Space and Aviation*. Developed and edited by a former Air Force pilot, it was a comprehensive series of 20 volumes, colorfully illustrated and written both as a reference and as popular history. It was authentic, but of little interest to the broader market it had to reach to recover the investment Morris had made. Further, space and aviation events were fast moving, out-dating the encyclopedia from the very first day of its publication. Just keeping up was expensive. Budgets came and went, but the task was already out of hand and dragging down the company. Morris needed help. Perhaps, he thought, he could negotiate a loan or, possibly, sell his company and concentrate totally on his legal activities.

I met him at our offices in New York. Martin, ever vigilant for new publishing ventures, had learned of Morris from the Encyclopedia's editor and decided Morris deserved an audience. Morris presented himself stoically, the sober lawyer talking, not the distraught owner of a sinking company. He spoke of his history, as youngsters Morris and Millard breaking social barriers, his talk immersed in modesty. About his business, he spoke as though dictating to a court stenographer, specifically and orderly, his facts marshaled and to a point. But for the Encyclopedia, went his argument, he had a profitable company.

It was not.

He suggested we visit his headquarters in Montgomery for a firsthand look. After Morris left, Martin said, This guy's the real thing. Let's fly to Montgomery for a day.

Plainly, Martin was emotionally struck by Morris's recounting of his legal victories and of Carter's involvement with Millard Fuller. Martin ignored the financial detail, the numbers that said the business, even after stripping out the losses incurred by the Encyclopedia, could not be sustained. It would fail in a matter of months. Instead, Martin heard compelling stories of social justice and, given his bias, deserving of reward.

This was late 1969. Alabama was not a publishing Mecca. Bull

By Way of Luck

Connor was still around, though upstate, with a leash in one hand and a fire hose in the other. The march from Selma had come and gone, and in the small towns of George Wallace country "colored only" signs were still posted where they'd always been posted. School children still walked the same paths to their school rooms, sat at the same desks and learned from the same teachers and books as did their parents and grandparents. Although Morris had driven the Ku Klux Klan underground and was solely responsible for the integration of the Alabama State Police, change was slow in coming. It would take time.

Martin and I returned from our Southern sojourn enthusiastic. I was partly responsible for that. I had campaigned TM's management to assess early a company's ability to market and sell books and then to evaluate its ability to develop and publish editorial matter. Having worked for two mammoth direct marketing companies, Doubleday and Curtis, I could see the simplicity of my thesis but found few willing to embrace it.

Martin and I had acquired Southwestern Publishing, a direct, door-to-door marketing company with little product. Southwestern's management accepted the direction we gave it, to their basic products of bibles and dictionaries adding cookbooks, homemaking books and reference books. Their sales soared.

Martin saw Fuller and Dees as having the same opportunity. Martin was in part correct, but did not accept that Fuller and Dees would need a large cash infusion to simply stay afloat and had no editorial resources to build on, nor the experience. Further, Martin did not see that Morris wanted to walk away from the company and devote his full attention to the emergence of the Southern Poverty Law Center.

Back at 280 Park Avenue, Martin called Al Casey, told him he and I wanted to acquire Fuller and Dees and asked for his blessing.

What happened next forced me to reflect on the continuing turns of my life. Was it so-far, so-good? I didn't think so. After leaving the Air Force, what had I done? A lot of admirable things, yes, creative and original I thought. But I was continually embroiled in conflict. How I worked, I thought satisfactory, but who I worked with and for I seemed always to find unsatisfactory. Clearly, I was my own problem. I pushed ideas relentlessly, at times mocking those who disagreed with me, with remarks I wished never to have made. Harry Abrams, always a blunt advisor told me, You scare people.

Hearing that from Harry was sobering. I recalled an instance at New American Library in a meeting with Sydney Kramer and his editor in chief, Ed Kuhn. We were reviewing the pictorial layouts of Svetlana, the diary of Joseph Stalin's daughter. To my eye the layouts were clumsy, the captions trite and uninformative, and I said so. Ed bristled. I said, you can't run a photograph of *Svetlana* standing in a furnished room that could be anywhere in the world and caption it with but one word, "Svetlana." A reader wants more. "When, where and what," I said briskly.

Ed appeared stunned. Sydney intervened, changing the subject and throwing me a ticked-off scowl. Ed was his respected man-in-charge-of-editorial. I was the guy from corporate. I should have known better. There were hurtful consequences.

When Ed was transferred to World Publishing, an assignment Ed did not relish, he outspokenly blamed me. When Christopher and Martin fired him at World, Ed blamed me. When *Playboy* shut him and his colleagues down, Ed blamed me.

What I learned, when you're feared or disliked — whatever the reason, the two go together — you become the one at fault.

Fuller and Dees, TM's newly acquired direct marketing company, even after an initial capital injection, was still struggling. Neither Morris nor his people knew how to source or create new books to be sold by mail, though they understood their commitment to do so. One project underway, a good idea as it later turned out, was stalled by a lack of confidence; it was called *The Life Cycle Library*. The company ran through the second infusion of cash and asked for another.

Martin showed panic. "You have to do something," he said, his manner demanding and decidedly shifting the blame to me.

By Way of Luck

I said I would fix the company. Martin was now keeping me at the fringes of involvement at NAL, Abrams and World, accepting my recommendations and acting on them himself. He was pissed that I had backed away from *Penthouse* and left him to deal with it.

Martin did not know how the finances of magazine subscription publishing worked, so he kept me visibly active in the forefront of the negotiations with the Popular Science Company, yet blocked my participation at the closing when all the brass convened to execute the purchase and sale agreements. Al, I was told, asked "Where's Jim?"

Whatever I might next do, I could not be Martin's junior partner. Without his support of me, I could not support him. Yet I had to prove I could not only run a company, I could fix one as well.

Give me Fuller and Dees, I said to Al, in fact pled for the assignment. I suggested terms: that I be given control of the company: that I be appointed its chief executive officer; that interest bearing TM loans to Fuller and Dees be capitalized; that I report to someone other than Martin; and that I continue to have a role with Times Mirror International, with the Southwestern Publishing Company and with Times Mirror International.

Martin stood aside. Al conceded Fuller and Dees to me accepting my requirements and assigning Matthew Birmingham, the CEO of TM's Matthew Bender Company, as my report. Matt was a gifted publisher, with substantial financial experience in both the magazine and book business, a stone-hard uncompromising sort, his history storied. Matt had been passed over in TM's search for the job Martin was given. He was qualified ever more greatly, the smarter of the two and with deeper insights. But his drinking habits and public rantings had become bothersome and there was understandable concern among upper level West Coast corporate officers.

Martin, seeing Matt as a competitor, open bitterness between him and Matt surfaced. In meetings, Matt spoke to Martin as he would a child, in one instance, in a hotel conference room, suggesting that Martin actually go upstairs to bed. Matt's quickness stripped Martin of his authority.

I moved to Alabama, to a farm in Coosada, a rural town just north of Montgomery. To drive there, one had to follow the road where the Coosa and the Tallapoosa rivers merge to form the Alabama River. My place, an ante bellum homestead, was located "just up the hill" about a mile away. My wife Maggie came south with me, but she did not stay long. Originally from northeast Iowa, she had agreed to put aside her advertising career in favor of mine, but she was ultimately fearful of one day returning to New York and finding no one who'd hire her, the gap in her work experience a disqualification. We got a one-day, no-hard-feelings Alabama divorce and she returned to the advertising job she'd left.

The downtown business community of Montgomery was suspicious of my intent, their small talk derisive and quickly getting back to me. That I was from New York was a complaint, that I was associated with Morris Dees was another, that I might close down the company and leave its employees without jobs was still another. I sought out the president of the largest bank in town, introduced myself, opened an account and immediately made a large initial deposit. The talk abated.

There was no nice way to set Fuller and Dees on a new course, though, without cutting and changing crew. I asked for Morris' resignation. He said he'd go but wanted to keep the revenue from the Coke machine. Was he kidding me? For his kids, he said, a scholarship fund. It was a test. I said no. He complied. I asked for the resignation of the company's president, George Seitz. He left. I took over the conference room as my office, using the expansive table and its many chairs as a way of bringing one or more people in for interviews, sometimes one on one, at other times by department and worked my way through an evaluation of the senior staff. Two women emerged as my keystone employees. Patsy Bogle and Marilyn Black. I leaned on them as would an authoritative Air Force colonel and drafted an employee reduction plan. The company was fat. Three weeks after my arrival, all at once we let go a quarter of the work force. With one exception, a coincidence, those departing were all vice presidents and all male.

At the end of the day, after the "pink slips" had been issued, I brought the remaining employees together in the Baptist Church next door. There was no other location big enough to seat everyone. Offering them an explanation for what I had done and giving them an encouraging picture of where we could take the company did not work. Most employees sat rigidly and emotionally frozen. As the meeting ended, I shook hands at the door with as many of them as I could. One of them, her look of contempt apparent, said, "You're no Morris Dees." I told her I didn't intend to be.

More Morris Dees

Morris was quick to seek political relationships as a way of advancing the mission of the Law Center and not so coincidentally to raise money. He had in 1970 managed the finances of the George Wallace campaign, Wallace successfully winning the Governor's seat he had previously lost. Morris attracted admirers. In 1972, Morris was George McGovern's national campaign finance manager, attracting more admirers. And in 1976, Morris was once again a national campaign finance manager, this time for Jimmy Carter. Through those year's, raising money largely by mail, Morris built a substantial data base of heavy-hitting donors from the liberal left and used it to assure the Law Center's long term financial stability. Morris had critics and he had enemies. His methods rankled friends and foes alike, but he was indifferent to their complaints and to the threats that often followed. He was undeterred.

To my dismay, I got caught in some of the anti-Dees rhetoric. Many notable Montgomery residents assumed that I, like Morris, was a radical, and was socially shunned by them as Morris was shunned.

Moreover, in fanciful, coming-to-realize moments, several former TM Los Angeles colleagues, including the company's controller, accused me of promoting the purchase of Fuller and Dees as a way of financing Morris's political ambitions, their acidic comments flying throughout the company. Whether it arose from Morris's politics or my quick successes, it was a rotten display of bad judgment on their part and I was hurt by it.

Unquestionably, I admired Morris. At times he could act the scoundrel or play the anti-hero, adept as necessary to win his way at every turn. Morris was an ultimate risk taker, leaving no room on the downside for failure. He had no friends. Only Leon Capuano, his longtime attorney and advisor, came close. Most of all, Morris was a negotiating phenomenon, smart, determined and brave, and eventually worthy of the recognition given him by the American Bar Association.

Moving Things Ahead

In succession: Up-grading order processing, turning in the Univac for an IBM 360-45, job descriptions for managers, setting up an incentive program based on both individual evaluations and over-all company gains, selling the print shop, keeping the presses where they stood and renting the facility to the new owner, putting systems in place and letting people know what to expect and what I expected of them. Marilyn was genius at smoothing busted egos.

Patsy and I and marketing manager Andy Swenson, the male exception, agreed on how to develop product: build on what we have that's working, abandon what's not, and seek fresh material. I formalized the Chicago editorial group that was working on the *Life Cycle Library*, hiring Jim Ertel, the former managing editor of *Encyclopedia Britannica*, to manage it. Jim was blessed — with talent and good humor. The Library was brilliant for its time, a guide for parents with children who had growing-up questions, about the changes they could expect and how to handle them, either for parents to use or for children themselves. We would market it not only to our own customer lists, but would wholesale it to other mail order companies as well, a novel idea.

I went on the road, attracting the attention of possible participants by promoting Fuller and Dees to marketing clubs in major cities as a luncheon speaker. I had two subjects, which to deliver

By Way of Luck

depending on the make-up of the audience. One, for senior executives: *Building Profits by Building Customer Satisfaction*. My New York City appearance was attended by Bob Clark, the president of Grolier and by Jack Cassidy, the Doubleday Vice-President who'd canned me. I called them out as model examples of fulfillment managers who'd benefited from artfully developed customer communication programs. Bob, whose company had committed to buying sizeable quantities of *The Life Cycle Library*, graciously waved a hand. Jack shot me a drop-dead look.

The other, *The Power of a Good Idea*, aimed primarily at mid to upper level managers, I told stories of how original suggestions — by themselves — and likely to be overlooked — could lay the foundations for corporate growth and personal success. (I did not realize at the time that I would become a beneficiary of my own story telling — which I'll write about later.)

Fuller and Dees had a division that developed cookbooks for sale to social and political clubs as fundraisers. There were thousands of recipes on file. I made a deal with The Progressive Farmer Company in Birmingham and its flagship magazine, *Southern Living*, to develop a 20-volume cooking series, overcoming the owners' reluctance to grant us the rights by making an offer difficult to refuse, a check for $100,000 as an advance against future royalties. Good food photography, archival and inexpensive, was easily available. And, of course, we had ample editorial copy. Jim Ertel and Patsy Bogle developed the interstitial text.

As we tested the market for *Southern Living*, by zip code we could identify the geographic areas where residents related to Southern subjects. From the obvious states of Georgia and Alabama, Mississippi, Tennessee, Virginia, Kentucky, the Carolinas, Arkansas and possibly Louisiana we could see the positive response to the cookbook series as far west as El Paso, inland to eastern Missouri and Kansas, as far north as southern Illinois and Indiana, as far east as Maryland, and south to the Florida panhandle and no further. So specific was the test, one zip abutting another zip could represent two different markets, we could reach our prime audiences — those who bought and paid their bills — most effectively. This at a time before the ubiquity of credit cards and before there was an abundance of software to draw on. Outside those areas, in spite of the response levels to our mailings, we would encounter a high rate of returns and a high rate of non-payments. We knew where to mail and where not to.

From the success of the *Southern Living Cookbook* mailings and supported by the experience I'd had at Doubleday with the Cookbook Guild, I concluded it was possible to build a sustainable business on cooking subjects. I learned of a cooking series developed by the British Printing Company, its text instructional, its inventory of food photography perfect for our needs. At an all-inclusive price, I flew to London and bought the North American publishing rights to the color separations and to the text, including the consultation required for translating British measurements and ingredients into their comparable American values, all for $25,000, less than half the value of the separations alone.

Readying a return to the United States, the food editors at British Printing eagerly gave me a package to deliver to Patsy. I held it in my lap on the flight back. It contained packs of various whitish flours, baking soda, baking powder and cream of tartar, being sent, I was told, to demonstrate their differences from similar American ingredients and with suggestions on how best to adapt the measurements for the recipes. On final approach to JFK, my curiosity finally engaged, I opened the package. In neat rows, tightly packed were see-through envelopes of white powder. If they had been packets of cocaine, they may not have looked differently.

Right away I feared being held up for hours, the possibility of being confronted by drug enforcement officers a reality. I chose not to take the risk. The package was unmarked. As I departed the aircraft I left it on some other seat, not mine. Patsy laughed it off. She didn't need the instructions; she had already figured out how the conversions could be made.

We retained Charlotte Turgeon, editor of the American edition of *Larousse Gastronomique,* as our consulting editor. Coincidentally,

By Way of Luck

Charlotte and I had history: she was on the board of directors of the Northampton School for Girls that had merged with my alma mater, Williston Academy, at a time I was involved with the school. Both in the publishing business and having an unusual commonality, we sought each other out. As a consultant, she oversaw our cookbook editorial staff.

The series came together easily. We sold it by subscription, the retention rate high and, given our low production costs, happily profitable. After more than a year, as the series waned, we made a one-volume edition and sold it to Nat Wartels, founder and president of Crown Publishers, for retail distribution. He had published the American edition of *Larousse*, a surprising best-seller. Nat felt comfortable taking on another major cookbook. Both Fuller and Dees and Crown profited.

Cookbooks as fund raisers had so far been marketed only to smaller groups, high schools, local societies and small town women's clubs. We expanded the programs reach, entering into contracts with major women's organizations, among them The National Committee of Republican Women, the Garden Clubs of America and the Daughters of the American Revolution.

We re-edited and up-priced the Fuller and Dees reference publications, directories produced in co-operation with the Junior Chamber of Commerce, annuals of the Chamber's award winning *Outstanding Young Men of America*, *Outstanding Young Women of America* and *Outstanding Young Athletes of America*. And along the way we sold the rights to the *Aviation* and *Space Encyclopedia* to Grolier and began aggressively renting our mailing list to non-competitive direct mailing companies. We were building a positive, consistent cash flow.

Data management, however, was a continuing problem. Glitches in the software we'd bought were popping up. We had no local competency to deal with it. TM sent staff to come up with solutions, but they were one-product, one-solution advisers and were stymied by the variety of products and pricings we employed. The problem was solved by an unexpected event: a young, German-born, former

Luftwaffe data processing whiz, arriving in Montgomery as a male war bride, knocked on our door looking for work. In days he began up-dating our processing systems and within four months was managing both order and data processing. Though initially gruff and short with his co-workers, he was respected for his experience and by the relief he brought to a troubled department. What luck!

By the end of the first year, the company was at break even. Swenson was gone, and two other women had emerged as competent and intensely committed managers, Cookie McDonald and Anita Capuano. By the end of the second year, we were profitable, our gross margins exceptional, our inventories manageable and with new products coming on line, altogether promising. Our balance sheet shone.

Auditors Ernst and Ernst, forwarded our year-ending financials to corporate in Los Angeles, noted that in their experience they'd never seen a quicker turn around. Al Casey called and read me the note. (Al was a supporter, why, I could not then understand. I was but another blip on a Times Mirror screen full of blips. All of them larger than mine. Though confused, I cherished his attention.)

Matt Birmingham, now a frequent visitor to Montgomery, was content. I did not know that on his visits he'd spent considerable after-hours time with our receptionist. Effectively, I had been given a free hand.

By the start of the third year, I was ready for something else. Fuller and Dees was profitable but its immediate growth rate would be difficult to sustain. Where could I take it from here? I had two choices, jump start the company by merger or acquisition...or break it up.

A merger with the Progressive Farmer Company loomed as a possibility. From the royalty stream earned from our sale of the *Southern Living* series, Progressive's President had strengthened his position with his Board. But there'd been a breech in our relationship. Whether from a suggestion or on his own initiative, Progressive's book department produced a cookbook designed in imitation of the series for sale to *Southern Living's* subscribers and in violation of our contract. I blew hot.

By Way of Luck

Southerners, I'd learned, if allowed small would grab big. By phone, I pulled him out of a Magazine Publishers Association meeting in Washington and, frankly, leaned on him plenty. He feigned ignorance. He'd fix it, he said, but he didn't. He said we'd have lunch when he returned to Birmingham.

We sat in his private dining room and explored ways of working together. There were none, practically speaking, except by merger or acquisition. I had a proposition. TM, I said, has expressed an interest in buying your company. I suspect you might have an interest in acquiring Fuller and Dees. If either possibility is of interest to your board, I went on, you would have the option to pursue whichever option appeals most to you. The proposition seemed doable.

Al Casey preferred acquisition. He had come close to scoring the acquisition of the Meredith Publishing Company. Discussions had gone on; agreements in draft had been approved. A new logo heralding the merger had been designed for the resulting corporate name, abandoning Times Mirror in favor of Times Meredith, the deal had moved that far along. Copies of the new logotypes were on my desk. But the Meredith family was cool to the proposed merger. Uncertainty set in, and the deal collapsed, in part because of the owners concerns, but also in part I assumed because of an unbudging TM refusal to giving Meredith future "kickers," that is, additional payments based on multiples of increased profits over the three to five years following the acquisition and sale.

TM had been burned by "kickers." The officer-owners of an earlier acquired company with a three year "kicker" contract period personally paid off an 8% reserve for bad debts, thereby sharply bumping profits and adding generously to the multiple to be paid. Wounds heal, but scars seldom go away.

Al didn't like loose strings. He and Martin failed to tie them together in still another transaction: during a "kicker" period, a key employee died, TM becoming the beneficiary of a large "key employee" insurance policy. Because such a likelihood had not been exempted from the "kicker" clause, given the multiples involved TM had to make an extraordinary payment to the prior owners, sufficiently large to effect a coincidental down tick in TM's stock price.

Undeterred, Al approached *Sunset*. He liked the magazine's strong regional presence and, given its physical proximity, it could benefit from the promotional positioning it might receive from The *Los Angeles Times* and from its Southern California community newspapers. *Sunset* said No. It was a growing, independent company and felt TM's structured management style would restrict its future opportunities.

Ordinarily, I did not think that TM's management would be interested in having a larger presence in the South. But its several losing attempts to add to its magazine division may have led to its decision to OK my effort.

Southern Living and its parent, The Progressive Farmer Company, had a profitable stable of regional magazines. TM liked what I was able to tell them about the company. Al advised me not to give anything away, that is, not to make promises that he had not previously approved. He was no less enthusiastic about acquiring new properties, but he had become more cautious.

Progressive's president was optimistic, he said. He liked the idea of becoming part of a larger publicly-held company and having the chance to make more money, lots of it, he said, through options. He and I worked on several scenarios. But none seemed satisfactory. The owners felt a sale premature; they could profit more by waiting more.

Matt, all along said he'd prefer that we sell Fuller and Dees to Progressive Farmer, but any chance of a deal, any kind of a deal, had run out of steam, the talks discontinued by mutual agreement.

For Progressive, it was a good decision, just as it was for *Sunset*. In later years, they were both acquired by Time, Inc. at purchase prices substantially higher than they might have gotten from TM.

For a while, I considered starting a magazine, *Southern Heritage*, hard cover, with six issues annually, later perhaps expanding to twelve. I understood the southern book market; we had a list of several million mail order buyers; we knew where they lived; we saw them as loyalists to Southern landscapes and to Southern history and family ways. Editor Patsy Bogle was from Talladega; Marilyn

By Way of Luck

Black from Montgomery; they were eager to do it.

I'd met a good many multiple-generation southerners including a lady whose forbearers went back to the early 1800s. Their money, old money, had been made in cotton, dealing with Corsicans whose packets sailed up the Alabama River to buy bales by the boatload for their weavers in Seville, Spain's only commercial seaport. Parts of downtown Montgomery are today still owned by Corsicans.

I was living in a homestead built in 1817, two years before Alabama became a State. But I was also living in a community half white and half black, each living poorly and keeping a distance from one another. I'd raised money for the renovation of a local library, learning afterward that only whites could use it. *Southern Living* was a white only magazine, not by design but by the affluence of its readership. Non-whites were rarely seen in its pages, except as menials. I had come to understand the 1970s South in deeper ways.

Southern Heritage was not a good idea. Its production would be expensive and even if it were successful, I questioned whether there was sufficient up-side to warrant the investment. I stopped thinking about it. Instead, I started thinking what I could do with Fuller and Dees. The jumpstart I hoped to find didn't exist. Simply moving it along, quarter by quarter, year by year, for me was not an option, however financially rewarding it might be.

I wrote an extensive memo outlining a break-up of the company, assigning its various operations to various TM subsidiaries where there were obvious fits. For the one least obvious, I had identified a reference book publisher and likely buyer. I included detail of how an accounting of the asset transfer could immediately boost the profitability of the involved subsidiaries, the market value of Fuller and Dees substantially higher than its book value. TM would retain ownership of the real estate, buildings and land. I sent the memo to Matt Birmingham and did not immediately hear from him. After a week had passed, I called him. He had conferred with Martin and with Al Casey. They disagreed with my assessment and rejected my proposal, Matt said. They asked that I continue the good work, and offered me raises, a one-time bonus and a pile of fresh incentives. I was quick not to respond.

Living with success, for me, was far more difficult than attaining it. Building on what I had so far accomplished, I saw an attempt to meet TM's growth requirements as too large a reach, the gamble great. I had been lucky finding good people, acquiring highly profitable products and developing strong supporting systems, but TM's rejection of my plan, and without an acquisition, growing Fuller and Dees and meeting TM's expectations would involve high risk. My confidence in management waning, I was not willing to take it.

10

What Next?

Doubleday & Company, my first employer, is now but a Bertelsmann imprint. Holt, Rinehart was devoured by one of its brethren; it appears merely as a Harcourt, Brace imprint in its catalog. A remnant of the Curtis Publishing Company, located in Indianapolis, is a shell, licensing Norman Rockwell bric-a-brac and publishing a medical magazine called *The Saturday Evening Post*. The Times Mirror Company eventually sold off all but its real estate assets, its book publishing subsidiaries dealt to various American and European entities and its major newspapers, the *Los Angeles Times,* the *Dallas Times Herald* and *Newsday* among them, sold to the Chicago Tribune Company. I had been scrambling up a corporate ladder that had no rungs, seeking a future that had no promise. Did I know in 1973, just 14 years after joining Doubleday that I would be jumping from one potentially collapsing company to another? I don't think so.

Nelson Doubleday must have known. He sold Doubleday & Company and with real estate developer Fred Wilpon bought the New York Mets from owner Joan Payson. The Murchison family must have known to sell Holt to Harcourt. The Chandler's must have known that books and newspapers were not safe long term investments. Curtis had been DOA, dead on arrival, and I didn't see it. At a steely moment in 1973, with little deliberation, I decided that

I was in the wrong business and, further, that corporate America held no promise for me.

Putting reason aside, with not an inkling of what I might do next, and indifferent to whatever consequences I might be opening myself to, certitude driving me, I submitted my resignation.

Within a day or two, I received a phone call from Al Casey. He was flying from Los Angeles to New York. Could I join him the following morning for breakfast. Meet me at Peacock Alley, he said, a restaurant on the main floor of the Waldorf Astoria Hotel, at eight o'clock in the morning. We should talk.

Al Casey had always been deferential toward me, adroitly defending me in budget presentations when I missed the knifing subtleties in seemingly off-handed questions, bringing me along when calling on investors, or sourcing possible acquisitions, whether making calls in New York, London or Paris. I don't believe it was a personal bias. He found me dependable; no more than that. Had he something in store for me? What could I expect? I flew in from Montgomery and checked into the Waldorf. I would know in less than twelve hours

Among those close to me and to Fuller and Dees, word of my resignation spread quickly, it could not be contained, my employees were passively upset, wishing me well in whatever I might do, but inwardly angry that I was abandoning them. One of our suppliers was cheered by the news, Florence Wolf, whose Chicago company ranked high among direct marketing data base managers. Listening to her lecture at a marketing association meeting in New Orleans soon after moving south, I tracked her down, interviewed both her and her partner, her husband Seymour, much impressed by them both, and gave them a contract to manage our mailing lists. The process was not complicated. Rent our lists to non-competitive users, and identify and evaluate owners whose lists we might rent. The results we would analyze in-house, a protective measure to insure confidentiality and to protect ourselves against theft.

The Wolfs appeared uncanny, their experience fresh, their knowledge unmatchable. We set the criteria, they did the rest. Our rush to profitability was accelerated by Wolf's list rentals. But for the

By Way of Luck

commission we were paying, the cash we received went straight to the bottom line. It was a high margin, unbudgeted and welcome windfall.

Florence called me from Chicago. Can I come down for a visit? she asked. With a predictable change in the management of Fuller and Dees, I suspected she was fearful of losing the account. I was wrong. She had a proposal, she said.

I thought Al Casey might have a proposal as well. I was wrong again. After we'd ordered English muffins and coffee, he asked, what company was I moving to? None, I said. After some time off, I'd look for work that would match my needs and not necessarily the needs of an employer. I told him that. You're brave, he said and added, I don't think I could do that. He said he was fascinated that I could.

Then he dropped a bomb, its shock wave immobilizing.

The same day I got your letter of resignation, Al said, I submitted my resignation to Franklin Murphy. He said it surely, as he might a public announcement he could not recant, adding, "I'm joining American Airlines."

(Murphy, the former Chancellor of UCLA was TM's recently appointed Chairman of the Board. He would succeed Al as CEO.)

Was I surprised, no. Numbed, yes. Stupidly, I joked, "Al, you're no pilot."

"I'll be President and CEO," he said with a glimmer of a smile. "I don't have to know how to fly."

We both laughed remorseful laughs. For the next hour or so we were gabbing innocents, guessing how we might fare, our different odysseys separating us widely, he taking charge of a visible, brand name company with a market cap in the near billions, and I taking charge of me.

Over the years, we stayed in touch by greeting cards and birthday remembrances. I didn't see Al again until 10 years later when he had left American and become head man at the Reconstruction Finance Corporation. I visited him again in Washington several years after.

Yet I was still puzzled why he had plucked me from the ranks of TM's corporate executives, overrode the layer of senior vice-presidents between him and me and gave me unearned operating room.

I found out in 2013 from an aviation broker, a buyer and seller of commercial aircraft who opened an Al Casey window that held the answer. Al, he said, while rebuilding American's financial foundations, pushed young men, the brightest and the strongest, into critical management positions, getting the work done and building a core to support the longer term success of the company. He had a reputation for that, the broker said. Click. Puzzle solved.

Florence Wolf

"Here's what I have in mind," Florence began. We were sitting on the screened back porch of the Coosada farm house facing the pasture where cattle were grazing. I had just come up from the barn, in hired-hand shirt, jeans and boots. Florence had arrived minutes ago, straight from Chicago to Montgomery, in full gear, the pearls, the cascading earrings, the diamonds and the gold, the watch that told of both wealth and time, a glittering sequined bodice, the silks, the sash, the aura and the aroma of a woman determined all enveloping, she could have been Estee Lauder.

"Coffee first," I said.

"It's hotter than hell here," she said.

"Ice coffee then."

"Gin on the rocks."

"Easy to do."

I poured. She took off her shoes.

Florence was older than I, by a dozen years or more, and had gumption, a word my mother used to describe women with the "powers of intimidation." By modest account, Florence was a soon-to-be heiress, her aged and stroke-ridden father living in Miami, her maiden name Green; she had graduated from Hunter College in mid-town Manhattan with a degree in psychology; and had recently been named Woman of the Year (in the marketing category, she was certain to tell me) by the American Management Association, receiving a certificate I could find mounted on the wall behind her office desk. She spoke proudly of her accomplishments and the

By Way of Luck

recognition she had been given by her peers.

She and Seymour had agreed I should move to Chicago. They'd give me an ample suite in their offices in the *Playboy* Building and secretarial support. "A place to re-start your life," Florence said. They were expanding, as marketing consultants to major consumer product companies. All they wanted from me was advice, perhaps a little help with their marketing materials. If at some point I wanted to join them, my call, they'd make it attractive. They could afford the investment it would take, she said.

She handed me current financial statements, both company and personal, as one. She and Seymour appeared flush, with ample cash, their only liability an office lease, their earnings history consistent and growing, their customers, which included Fuller and Dees, a list of well-known names. I wasn't surprised. Florence was famous in her niche of the direct marketing industry, and more than held her own in the tumult of the mailing list business, her story told without blemish, confirmation of what she had told me coming in a letter from her attorney.

I bit.

My luck had changed.

Within months Florence would be facing bankruptcy.

After hiring my replacement at Fuller and Dees and given a generous, no-hard-feelings bonus, I moved to Chicago. The decision was easy: I had friends there; I liked living there; my children liked it there; the city was central to my interests, I could build a business there, London as available as from New York; San Francisco and Los Angeles a half day closer, I could resume flying out of Midway or put a boat in a downtown harbor, cruising the Great Lakes always vigorous and welcome. The assurances I sought were at my feet.

Florence had located an apartment for me, on the near north side, overlooking Lake Michigan. I bought it. She'd furnished the promised office. I moved in. I called people I knew, the dinner invitations mounted, the Kessie's, Jack and Carol, came by with bottles of wine and fruit, Jack careful to distinguish which went with which, Maggie flying in to say hello and to mingle with lost friends, the maître d' at the Tavern Club nodding in recognition, Susan, my eldest daughter, asking whether she and her sisters might still use Hefner's pool — could I have felt any more at home?

But home wasn't what I was feeling. Around the Wolf offices there was whispering, sales reps looking askance, Seymour walking hurriedly past me when I had questions, muttering, don't ask, don't ask, Florence's door shut against shouts muffled and indistinct. Yet Florence appeared unperturbed, late one morning laying on my desk a purchase order just received, she said, that would net her a hundred thousand dollars for "just a few hour's work."

Why was she being defensive? I had to find out. I was making calls, lining up appointments, fishing for information that could lead to something, I wasn't sure what, but I knew the something would come along, it always had. The luck thing. But were it to come, I couldn't be embroiled in what I guessed were financial disputes, closed doors the give-away.

One of Florence's sales reps sent me warning signals, bumping eyebrows, look-away glances. I didn't see them until my suspicions were roused. I met the rep outside the office for coffee at an Oak Street deli.

The Lie

Florence is broke, the rep told me. She owes me commissions. If I leave I'll never get them. So I stay. She owes everybody.

I said I was surprised. She wears expensive clothes, the jewelry, the big apartment overlooking the Lake, the cars, the travel, she has to have money.

The rep shot back, You don't get. The company earns a 20% commission for what it sells. She's not satisfied with the 20%. She thinks it's all her money. She comingles; it's all in one account, her money and their money. She shorts the list owners. Issues phony reports. She pays out just enough to keep competitors and clients from shutting her down. And the financial statements? Phony, too, he said. We all knew that.

By Way of Luck

Florence always paid Fuller and Dees in full, I said.

Surprise, surprise, the rep said. She likes you. She wants you to straighten out her mess, be her partner. Seymour's leaving her.

I tried not to appear angry. At whom? At the rep's story? At myself, if the rep's story were true? There had to be a more valid account than what I'd just heard. I returned to the office and made phone calls.

What letter? Sam Pfeffer said. Sam was Florence's attorney, his letter an assurance of her financial condition. I read it to him. He didn't hesitate to say he hadn't written any such letter. If she's used my letterhead, he added, she's got trouble from me.

I reached an administrator in the Hunter College alumni office. There was no record of either a Florence Green or a Florence Wolf in its files.

A lady at the American Management Association told me there was no Woman of the Year award. Sinking fast, my pulse racing, I asked her to look again. Look for what? she said. We don't have files for things that aren't there. She hung up, angrily it seemed, the phone clattering and slow to find its cradle. It was late on a Friday, I remember so clearly. The lady had hurried to leave.

I walked home and called Florence's apartment. The ringing of her phone was coming as if from a distance. My systems were shutting down, the humiliation enveloping me, nothing was working, not my ears, not my eyes, not my mouth, only my voice and that just barely.

She anticipated what I might say, interrupting me before I could say it. Seymour and I want to talk with you, she said. Please. Can you come over? I said no. Tomorrow then, she said. Maybe lunch. I said, at the Drake Hotel, the main dining room. 12 noon. There was a pause. OK, she said but we could eat here just as well. At the Drake Hotel, I said. 12 noon. I hung up.

There would be an explanation, an argument, a denial and worse, an explosive, accusing retort, all rumors, she would say, truthless and driven by her competitors, I could feel it coming. I would bring it to an end, but in a place where I had the control. I booked a lunchtime table, asking specifically that it be in the middle of the dining room where Florence and Seymour would hesitate to be loud and where I could easily leave.

Seymour and I are divorcing, Florence began. He's been unfaithful.

Opening a potentially clamorous conversation with a deliberate diversion was a chess master's move and worth remembering. Had I a tape recorder, I would at that moment turned it on for the brazenness to come. Florence was a crook, of that I was sure, and skillful. No big deal, Seymour said. No reason for a divorce.

He's got a girlfriend, Florence said.

Not a girlfriend, Seymour said, emphasizing friend, as if anticipating forgiveness. Just a girl. He then uttered a remark I recall most vividly. "I was only sport fucking," he said, his eyes alight, looking for a laugh.

Florence moved adamantly on, ignoring him. I'll give you Seymour's share of the business. He's leaving and I won't let him take it with him. Anyway, she added, I own the whole company. I say around he's a co-owner as a face saver. She started to ramble.

I got up and walked away.

Her creditors took over her company and paid off her debts at a discount. As a group, the creditors wanted to avoid the financial confusion of a bankruptcy and to sustain the credibility of mailing list and database management suppliers. They were angry yet remained smart.

I saw her but once many years later. Unnoticed, I passed her in the lobby of the New York Hilton. From her dress and her adornment, I could tell she had reestablished herself somewhere with somebody. Seymour moved to Los Angeles, I heard, with his girlfriend whose ex had given her an interest in a Beverly Hills Hotel. Florence and Seymour were survivors both.

One more lesson learned from the school of hard knocks. I'd heard that said many times, never thinking I'd one day be in attendance there. It's a lesson that does not come without pain and embarrassment, nor does one forget it, an unwise decision at a time of change, making me most vulnerable and questioning my strength

By Way of Luck

and purpose. I was sorely chastised by my decision — to leave TM and to accept Florence's proposition — and having to remount my enterprising spirit. I was ashamed and feeling low.

Meantime, Matt Birmingham and the Times Mirror Company executed my proposal for the break-up of Fuller and Dees. To the letter.

Patsy Bogle took the larger asset — the general book group — to New York and merged it with the Popular Science Publishing Company, taking her two children with her and starting a new life away from Montgomery where, two years earlier, her husband had been murdered.

11
GRT

General Recorded Tape, located in Sunnyvale, California — today the heart of Silicon Valley — in the late 1960s grew out of a new technology: audio tape. Recording companies had been cutting music on vinyl for several generations and distributing singles and albums at retail by way of wholesalers. The occasional best sellers aside, it was a business made marginal by the production costs and by maintaining large inventories in as many as 20,000 outlets in the United States. Further, the music studios had substantial investments in the machines, the order processing and the shipping. A move from vinyl to tape, a shift to a new technology and to a different business platform, looked risky.

GRT was formed by a handful of entrepreneurs in the Valley. With the support of private investors they ignored the risk, acquiring rights from the studios to re-record from vinyl platters to far less expensive tape stored in plastic cassettes, to manufacture and market their titles. For the music studios, seeing tape as untested, they eagerly signed royalty contracts.

GRT's cassette sales jumped quickly. Vinyl sales shrunk. The cassette margins were robust. The investors took the company public and the entrepreneurs and the venture capitalists made money.

The company attracted competition; defensively, GRT looked

By Way of Luck

for ways to expand its base as a music distributor, lessening its dependence on the studios by seeking new markets and developing products that could be sold direct to the consumer, by-passing wholesalers and retailers by direct mail and television advertising.

Jim Levy was recruited to build out GRT's direct mail business. Originally from Baton Rouge, by way of a college degree from Carnegie Mellon, he'd landed a job at Time, Inc., in its New York City subscription department, successfully handling an assignment that got him moved to the San Francisco Bay area with Haverhill's, a Time, Inc. subsidiary, as the "big guy from back East" selling household merchandise by mail.

Actually, Jim was a "little guy," youngish in years and experience and not long enough in direct marketing to qualify for a senior management responsibility. Before Haverhill's found him out, the publicity accompanying his move West attracted the attention of a head hunter who, finding Jim low-key and steady, his strongest qualifications, introduced him to GRT. That Levy was a musician and played riotous doo-wop piano won over GRT's management.

Less than a year later, by 1973, he'd spent $600,000 on a record album mailing assembled by a Chicago merchandising company specializing in oil company billing inserts, and had nothing to show for it. He'd hired the right experience in the wrong end of the business. Now, he was in Chicago picking up the pieces, and seeking help. Agencies in the loop and on the North Side ignored him. He had no budget; he had both a business and personal disaster on his hands. Were he to lose his job, every employer in the Bay Area, a tight community rank with gossip and innuendo, would know of his failing in unending instances of phone calls and water cooler chit-chats. He would be a doomed man. Jim Levy had to find a savior.

Several months before, in Florence Wolf's office renting lists from her, I'd met Jim Levy. Jim had made a note of it and called me. Plaintive and polite, he said he needed help. Could we meet? I had just taken space on a high floor of the *Playboy* Building. I had no income. Just a phone number, a couple of desks and Sharon, an indelibly inventive assistant willing to take a chance on me.

Jim Levy told me how the new GRT start-up had come apart. Bring me the pieces, I said. It was mid-summer. Sorting through the baggage he handed me, I could see what had gone wrong. Though the music was not to my taste, a collection of Lawrence Welk favorites, there was an audience for it, I was sure. The offer was weak, there was no inducement and nowhere could I find the word FREE. The whole package, expensively produced, reeked of unimportance. Worse, list selection had been based on the results of mailings for cameras, kitchen appliances, and automotive accessories, a compilation of names and addresses of no relevance. Bad decisions outweighed good decisions by a wide margin

After a couple of hours of morning talk, Jim offered to buy me lunch and suggested a bar and grill down the street, a gathering place for high-rollers. I took him instead to a nearby luncheonette at the Oak Street beach a short walk from the office. I bought us each a hot dog and a Coke. We parked our butts on the warm sand and watched girls playing volley ball.

What are we doing here? Jim Levy asked, his grin questioning.

Learning not to spend money, I told him. You owe me two dollars for your share of lunch. Jim got the message and agreed to my proposal. I would take the lead in explaining to his management what had taken place and how we could build profitably on it. I insisted on Jim's agreement to that. He had no more to lose. If his management didn't like me and what I could do for their company, I'd be the one escorted out of the house, perhaps saving Jim from a similar fate.

The next day we flew out to Sunnyvale to meet GRT's chairman and his CEO, K. White Sonner. Sitting at opposite ends of a limolong, loosely cushioned couch, they assumed skeptical postures, arms folded, legs crossed, doubt etched into their faces. I took the lead. The loss is characteristic of new mail order ventures, I explained, giving them examples of specific promotions that grew successful out of the ashes of a seemingly bad experience. Now, you can write off your so-called disaster or you can build on it. Here's how.

Our case went something like this, not word for word, but

By Way of Luck

accurate: We will package not by performer but by category. Jim will source and acquire the music. I will produce the packaging and promotional materials and handle the mailings, starting with a remake of the Welk album. Whatever GRT has in it is a sunk cost, so the additional expenditures, except for marketing costs, will be relatively minor. Beginning with the remake, each album will have a FREE book, yours to keep whether or not...etc. I will produce the books, 32 pages each, all about the music and the performers the album contains, heavily illustrated and inexpensive. Each will have a distinguishing characteristic. (Example: For few dollars, I got permission, from the new owners of *The Saturday Evening Post* to later headline an album of movie music *The Saturday Evening Post Goes to the Movies*. We would look for other similar "sponsorships.) Each album will feature "keepsake" cover art. Our audience is small town America. We will fill a unique gap in the music market with albums that can't be found anywhere else. We will fill it with organ music, with accordion music, and with polkas, with songs of faith, and with music played at hoe-downs and barn raisings and at rural family picnics and with music the whole town will gather at the bandstand to hear played.

Whew! I was selling hard. I had no business nor the prospects of one.

I went on. Our research has shown us that a yearning for old time tunes is out there. We'll find it. We'll sell it. And we'll make it available on vinyl as well tape, either in the regular or deluxe edition.

Jim and I defined the sales strategy, both of us staying up-beat and positive and ignoring the looks of disbelief that faced us. In time the arms un-folded, the legs came uncrossed, the questions got answers and, by invoking some of the stuff Time, Inc. had taught him, Jim presented a convincing case for approval.

He got it.

I got what I labored for.

That evening at dinner, I ordered celebratory drinks for Jim and me.

What's a deep-dish juniper berry pie? Jim asked.

The experience of selling an outlying idea to a pair of hard-liners brought Jim and me together. He was happy. I was happy he was happy and he was happy I was happy. I stopped calling him Jim. He was Levy. He stopped calling me Jim. I was Perkins. That way no one around GRT would have to guess which of us was the real Jim.

For me, landing GRT was the start of my business, revenue enough to bring in another hire, Linda from Tulsa, who with Sharon could handle the detail, coordinating production and managing payables. I could freelance everything else, writers, artists, researchers, directors. Exhilaration surged through me.

The strategy worked as we said it would. Levy's flowering career bloomed in full. He became a star and a GRT vice-president. We were a team for almost three years.

With the exception of K. White Sonner, the company rallied around the new venture. White could be boorish and remain so indefinitely, likeable only from a distance. His job was to ask the tough questions, he said, a trite expression common among executives deflecting responsibility.

Sometime in late 1974, when I was in Sunnyvale, White's boss, the company's chairman and CEO, invited me to dinner. He had so far kept me at arm's length. White was on his agenda. He was firing White and said I might want to consider replacing him. Oops. I was up against a rock. I told him that. Take your time to think on it, he said. He had a board meeting the following morning and would get its concurrence on ushering White out the door. My decision could wait, he said.

At noon the next day, White came by the conference room where I was bundling materials to take back to Chicago. Some news for you, he said. Thought you might appreciate knowing at a meeting this morning our CEO was fired by GRT's board of directors.

He said this with such innocence I knew he could not have known of the dinner meeting I'd had the night before. He also said, with his need to assume more responsibilities, I'd need to take on more work. He increased my retainer.

I had unwittingly been in the middle of a power struggle and

By Way of Luck

whichever way it might have gone, luckily, I was a winner. I extended the lease on my Chicago office.

Post Script

The same head hunter who'd found Levy nearly four years earlier moved him to another company, a start-up video game venture, Jim's success at GRT a credit that resonated with the investors. The venture was called Activision, after Nintendo becoming the fastest growing, most profitable video game companies of all time. Jim Levy was the founding president, an instant high-tech super star and, when Activision went public, a very rich man.

12
Beurt and Cory SerVaas

My fledgling business took on a shape I could not have predicted. Following up on my initial meeting with the *Post* in Indianapolis, the owners, Beurt and Cory SerVaas, asked that I lend them a hand in reviving the magazine and developing books derived from archival materials. I was a perfect fit for them. I had edited several *Post* anthologies. I knew the inventory.

Fred Birmingham, once the editor-in-chief of *Esquire*, was the SerVaas's editorial director. Fred was in his retiring years. And immediately wary of me. I reminded him that we'd met once before. He was a Williston Academy alumnus, as I was. On a visit to the school, he'd addressed our publications staff. After the talk, I chased him down and interviewed him for an article in the school's newspaper. Politely, he said he remembered the event. The wariness faded. He became my in-house advisor on all things SerVaas.

Beurt and Cory were industrious people and gifted. In their 40s they went back to school, part time, at Indiana University School of Medicine, each earning MD's, all the while building a business empire encompassing more than 20 companies, Curtis Publishing among them, either by buying them or starting them.

Beurt was President of the Indianapolis City Council for over 30 years and a political stalwart. He was the State's "Mr. Republican."

By Way of Luck

He and his wife Cory were close friends of Patricia and Richard Nixon; they accompanied the Nixon's on their famed trip to China.

Our relationship was informal. When they had something for me to do, I'd drive to Indianapolis and do it, or take it back to Chicago if I needed more time. When I stayed over, I always had a room at their home. With the coming bi-centennial in 1976, I told Beurt and Cory there was sufficient material in the Post archives to produce a glamorous, coffee-table-sized book on the 200 year-old history of the United States. I called it *The American Story*.

Beurt and Cory gave me an immediate Yes! I assembled an editorial and production team. As we progressed I offered Beurt some thoughts on marketing the book. Beurt said he'd take care of it. With layouts, Beurt and I called on Sears and pitched a senior buyer on building the company's 1976 marketing strategy around the book. Beurt, I discovered in an office high in the Sears Tower, was a bold and fearless salesman. He asked for an order of 100,000 copies; in but a few weeks and after little dickering, he received in the mail, at the price we had proposed, a purchase order for 100,000 copies of *The American Story*. All other sales Beurt and Cory might generate, book store and by mail, would be incidental.

Cory introduced me to Julie Nixon Eisenhower and her husband David Eisenhower who were visiting. Cory thought I might assist Julie in her effort to produce one or more children's books, or cook books, she wasn't sure which. Julie did not need any help. A strong woman and sure of herself, she knew what she was doing. I think Cory just wanted to show her off to friends. OK by me.

Over time, Beurt, Cory and I constructed a warm relationship, mostly business, but close and sometimes personal. They knew my story, I knew theirs. On occasion, they'd make up projects for me, unnecessary and small, but enough to encourage a trip to Indianapolis.

On one visit Beurt and I played a pitch and putt game at his golf course. I beat Beurt, one-putting eight of the nine holes, all lucky. But Beurt had no way of knowing that. A week later he was in Chicago, in my apartment. He suggested I move to Indianapolis. Get married there. Have kids. Become part of the local community, he said. Move into his offices. Join him and Cory in the management of their businesses. He was in his sell mode. He valued me, he said, addressing me in the manner of advisor and mentor. He was not convinced I could make a living peddling creative services. Slow growth and risky, he said. I sensed in him, there, where I lived, in my apartment, he drinking tea, I coffee, he as compulsive as I had witnessed at our meeting with the Sears buyer. He was relentless. He wanted a win. Were I to say yes, he would have it. I said no. He didn't need me, I told him.

I think the eight one-putts complicated his fondness for me.

13

Queen's Way

A half block from my apartment were two classic Chicago restaurants: At the Hotel Ambassador East, the Pump Room. In an adjoining apartment house, below street level, Maxim's, an acceptable replica of the original 1800s art nouveau restaurant on the Rue Royal in Paris. Augie and Theo Spectorsky routinely entertained out of town guests there. The plush décor, the red on red layering of fabric and mottled wood, the pretense to an age long past tolerable, Maxim's played to its image as a sophisticated watering hole. I joined them happily when invited. But the Pump Room was occasionally for me the start of an evening.

On a late afternoon at the Bar, an office party in progress, waiting for a friend to show, a mid-sized fellow dressed preppy said hello and began talking as if he knew me. His name was Jim Davis. His card showed he was president of Queen's Way to Fashion, a lady's apparel company. We'd met at an industry convention. A week later, he was on the phone asking me to visit his complex. He'd like to show me around. He gave me an address in Evanston, a northern Chicago suburb, and said I'd recognize the company by its sign. As I approached, I could see Queens-Way writ in large black letters.

We walked the plant together, design and manufacturing, order processing, shipping, marketing, sales, and finance, Jim introducing me to managers as we moved along. Nice business, I said. Thanks, he replied, but our revenues are flat. We talked. I learned that Queen's Way was family owned, Jim the outsider son-in-law working part-time on an MBA from the University of Chicago and obviously a capable executive. But he needed ideas. He suggested a consulting assignment.

Jim had convened a committee of his senior people to meet weekly for an hour or two to identify new directions Queen's Way might take to bolster sales. His senior managers were reluctant participants. They were comfortable with the status quo and feared change, a reorganization perhaps, and possibly leading to something that none of them wished, a merger that could be followed by a house-cleaning. I'd like you to participate in the meetings, Jim said. Stir things up, figure out what's holding us back.

This was late summer 1973, Nixon had just resigned, on my fortieth birthday, August 9, the economy was hovering in mid-air with no landing field in sight, I had three children in private schools and still guessing where my next dollar was coming from. Did I truly want to have as a client a woman's clothing company that sold its products at parties in the home?

For my attendance at each of his one-hour meetings, Jim offered me a thousand dollars and expenses. He got my attention.

I sat in on several, unproductive sessions, loitering about the premises afterward, chatting with managers I'd met on the initial tour, and in a few weeks came to conclusions I knew would not change should I spend months on the assignment.

I told Jim three things: 1. Your organization is over staffed, yet qualified; I see three employees doing the job of two. 2. Your market is not well-enough defined; it should be segmented, with products to match. 3. Your managers are dug in against change and their attitudes are assumed by the middle and lower level managers and employees.

Jim Davis interrupted. Give me an example of market segmentation, he said. Women come in all shapes and sizes, I said, yet your product line is uniformly the same. A designer starts with a size

By Way of Luck

7 and scales it up from there. By the time it gets, say, to a size 24 the styling is compromised, the fabric balloons, the garment no longer fits. You must cut to the size and also to the cloth. Larger garments exaggerate design; a floral pattern on a size 7 may work for a younger, more petite woman, but on a larger, possibly older, woman, florals appear outsized and ridiculous. I had concluded this, I told Jim, by watching his best customers, the larger, fuller figured women working in his company. Their ample bodies were draped in swaths of material, much of it bunched under their arms and hanging like parachute cloth. I suggested he develop a line specifically for the fuller figured women.

Mmmmm, Jim muttered. No more weekly meetings. Thanks. I'll get back to you soon.

In a few days he made a novel proposal. I accept your analysis, he said. But I won't get the cooperation of my managers to execute the changes we'll need to make. He then revealed the road block he suffered. Two of his most senior people, the executives in charge of marketing and manufacture — and the most argumentative in our meetings — were on Jim's board of directors and relatives of the company's owners. They'd have their say. Jim would not have their cooperation.

Here's what I want to do, Jim went on. Start a new business for me. Distant from Queen's Way's, perhaps out of your offices. Develop a wardrobe for the fuller figured woman, do everything, design, manufacture, marketing, even accounting, the product line to be sold by catalog. If it works, Queen's Way will absorb it, a going business, that way we avoid the uncertainty of a start-up and the internal bad-mouthing that would come with it. If it doesn't work, we cut it loose. In either way, it will not be a drain on our established business. Frankly, he added, I can convince the family to give it a try.

How distressing, I thought, a capable guy like Jim having to go to the in-laws for OK's. A sympathetic shake of my head Jim mistook as a negative signal, a rejection of his proposal. I'll make it worth your while, he said, fearful I'd refuse. I'll pay you six thousand a week and a mark-up on all promotional expenses. Build a budget for me, define a success bonus, just tell me what you'll need and I'll finance it. What do you say to that?

Was Jim daffy? I was a media guy. Why did he think I could run a clothing business. But...wasn't I already in the music business?

I demurred. But not for long, assessing whether Jim's offer might lead to a new, perhaps better, definition of my life, my career, my work habits, and my ethic...uh, uh...I stopped my irrational meandering. It was all bull shit. I needed the money. I agreed. I leased adjoining office space.

Most businesses come together substantially the same: a market need or opportunity is identified; a product or service is required, as is its development; a method to market and sell is chosen, as is its management; a regular accounting is put in place to track expense and income and the management of payables and receivables. And having money in the bank. Which Jim did. Hiring the right people, all else falls in to place. Usually.

My immediate need: a designer and a manager to handle manufacture and inventory management. We were committed to sell by catalog. I'd take on the hiring and the marketing and, with Jim as my overseer, the responsibility for making happen what we wished to happen.

So...how did it turn out? Luck, coincidence and the evolution of an idea took over.

Following a divorce and looking for a change in her life, the fashion designer of a German retail chain had just moved to New York. I found her, interviewed her by telephone and invited her to Chicago. She brought tear sheets from various catalogs featuring her designs, her models ample and fully figured. I hired her.

Jim called with a recommendation. His senior people had fired a long-time Queen's Way employee who had run purchasing, warehousing and shipping, a squabble apparently getting in the way of better judgment. You won't find anyone with more experience, he said. I had another hire.

Retaining the direct marketing division of J. Walter Thompson's Chicago office, its staff among the best in the city, we put together

By Way of Luck

a test. We would call ourselves The Fashion Coalition. Our catalog, combining editorial and promotional content, would be named Woman. Thompson would produce and manage the mailing. My office would produce the catalog.

One by one, the pieces came together. The test response met our goal. The follow up mailing of the catalog was marginally disappointing, a guess, as there was nothing comparable by which to measure results. There would be further tests.

J. Walter decided to make an end run on me. To its way of thinking, a one-man shop with a sizeable promotional contract was ripe for plucking by a larger, established agency. The Chicago senior vice president who headed J. Walter's direct marketing division, Bob Bobowski, called on Jim Davis at the Queen's Way offices and pitched him for the account. Jim was offended by Bob's visit and told him so. The next day, by messenger, I received J. Walter's Fashion Coalition project files, including the production materials for the mailings. J. Walter was canned.

Jim told me to hire however many people I required to manage the promotions out of my office.

In the months ahead, we built a product line, developed a modest mailing list and published two catalogs. The catalogs were roughly designed and, to my way of thinking, inadequate, a responsibility I managed badly. I hired magazine people, Don Myrus and a freelance art director, believing we could assemble not only an excellent selling catalog, but an interesting one to read as well, a combination magazine and catalog. I was wrong. Don and the art director performed well enough, but I did not. I was not satisfied with what we'd done. Time ran out, we hit a mailing deadline, still not fully confident, I nonetheless just let it go. A bad decision. After fourteen months of what I considered ground breaking work, I found myself hoping for a miracle.

The miracle rose like sunshine in the morning. From a distance, Jim's senior executives, the in-laws, were tracking our progress, their criticisms a loud annoyance. As the weeks and months went by, as new product moved into the warehouse, as the promotions proceeded, as the first catalog was published, bit by bit voices from the executive suite hinted at envy.

They wanted the product line for themselves and went to Jim begging for it. Regardless of the shape it was in!

Jim Davis got what he wanted. His senior employees were once again happy. And after a peaceable transition, I was off the hook.

A Turning Point in the Tax Laws

Jim and I stayed socially friendly, close enough for him to share the details of a law suit he was planning. Its outcome, either way, win or lose, would have a game changing impact on the direct selling industry made up of such giants such Avon, Amway, Stanley Home Products, Tupperware, Rubbermaid, and Mary Kay Cosmetics. The Internal Revenue Service had decreed that the Federal Insurance Contribution Act, known as FICA, applied not only to full time employees but to part-time, independent contractors as well — substantially all direct selling sales people.

Independent contractors, self-determined and self-employed, work at places and times of their own choosing and not at the direction of the companies they represent. How and what they earn and how they present themselves is solely at their discretion. FICA's new rules would require that contractor earnings be taxed and matched by their "employer." Further, contributions to Medicare would also be deducted. The requirement ran counter to labor laws, would be costly if not disruptive, and would effectively take away from sales people the independence that first attracted them to direct selling. The industry could be permanently crippled.

Industry leaders, groping for what action they might take, wrote letters, hired lobbyists, and rallied their Congressmen, learning only that little could be done until the requirement be enacted, that is, until they had been aggrieved. Jim Davis and Queen's Way took a more direct course. For the most recent 12-month period, the company paid in full a sum that amounted to what his company might have contributed to FICA, writing a check for the total, and sending

By Way of Luck

it to the IRS. When the check was cashed, Jim and the IRS had crossed a legal threshold. Queen's Way had been aggrieved.

Jim, on behalf of Queen's Way, sued the IRS in Federal Court — on too many counts to be documented in this narrative — the IRS decision was reversed and Queen's Way got its money back, plus interest. Without the fuss industry leaders were exploring, like Mighty Mouse, Jim's small company accomplished what his larger competitors were fearful of confronting. Expressions of gratitude from both friends and competitors flooded his office.

Jim died in his mid-fifties from an irreversible cancer, an unexpected and sad event.

In the meantime, by bringing on two additional clients I was making sufficient money to pay the rent, cover tuitions and in a fashion indulge my wants and needs and find more time for my children.

Complaining to myself that I was not in a business I wanted to be in, I had to ask, what business do you wish to be in? I had no answer. I was seen, though, as being in advertising, introduced to new friends by old friends as Jim, he's in advertising. I could not quarrel with that, so I merged my business with an established advertising agency, Bernstein Associates, for twenty years representing clients in direct marketing, direct selling and general consumer advertising, Ron Bernstein its owner and president. The newly formed company was called Perkins Bernstein, Ron and I were equal owners, he would manage the company as its CEO, I would be its Chair and Creative Director and together we would manage our clients and seek new business.

Ron was the antithesis of the popular picture of an ad guy, unassuming, eschewing spoken words, preferring to communicate by gesture, a barely perceptible shake of his head, or a nod, a thin scowl for disapproval, an up-ward jerk of his chin a big OK, and when a show of enthusiasm was called for, he'd compose his remarks redundantly and deliver them with expletive force. At our attorney's office, signing the contract that formed our company, Ron roared, "Let's make a fortune of money!" On another occasion, "Our future is ahead of us!"

I moved from my offices in the Playboy building and into office space adjoining Ron in the John Hancock Building, a landmark on Michigan Avenue's Miracle Mile. After breaking through the walls, his people and my people were one.

14

Perkins, Bernstein, Inc.

For three years beginning in 1976, listed in the Chicago telephone book, at the best address in town, with a basket full of clients and making money, there was an advertising agency named Perkins, Bernstein, Inc., its fourteen employees producing art and copy, buying media, buying printing, offering a slew of supporting services and holding hands with a dozen or more clients including its founding accounts, GRT and Rubbermaid's party plan. With our experience in both direct marketing, meaning by mail, and direct selling, meaning by knocking on doors, Ron and I occupied a rare niche as an agency, rare enough to claim we were unique and our talents valid and worthy of consideration.

We could open new doors for our clients, we said, leading them to new, untappd business opportunities. We earned assignments from Amway, Duraclean, Beeline, Prentice-Hall, Thomas Nelson Publishers and the Direct Selling Association, the latter hiring us to produce a new logotype, an identifying corporate insignia. We soon had a modest, profitable stable.

I sought something more demanding and more rewarding. My eye was on Meredith Corporation, publisher of *Better Homes and Gardens* and seven other national magazines and publisher of homemaking books, among them, notably, the *Better Homes and Gardens Cookbook*, a Meredith mainstay for over 75 years.

Better Homes and Gardens

The magazine's home town, Des Moines, had a Marketing Club that met monthly and featured guest speakers. By phone with its president, I wangled an invitation to address an upcoming monthly luncheon. I would tell marketing success stories, specifically about direct selling companies: Avon and Amway, Mary Kay, and Home Products and Gifts, self-described door-to-door retailers our agency had close ties with, and asked the president to be sure the lunch had a good turnout of *Better Homes* and Meredith people. The Club's bulletin, reminding members of the date and headlining the speaker, did its job.

I spoke to a crowded room, enhanced largely by the attendance of a large assemblage of *Better Homes* marketing managers, one of them, Terry Warder, seeking me out after the meeting came to a close. Terry said he'd given some thought to selling direct one of its popular mail order products. Could we talk?

During the weeks that followed, Terry and I constructed a proposal that would have *Better Homes* sell its do-it-yourself needlecraft kits — then available only by coupon from Meredith magazine house ads — directly into the home. We'd adopt a party plan format, exclusively recruit managers with substantial needlework experience, and promote in-home attendance by offering party participants a valuable learning experience, whether in crocheting, sewing or knitting, needlepoint or cross stitching. The *Better Homes* brand would drive recruiting. Kit sales, we felt, would follow.

Terry was a smart manager, young enough to be fearless, old enough to be credible. Within days, it seemed, and excited by the proposition, Terry scheduled a meeting with two corporate senior vice presidents. They'd reviewed the proposal. They liked it. Obviously they liked Terry as well, his many talents having been acknowledged by his upper echelon managers. My goal was to sell them our services as an advertising and promotion agency, counseling them on tactics and producing the advertising. They had other ideas, Terry said. Uneasy, Ron travelled with me to Des Moines thinking we might have to pitch the business all over again.

By Way of Luck

At the onset of the meeting, in corporate dress, button down shirts, striped ties and tweedy jackets, the two VP's asked bluntly, would I write the Business Plan? Whoops! The proposition had taken an unexpected turn and I was given little time to evaluate it. Usually the client prepared such a plan. The Meredith people wanted an immediate response. I had to say yes, having come this far, but I first had to establish the parameters. So we chatted. What were they were looking for in the Plan, how Terry and corporate would contribute to it, and so on, a comprehensive document that could justifiably give them reason either to accept or reject the project. I set a price for the Plan, high enough to be seen as significant, low enough to be acceptable, payable in two installments, half up front the other half upon completion.

Across the table, eyes shifting one side to the other, the two VP's asked to be excused for a few moments while they conferred in the hall. Their exit gave me and Ron time enough for second thoughts. We had none.

Ron had a long standing relationship with Rubbermaid's party plan and saw perhaps more clearly than I what the upside could do for Meredith and for our company.

On their return, the VP's gave us the go ahead. We had a contract. Terry pulled together the financial information I requested and readied himself and his staff for whatever else I might need. After a couple of weeks of study — gathering through interviews and dogged research on just how direct selling companies worked — I locked myself into the Perkins, Bernstein conference room and started compiling and writing.

I was driven by one affirming discovery. Women I interviewed, all with years in the field, recruiting and selling direct by party plan, agreed — enthusiastically — with the tactic of recruiting women managers who sewed, knitted, tatted, wove, and so on, what were called the "needle arts." Why so? I asked one. Because, she replied, they like to teach. *They enjoy the satisfaction of passing on their skills to others.* "And that's a fact," several women added in unison, "you can take to the bank!"

Hearing their advice lifted my spirits. Clearly, a *Better Homes and Gardens* craft party, with no obligation to buy, could be built around the prospect of receiving, free, a valuable learning experience. After a "class" attendees would receive a catalog and order form and have the "privilege" of ordering craft kits for practice, for their own use, or as gifts. The offer, coupled with the assurance of the *Better Homes* name and the high quality of its needlecraft kits, my interviewees had assured me, had built-in value.

Instead of focusing on the earnings opportunity as a recruiting method, as did most other direct selling companies, managers would be attracted by the chance to teach. Further, speculation went, a *Better Homes* "teach in" would attract a high percentage of repeat customers already disposed to its products and produce a higher percentage of sales per party, hence a higher dollar per sale. I thought the speculation excessive, but we'd see.

The first draft of the business plan I completed in ten days, let distance set in for a week, and took the following week to edit it, build out pro forma financial projections, and ship the plan to Terry.

I was exhausted. I had been at typewriter and calculator, laboring 12 to 14 hour days, through the weekends and my own birthday. I thought spending a few days working on my boat would clear my head, but I had run out of time.

Terry had not a single negative comment to make about the Business Plan. Could I come to Des Moines right away. The plan had been accepted. Management was eager to proceed with the test. The VP's wanted a discussion to "sew" things up, they said. So did I.

I had outlined the test parameters pretty clearly, but I wasn't certain I had sufficiently emphasized one of the variables. Direct selling companies recruit independent contractors who in turn recruit independent contractors, the more senior managers building their own sales organizations within the greater corporate organization. Largely for tax purposes, as we knew, management cannot directly control independent contractors. When a direct selling business offers a new and untested product, recruiting and sales are difficult to predict, with either the potential to overwhelm order

By Way of Luck

processing, billing and the documenting of commissions or to stick the business with unsalable inventory and an expensive write off.

The *Better Homes* craft business would be working almost exclusively with independent contractors whose efforts we could manage but couldn't control. If the test were to fail, it would be obvious. But if the test were to succeed...the company had to be ready to support it.

A Word about Direct Selling

Party plan and in-home sales, including the recruiting process, commissions scaled in hierarchical order, those at the top making more money than those at the bottom, and so on, have borne a larger share of criticisms from on-lookers than have more traditional retailers, Target, Kohl's, Macy's and so on. Why that is, I don't know, because the process is much the same — a knock on the door is akin to an ad in a magazine — only the medium differs. When I was a kid, at our house knocks on our door were welcomed, my mother often counting on them, coming from a local farmer with produce to sell, from our dry cleaner asking whether we had clothes to pick up, from a dairy farmer calling out that he'd left milk on the back stoop, from the butcher in his horse-drawn meat wagon, from a neighbor with home-made root beer to sell, and from doctors, too, carrying a weighty black bag, a pharmacy of the times, and making house calls.

Not yet a teen-ager, I once went door-to-door. Responding to a comic book ad from a Chicago company with a free gift offer, I was sent a punch board. I'd rap on a neighborhood door and ask the woman of the house whether she could use a set of new pans or a camera or a pair of binoculars, the offers varied. If she said yes, I'd tell her about a drawing and for a quarter she'd get a "punch" with a number that "could be the winner." When the punch board was punched out, I'd select the winning number by punching a "secret" hole, send the money I'd collected to the company which, in turn, would send me the winner's prize along with my free gift.

I learned to call on stand-alone households where during the day most women were at home, ringing the bell, making my pitch, chatting about nothing while holding my hand out for the quarter, from the winners seeing the smiles, enjoying the shrieks of surprise, earning the notoriety one neighborhood after another, even from the non-winners, and forgetting the calls that ended with a door pushed angrily closed. The social interaction was more rewarding than the free gifts.

On a visit to Rubbermaid, I told my punch board story to a highly placed manager. She had a story of her own. She had been widowed young, she said, and in her grief became a recluse, her shades drawn, with only a radio to break the silence. A lady "down the street" shopped for her, sometimes leaving a box on her porch, another twice helped her clean and do laundry, another trimmed her hair every few months, the trio the only human contact she had for nearly five years. A stranger knocking at the door changed all that, a jabber-mouth, the manager said, an insistent woman who talked her into attending a Rubbermaid party. She took hold of my life, the manager told me, helping me make new friends, in time training me as a sales agent, and day by day, week by week, teaching me to be a responsible person, for my customers and for my own well-being.

I met the manager at Rubbermaid's headquarters in Chillicothe, Ohio. She was vibrant in her dress and her manner, and proud, there to be recognized as Rubbermaid's Sales Director of the Year.

I've heard similar stories. I've also heard stories that ridicule direct selling, the belittlements and disparagements from people who disrespect salesmen and saleswomen and I fail to see why. At last count, during 2012 more than sixteen million direct sellers made a living knocking on doors and representing an industry with annual sales exceeding $35 billion. Their entrepreneurial spirit is not to be chastened, but to be applauded.

Further, direct selling is primarily a woman's occupation, and for many women, regardless of age, color or religion, it can be a liberating experience, a way up and a way out, an opportunity to make some money on their own, to support a family, to attain self-esteem, and to experience a measure of independence they could find nowhere else. All that's required is a willingness to take a chance on themselves.

In my book it says, Ya gotta respect that!

By Way of Luck

Another Surprise Proposition

We reassembled, Terry and the VP's, Ron and I, sitting around an oval conference table in an otherwise bare, sun-lit room, for a few moments fumbling to see who would speak first. Terry spoke up: We've got the OK to move this project along, and do it jointly. The VP's interjected. Terry's group, they said, will manage product sourcing, order processing, warehousing and shipping, collections and the payment of commissions. Perkins, Bernstein will be responsible for marketing and sales, which includes hiring and recruiting, managing the incentive programs and integrating its promotional effort with Des Moines.

Essentially, the VP's were rubber-stamping the business plan I'd produced and never expected them totally to approve, our piece of the pie intentionally big and Ron unable to stifle a giggle, the promise and the potential outcome so great.

How we put the business together, I'll skip, except we did it, carving out eastern Iowa, northern Illinois, southern Minnesota and all of Wisconsin as our test market, hiring good recruiters and capable sales people and training them in the "Better Homes Way." When Terry was ready, we launched. It was the fall of 1977.

For nearly three weeks, recruiting reports hit my desk with growing regularity, but Des Moines had yet to receive an order. Terry was anxious, his experience limited to direct mail — running the ad, getting the coupon, shipping the product and receiving prompt results. He had people standing by, he complained, a warehouse with inventory that could easily fulfill the 2500 orders we expected to receive from the test effort and an experienced order processing and shipping crew. The VP's were also looking for sales reports. I imagined hearing their impatient snorts.

Two weeks later, Terry called again, panic now in his voice. We're flooded, he gasped, mail pouring in, most orders in multiples, that is, a buyer ordering two or more kits, the post office making two-a-day deliveries to the Des Moines warehouse. If this keeps up, he said, we'll run out of inventory.

It kept up.

We — mostly me — had underestimated the power of the *Better Homes* name and the ripeness of the offer. Loudly, homemakers were saying Yes at every party, not four out of ten, an industry wide ratio, nor six out of twelve, but an across the board ten units sold for every ten party attendees. The realization of what we had done hit at once: we had a bang-up success on our hands. Yet by running out of merchandise, to our sales people and their customers we would be seen as a flop. In the field there would be scores of grumpy buyers and sellers.

Terry ordered everything stopped. The VP's had demanded it.

To begin the patching up and, I thought, preparing for a restart, Terry and the VP's invited our senior sales people to Des Moines for dinner, a way of saying thanks, and explaining what had taken place. Smartly, they put the apology on themselves. The next morning the VP's took the sales people on a tour, first the *Better Homes* kitchens, then the printing plant where the presses were thumping along at high speed and dropping color sheets in a growing pile located right on the aisle where they could be seen. Expecting typical *Better Homes* editorial matter, pictures of kitchens and quilts, instead the onlookers saw photo spreads of nude women and didn't know whether to laugh or retreat in horror. Meredith, *Better Homes'* parent, the reader may recall, had contracted with Bob Guccione to print and bind *Penthouse* magazine. On the day of the tour, next month's issue was being printed. The tension was broken when one of our managers broke into hilarious laughter.

Later the same day, after our sales people were on their way home, expecting, as was I, that Meredith would decide how to proceed, I was told that the project had been stopped, not temporarily, but for good. Neither Terry nor the VP's could tell me why. They had a call from the CFO who told them to stop. Like in STOP, the CFO reportedly said.

I sensed something screwy. For such an abrupt decision, without discussion, even "screwy" could not be explained. Running out of inventory may have been a game changer but not a game stopper.

By Way of Luck

The sales results, whether orders could be fulfilled or not, unequivocally demonstrated we had a hit on our hands. With the VP's blessing, I sought an answer.

The CFO couldn't give me one, he said. And he wouldn't. He'd gotten orders from the boss, Bob the CEO.

I made an appointment to see Bob. The VP's were upset I'd done so. An hour before the scheduled meeting they sat with me over coffee and briefed me on what to say, how to say it, and what I should wear, Bob known for dressing casually in his office, suit jacket off, a shirt button undone, a loosed tie and maybe both feet on his desk. Try not to match his wardrobe, they cautioned. They were fearful I might assign blame to them, one of the VP's actually wringing his hands. I assured them I was looking for answers, no more.

Brilliant, Bob said, a big man sitting at a big desk. A great job. Remarkable. His gushing compliments, I gathered, were an off-putting ploy and put me on guard. You're here to learn why I've put the kibosh on the craft thing, yes? He went on to describe at length another business *Better Homes* was contemplating, selling endorsements to household real estate sales companies. Meredith couldn't manage both propositions, he said. He had to make a choice. He appeared hopeful I would accept his explanation and leave.

Was he expecting I'd back away with a dutiful bow? He knew and I knew the craft business had far greater potential than putting the *Better Homes* logotype on For Sale signs stuck on suburban lawns. My brow wrinkled, my cheeks squeezed, I could feel it happening, my question ridden face told him, Stop the bullshit.

He took my look as a rebuttal. His body stiffened, like a boxer waiting for the bell to ring, he sat silent, forcing me to take the lead. I had no choice. I said I'd manage the project if cash flow was his concern. Perkins, Bernstein would fund it, taking the losses if any and sharing the profits equally with Meredith. It was more than I should have offered, or could afford, but I had to draw him out. Would I get the response I sought. I did. I couldn't have guessed his real reasoning.

In an accusing manner, Bob said, You're persistent. There's more to my decision. Then he went blunt. I had irritated him. A *Better Homes* party plan, he said, featuring needle work taught in the home by practiced sales agents offering our kits — he paused for a half sec — would engulf our entire company. It could be that big a deal. We'd no longer be Meredith, a magazine and book publishing company, he said, his voice rising. We'd be a party plan company with a publishing business on the side. I can't let that happen, he concluded, shouting.

I was incredulous. I thought his remarks an exaggeration. He went on, angrily. I know what it would do to our company. I know the door-to-door business. I don't like it. Meredith doesn't need it. We have a reputation to maintain. He placed his forearms on his desk and hunched toward me in a challenging pose.

I could have argued that Meredith was already a direct selling business, its magazine subscriptions and books sold almost exclusively by mail, its television sales reps calling directly on ad agencies and advertisers. But Bob left no room for argument. Direct selling, in his eyes, was socially unacceptable.

I backed off. There were other Perkins Bernstein assignments to be earned at Meredith. I chose not to jeopardize them. I thanked him for being straight with me.

As I left his office, my thoughts went to Al Casey's encounter with Meredith and the failure of a Times Meredith merger. Al hadn't grown shy during the negotiations as I'd guessed. I now knew it was Meredith who'd backed off. Its owners and its management were comfortable in their insular location in the middle of middle America and feared being dislodged by another company...or by a new business that might alter the company from within. Meredith suffered from a *prima donna* effect.

Over the next thirty-five years, accounting for inflation, in real dollars Meredith's revenues shrunk by half.

Back to Work

With six sustaining clients — and several smaller ones we were grooming for the longer haul — Perkins Bernstein was a busy place,

By Way of Luck

hiring two account executives, a media buyer, and a creative director formerly in *Playboy's* promotions department and managing our expenses and our payroll. Ron and I set up a profit sharing plan, had a martini lunch every Wednesday, drove new cars and lived comfortably in the same apartment building, often walking to our offices while conferring the day ahead. I was bringing in the business, and managing the agency's creative effort, sharing the management of accounts with Ron and Ron handling everything else, administration, production and personnel included, each of us in easy agreement on most everything. Then the unraveling began.

Ron overdrew our account at the First National Bank of Chicago. How could he have done that? He was sitting in my office asking what we should do. Without answering him, I called Joe Migley, my Delta Kappa Epsilon fraternity brother, a vice president of the bank, and told him the amount of the checks coming in and asked him to cover, which he did, for a few days he said, but don't leave me holding bad paper. I'd write a personal check if I had to, I told him.

Billings and the management of payables and receivables were in the hands of the business manager Ron brought with him when we consolidated our companies. Ron vouched for him: He's been with me five years, never a complaint. I sought out the Business Manager. He balked at my intrusion. He reported only to Ron, he said. I told the Business Manager to take off a couple of days. I went through his books, through the drawers, through the files, through in-baskets and out-baskets, opening unopened monthly bank statements and blaming myself for being so trusting and unknowing. There were expenses unaccounted, expenses and work unbilled, expenses unapproved, delinquencies forgotten or arbitrarily forgiven, and checks made out to suppliers I'd never heard of. Our records were a mess. And so was I.

At my insistence, anger pent, I told Ron to fire the Business Manager. Call him at home, I said. I don't want him here. I pushed my work load on to a dependable trio and assumed the task of figuring where we were, how we got there, and where we had to go. I was pissed by what I had to do, but I had no choice.

The Women in My Life

Judy Woodard and I were introduced by mutual friends, Bill and Joanna, a Chicago couple newly engaged and seeking pre-marital support from other couples, married or not, for their declared intentions. They reached out to two people, unknown to each other, they felt certain would help them seal their commitment. A match-making. Here's how it went:

Bill invited me to lunch in his office, a Chicago ad agency, telling me disparaging stories of the women I dated and magical stories about Judy Woodard. Joanna, Judy's co-worker at IBM, matching Bill's tactic, lunched with Judy in the IBM cafeteria and promoted the idea of meeting this "great guy" named Jim Perkins. We should all get together. A time and date was picked, and a place, in the loop, at a hotel lounge, many days ahead.

Judy balked. She didn't do blind dates. But she was curious I soon discovered. I was in my office. My receptionist buzzed. There was a woman asking to see me. Ms. Woodard. With IBM.

Uh, oh, cuckoo, my first thought. She just barges in? Reluctantly I left my desk and headed toward reception, making up excuses as I went, why I had time only for a hello, and readying an angry call to Bill. Damn him!

Ms. Woodard stood. She wore a beige suit, skirt at the knee, jacket wasp-waisted, a silk scarf tucked just right, hair mixed blonde, tall, willowy and creamy all over, smoothly stunning and sure of herself, my first take, more woman than I had ever met or seen at first sight. Wow!

Extending a hand, she said she was on a sales call in the building. Joanna told her I had an office there. What next she said I could not hear, this exotic creature turning me to stone. I suggested lunch, told the receptionist to hold my calls, took Judy by the arm, guided her to an elevator, and up we went to John Hancock's roof-top restaurant. We were there for over three hours, slow to leave, each of us quizzing the other, talking in code, concealed words of emerging acceptance and affection, and spontaneously asking, What do we do about Bill and Joanna?

By Way of Luck

We plotted a plot. A comic stunt actually. We decided to make the date a pretense, never telling them we'd met, sit with them and in mere minutes faking falling-in-love noises and gestures, and after a while leave holding hands and by our body language suggesting we were headed for a close-by bedroom. We saw it as a practical joke the four of us could remember as great fun.

Judy and I followed the script, every move we had imagined. Our act was so real, Bill and JoAnn didn't catch on. We threw them a wave of gratitude as we departed. And never told them we had played make-believe on them, saving them the embarrassment of learning they'd been had.

This all happened nearly forty years ago. Judy and I have been together since, each of us now aged. She has been step-mother to my children, though more the friend, helping them grow as their true mother could not. Judy is still creamy all over and smoothly stunning, a companion I treasure having by my side.

Macedonian Prescience

Born in Thessalonika in 1867, a rough date, my paternal grandfather, Demetri Pisperikos, was considered a businessman by his rural relatives, a disdainful commentary coming from mountain sheepherders, but an estimable characterization from the urban side of his extended family. Long before trains and paved roads, he moved freight across the Macedonian panhandle between Salonika and Istanbul, his locomotion a four-wheeled oaken wagon and a team of four hardy mules, his road an ancient pathway of crushed rock and rough cut stone bridges, passing through Alexandropoulos and Komotini, both trading centers, as he went.

His eldest son, my father, grew up in Samarina where his mother lived. His two younger sons, coming along when their father had money, were educated in the city, Tom, becoming a lawyer and John, an officer in the Greek army. But their father did not survive long. He was killed on one of his trips, by a mule he was attempting to harness, it was presumed, and buried along the road. His first born grandchild, my name is an Americanization of Dimitri.

My maternal grandmother, Chaimo, from the Brajituli family and married to John Tegu, was a mystical being, uneducated yet knowledgeable, her life circumscribed by Macedonian traditions, aware of people, sensitive to their nuances, and from the stories told by her elders acquiring an oral history that she passed on to her children and their children, my sisters and me, my cousins, nieces and nephews. I learned from her of my birth. I was found in a cabbage patch.

Her other teachings were more practical and honest.

She predicted events, warning her husband in 1910 of a war that would devastate their family and hurrying their emigration to the south, to Athens and to what lay beyond. Her husband, with his two eldest children left immediately. She stayed behind with my mother and two siblings and was trapped in the Pindus Mountains along the Albanian border until 1920 when the war had eased and her husband could bring them to the United States.

She saw the coming of moving pictures, people on a large wall, story tellers she called them, and urged her husband to find out who they were. Acting on her vision, my grandfather and his eldest son, my Uncle Andrew, built one of this country's earliest movie theater chains, eight across New Hampshire and Vermont, naming them after prominent international theaters, Tegu's Palace, Tegu's Bijou, Tegu's Rialto, Tegu's Strand, Tegu's State, Tegu's Orpheum, Tegu's Premier, and Tegu's Odeon, preceding the Pantages and Warner Brothers chains by several years and, like them, their interiors elegantly ornamented in the art deco style.

My youngest daughter, actress Elizabeth Perkins, is the only child in our family to adhere to the Tegu's movie traditions, from her earliest years performing in school plays and exercising her skills in dramas of her own making. She has appeared in over fifty films, opposite Tom Hanks in *Big*, as Wilma in *The Flintstones*, and replicating Maureen O'Hara's role in a remake of *Miracle on 34th Street* and starring in leading performances in *About Last Night*, *Avalon* and *He Said, She Said*. She's been busy on stage, *Brighton Beach*

By Way of Luck

Memoirs, Four Dogs and a Bone, and in television, most notably co-starring with Mary Elizabeth Parker in *Weeds*.

Her older sister Karen, deciding as a teen she would become a scientist, made it through her Ph.D. in bio-chemistry, got funding from the Damon Runyon/Walter Winchell Foundation that underwrote a five year fellowship at U.C. Berkeley, and moved on to an Assistant Professorship at Johns Hopkins Medical School and Hospital. She now teaches science at Pacific Palisades High School, a charter school whose Board of Directors she chaired for a three-year term, and following that, under the auspices of the Los Angeles School District, started a STEM (Science Technology, Engineering and Math) school in Beverly Hills. Because of her extraordinary contributions to cancer research, she was for several years the face of the American Cancer Society's many annual appeals. Karen refers to herself as her father's favorite daughter.

The oldest, Susan, my first born daughter, earned an MBA at NYU and managed other people's money until she retired at age 46. She lives in Massachusetts, owns a sky dive center outside of Tampa, Florida, and is just finishing up law school. She busted a glass ceiling early in her career. Finding herself the only woman in an institutional department of a major brokerage firm, she was cut off from the usual interactions that allow colleagues to exchange information, seek advice and build upon mutual experiences that were not available to her. She concluded, were she to succeed as a manager, she had to differentiate herself. She took up sky diving.

Forbes took notice and published a story in its FYI Magazine entitled the "Sky Diving Stock Broker," featuring Susan on the cover in exotic sky-diving regalia and inside, adjacent to the copy, and on three double-page spreads appearing in gowns styled bird-like and designed exclusively for her by Bob Mackie. Susan was instantly visible throughout the investment community. In a single dramatic swoop she had acquired both credibility and value. Susan has become the go-to person in both our close and extended families.

Removing Perkins from Perkins, Bernstein

On forming our company, Ron and I agreed on a dissolution plan, should we ever need one. I decided I needed one. We had both made some money, we had a sustainable business, but I wasn't doing what I wanted to be doing. Worse, I didn't yet know what I should be doing. I just knew that what I was doing wasn't it. I'd have to break with Ron. It was not an unreasonable decision for me to make. Attracting and managing clients, and managing the creative work was, to me, the heart of the business, where one could feel its beat. The rest, media buying, production, and managing our billings and the people who worked for us, though important, was an area less demanding, yet Ron had shown he was incapable of handling it. He worked best when sitting on his hands.

Had I twenty years earlier accepted General LeBailey's offer — had his prediction been realized and had I not been killed by the Viet Cong, or worse, by friendly fire — I would be an U.S. Air Force Colonel. Or so the General promised. At Perkins, Bernstein I felt like a Military Police sergeant.

The dissolution plan was simple. Should one partner either wish to leave or wish the other partner to leave, the one partner would put an offer on the table. The other partner would then have the option either to accept the offer and leave the company or to buy out the one partner for the amount offered. The size of the stake would be a deciding factor: if it were low, the other partner would be encouraged to buy out the one. And if too high, the other would take the money and walk away. I made a low offer. I wanted Ron to have the company and to run it his way. He complied, handing me a check. I took an empty office down the hall, rented some furniture, brought along my secretary and an art director, Barry Parks, who chose to leave with me, and found myself once again having to guess my way from here to whatever's out there.

Am I the idiot my reader must think me to be, so unstable, so ungrounded, so arrogant as to believe that moving from one business

By Way of Luck

to another constituted a career path. My children were on the way to being who they decided to be and, as it turned out, stuck to their game plan. Obviously, were I a guiding influence in their lives, as they have said I was, would I have told them not to do as I do, and expected them to respect that? Hardly, their decision making has been much sounder than mine.

Or did I believe then as I believed as a child that I was a character in a movie with a convoluted plot fraught with unknown dangers though for me there would be a happy ending? If not, what other explanation is there for my mixed behavior and for my impulsive decisions to move on to the next thing, and the next. I had no answer for that, and I still don't.

Was the nomadic existence of my parents forebears somehow instilled in me? Was it my apprenticeship with writer Corey Ford whose assignments took him from article to article, book to book? Possibly, but to affirm either supposition is a way of absolving myself from my conduct; some sort of reasoning was demanded.

Or had I begun to count on it as luck?

15

Not One, Not Two, but Three New Cable Television Networks

It was 1980. A recession was upon us. Wall Street pundits were predicting a deeper drop in the markets than the Great Depression of the 1930s. Three slow years would pass before investors could expect a rebound. I had sold my interest in Perkins, Bernstein mere weeks before the economy turned sour. I had cash from the sale, but little income. Aside from an occasional assignment I was at loose ends and figuring what I might do next.

The figuring didn't take long. Broadcaster Ted Turner was everywhere in the news, getting favorable if not adulating reviews for transforming his local Atlanta UHF television station TBS into a national entertainment network, delivering his programming by satellite to cable operators and over the air to independent broadcasters. Was the promise of cable television about to happen or was it a novelty? Either way, with few prospects and the economy in descent, beyond the noise Turner was creating, curious, I had to assess what might be real, what wasn't.

The outlook appeared dim. With a spending down-turn underway, few cable operators were willing to take on the debt to download Ted's network, to invest in the antennas and switching equipment,

By Way of Luck

to lay cable in freshly dug ditches along streets and highways and to spend what little cash they might have left to switch reluctant viewers from roof-top rabbit ears to table-top converters. The promise Ted was promoting seemed risky. Yet his billboards promoted success, a smiling picture of Ted, with a single copy line: "I Was Cable When Cable Wasn't Cool." He was challenging the cable industry to join his jihad, his holy war.

Likely investors saw only high risk, the cost of re-wiring America versus the promise of an adequate financial return too improbable. Advertisers and their agencies doubted cable television would be attractive to its advertisers and, further, viewers would be indifferent. For many, it was just more CATV (Community Antenna Television), wires hung from a nearby telephone pole, strung through the trees and finally connecting to a TV set where rabbit ears once connected. The potential of more channels stirred little interest. ABC, CBS and NBC and PBS seemed quite enough.

Further, Ted's talk of cable one day delivering home shopping, home banking and a 24/7 news channel sounded like so much science fiction. CATV was by then making available as many as five or six channels, adding nearby over-the-air stations to local cable programming line-ups and offering home-town producers their un-used channels to fill in the blanks with crudely produced original programs. Otherwise, there was little evidence that additional TV programming would be an attraction or even worth watching. Whether it was a business I might get into I soon found out, not because of my curiosity if not eagerness, but because of two unexpected events.

Chicago law firm Winston and Strawn was retained by Warner Amex, a joint venture of Warner Communications and American Express, to assist in the acquisition of cable television franchises in the greater Chicago area. WarnerAmex had its eye on Evanston, a northern suburb. Facing competition from Cablevision and Comcast, it needed local legal and marketing support. The firm detailed attorney Joe Mathewson to handle the assignment, his boss suggesting he find a marketing guy to partner with. I was the guy, Joe told me over the phone. Cablevision was already on the scene.

Why did Joe choose me? He had a fat Rolodex of area friends and colleagues, professional people with known accomplishments and long-time political connections. He had better choices. We were not close. I saw him from a distance — urbane, yet restrained; giving, yet guarded; stylish, yet understated, at Dartmouth admired by many, envied by some, and rousing the jealousy of the remaining few. He seemed aloof, if not indifferent, marginally generous, and possibly lacking sincerity. I was not one of his fans.

Yet over the years that followed college, Joe and I became friends, extraordinary, thinking back, as I've had few dependable friends: Bob Rowe, a commercial real estate broker, whom I've known since we were in the first grade; Jack Rafferty a silver haired, New York City fireman with the off-duty job of posing for Grecian Formula commercials; Ron Ladden, a Chicago lawyer who helped me through a custody suit; Haines Gaffner, a brilliant quirk, a gatherer of people, his energy unstoppable; Eldon Sellers and Bob McKenzie, friends from *Playboy* days; George Hetson, a dentist whose practice takes second place to golf, his handicap a three, and my occasional ski pal; each of my two sons in-law, Jon and Julio, a friendship we've toiled diligently to bring about and maintain. And Joe.

For the next three months Joe and I met in Evanston with local businessmen, city officials, school superintendents and their boards, church leaders and most of the city's not-for-profit organizations. We attended public meetings, perhaps two a week, with other cable company representatives sitting in our midst. We asked and answered questions of cable committee members and helped WarnerAmex reps position their arguments.

Many of the reps hadn't been trained, nor did they have the experience, either in marketing or legal issues, that Joe and I could provide. One of the more ludicrous propositions we heard was a cable rep's response to the question, how do you intend to provide cable service to families who may need it but can't afford it?

The answer, I am embarrassed to report, came from one of WarnerAmex's own people. "Like food stamps," she said, social fervor in her voice, "WarnerAmex will provide the poor with cable stamps!"

By Way of Luck

Evanston was seen as the linchpin to the suburban area abutting Chicago's north side. As it went so, too, might the neighboring communities and eventually Chicago itself. Chuck Dolan, Cablevision's founder and earlier the founder of HBO, was personally canvassing the area, believing it too important to risk losing. Former New York City Deputy Mayor Dick Aurillio, WarnerAmex's senior executive in charge of the national franchising effort, made an in-and-out one-day visit asking Joe and me whether we had any evidence that his local WarnerAmex representative was forcing kick-backs from paid consultants. No, Joe and I both answered. After making penciled notes on a pad he'd pulled from his chest pocket Dick went away, leaving us in semi-shock by his question, and wondering what had stirred his visit. He never again returned to Evanston.

Eventually Dolan won the franchise. Noticing our disappointment, the chair of Evanston's cable television committee told us in an aside that the WarnerAmex proposition easily matched Cablevision's. The committee, said the chair, simply liked dealing directly with the person who'd be signing the checks.

Joe and I saw the decision differently. For Joe it was liked losing a case. For me, having a ground floor view of how cable television was coming together as an industry, I could feel the excitement.

One Door Closes, Another Opens

Only days after the shut-down of the WarnerAmex campaign, the second unlikely occurrence took place. With no knock on the door a fellow walked into my sparse office in the John Hancock building and plunked into a chair by my desk. His name was Dan and he needed help, he said. Dan didn't appear threatening, so I listened. He had started a direct response cable show called Shopper's Showcase. It was working, he claimed. He flashed a handful of checks he'd received from viewers as proof. He asked that I get involved. How, he wasn't sure.

He had tapes to show me, produced at little cost in a television studio in Peoria. He was the writer, director and producer. He'd make copies and send cassettes to cable operators to run, giving them a cut of his sale. He was stumped by the same question I was asking of myself, what next to do?

My curiosity rising, Dan still by my desk, I called a former client in Des Moines, a *Better Homes* manager responsible for its direct mail sale of books and magazine subscriptions, told him what Dan was doing and suggested the three of us concoct a half-hour *Better Homes* show and meet in Peoria to produce it. Which we did. How better to test a proposition than by doing it?

I'll skip the detail of what went on from there, except to say that *Better Homes and Gardens* wasn't interested, the orders they'd gotten were scant, they said, flatly ignoring their own patterns of building the worth of a mail order product.

Dan disappeared — I tried diligently to locate him — eventually assuming the checks were phony and he had some sort of scam in mind — but I was by then smitten by the prospect of actually producing and selling a direct marketing show. Like Ted Turner, the Evanston assignment gaining me a taste of the business, I was becoming a cable believer.

Contracting with a Chicago studio — later acquired by Oprah Winfrey as home for her syndicated daytime show — I could produce a half-hour for under $1500 — if I taped and edited four half hour shows in a $6000 eleven hour day. Without attempting to replicate broadcast network quality, estimating how the shooting might go, I thought I could do that.

MSN, the Modern Satellite Network, a distributor of institutional programs, agreed to sell me time by the hour, scarce but available. Until multiple communication satellites were put into orbit, it was my only option. A GE satellite that would reduce the scarcity had just launched...and lost...$365 million of orbiting hardware, vanishing in less than eleven minutes. New satellites were under construction, both GE and RCA assured the industry.

And I recruited Avis, the car rental company, to manage incoming 800 number calls on its Wizard system. Our projected daytime telephone responses fit nicely into its heavier early evening and nighttime traffic.

By Way of Luck

The pieces were coming together, an enterprise was taking shape. Operating by myself, I got caught up in my own momentum, never questioning whether it was a business I should or should not be investing in. Once started, my behavior turned compulsive. It would be difficult for me to abandon should the need, obvious and costly, ever arise.

Unexpectedly, I had a volunteer: My wife Judy, a long-time marketing manager with IBM, quit her job to work with me. I was surprised. Like her father, I thought she was an IBM lifer. "You're having more fun than I am at IBM," she said. Had she been anyone else, I might have had a brief heart-to-heart talk with her and led her out of my office. But she was my wife!

"What can I do," she asked?

"You can be a producer," I said

Neither of us had ever produced a single minute of television. But that seemed not to matter. We would find our way.

Our concept differed from Dan's and from what The Home Shopping Network eventually became. Conventional network television, because it was carried on publicly owned airwaves, was controlled by the Federal Communications Commission which restricted on-air advertising to run no more than four minutes per half hour. That restriction gave birth to the 60-second commercial, and later to 30-second and 15-second commercials, tightly scripted modules run frequently and designed to produce an emotionally positive image of the product being advertised and staying within the restricted time.

If an ad made a viewer feel good, agencies and their clients also felt good, assuming that feel good advertising created brand awareness and drove shoppers to market looking for their branded products and, thereafter, becoming brand loyalists. Which may have been true, but there has never been a calculated correlation between advertising dollars spent and retail sales produced. If a product does not fulfill a buyer's expectation, no amount of advertising dollars will change his or her mind.

I saw cable, its signal delivered not by government regulated frequencies but by regulation-free satellite distributed into the home by regulation free wire, as an opportunity for advertisers to demonstrate their products in long form commercials. We could in a single segment of five or six minutes give viewers solid product detail, as most direct marketers have always done, through detail and demonstration, and provide end-user evidence of the inherent values of an advertised product. I considered it to be a good proposition, and it was.

Structuring the Business and Making the Sale

There were no established protocols for selling long form commercials on cable television. Middle management media buyers had no budgets and no immediate understanding of the medium. We had to attract senior decision makers, as high up on the management ladder as we could find. I retained a public relations firm. The assignment: to tell our story. Our strategy: with two hired sales persons and me, we'd cold call likely clients. We found we could easily reach the secretary of a CEO of a major US company. We would introduce ourselves as producers of a new television network and wanted to highlight her boss and her company in an up-coming television series. Inevitably, I'd be put through to the CEO or, at the very least, to the Executive Vice-President Advertising or the Executive Vice-President Marketing.

We had a product to demonstrate: tapes of our shows. And a powerful brochure produced, of course, by the former Creative Director of Perkins Bernstein. Our PR took hold immediately. The novelty of a TV channel that carried only commercials cornered media interest. Articles were showing up in major news outlets — in the *Wall Street Journal* and in the *Chicago Sun Times*; an entire column, including my picture in the *New York Times* business section, and a brief comment in *Time* magazine. *The Chicago Tribune* featured the Show in a full page article on the cover page of its Sunday business section labeling me as "King" of the infomercial. And the CBS Evening News gave us a full 90 seconds. Syndicated stories were running in hundreds of newspapers. Late night radio talk shows

By Way of Luck

were calling for interviews with me and our hosts. Morning TV shows found the whole concept sufficiently amusing to run chunks of our programming. Paying our PR agency $3000 a month brought me the best advertising I could have gotten at the least price I could have paid.

We had a strategy: make it easy for companies to say Yes to the promise we offered: we bundled the buy...creative, production, time, an 800 number and an accounting of results, all for a single price. With Judy producing, bless her brilliance, Revlon showed Home Shopping viewers how to use its home permanent kit. Amana promoted interchangeable decorator panels for its dishwashers and ovens. Volvo explained rack and pinion steering. Pillsbury threw a birthday party making "Ice Cream Around" sandwiches with its refrigerated dough. Hager's slacks went into the washer-dryer soiled and on camera came out clean, wrinkle free and immediately wearable. Vita-Mix and Gensu knives were regulars. We were a hit, or so it seemed.

But financially The Home Shopping Show wasn't working. Our business model seemed sound. We were gaining sales and advertisers, and I could see my way to breakeven but the anticipated growth in the number of households able to receive cable was sluggish, mired at less than 20%. Until we were at 33%, my numbers said, we'd be hurting. Further, our advertisers considered the Show a novelty, a new medium to play with but not to take seriously.

Meantime, cable operators were building systems but much too gradually, unrealistically expecting their build-outs to be financed by programmers' carrying charges. Risk averse, they wanted a cash and carry payment system. Programmers were equally cautious, their business models depending on cable operators to pay for the programming. The two, taking contrary positions, were stalled in negotiations played out largely in the press, neither taking responsibility for driving viewer growth.

Nor was distribution working the way I'd hoped. MSN treated us badly, dropping us into odd slots, for a while positioning "Modern Danish Agricultural Methods," not exactly an audience builder, as a lead-in to our show. Further, buying time as it became available precluded us from publicizing a program schedule. Viewers could only see the *Show* if they stumbled upon it.

Getting to cash break-even now seemed a longer reach than I had anticipated. In my mind the prospects for cable and all the subsequent applications of wide-band video delivery, shopping and banking, were sound as they were eventually proven to be. But there was an important consideration: I was financing our development and operating costs out of my own pocket. To bridge the gap, I had to find outside financing, not just to carry programming, but to acquire a UHF station as well. I wanted to replicate the Ted Turner model.

Judy meantime was proving herself a valuable employee, managing production for our clients, on the set and in the control room, and handling the inevitable screw-ups which, she said, were equally common at IBM. She also had her eye on the business decisions I was making. "Where's the money coming from," she asked? We were spending far more in developing what we hoped would become a network staple than we were bringing in.

We had a fee structure. We'd produce a commercial of up to seven minutes in length and provide our clients with five airings on the network for a fixed fee, and thereafter charge for further airings on a cost plus basis. It was too little, but we saw the necessity of making the investment. I had a vision of the future, if I may say so.

"You're spending our money," Judy said. It was not a question.

In 1980, Judy and I had been married less than two years. She could see we had a tough sell. Uncertainty set in. Major companies, advertisers all, were ignorant of cable's potential. For every sale, we'd have to educate the buyer. Cable was not a household word. I thought the companies we had so far featured would serve as endorsements. While their interest appeared sincere, they saw cable as no more than a game to be played. With few repeats, we were a one-night stand.

And there it would most often stop, with a "tell us more" response that might lead to a renewal, or halted by one killer question: "What's your cost per thousand?" Media buyers, the agencies

By Way of Luck

and their advertising clients, were bound by the soon to be outdated measuring standards, Nielsen as an example, common to network television.

At a Chicago conference produced by *Advertising Age*, the weekly bible of advertising, I addressed a hall packed with agency and advertiser people. My sponsor there was a Northwestern University Marketing Professor, a one-time principal in an advertising agency. He understood the promise of cable. During my presentation, talking marketing futures and demonstrating actual long-form ads, I could hear the giggling. "Do you actually think," one attendee asking, "that people will be buying merchandise from an all ad network?" He looked around for support, playing the audience. There was derisive jeering.

My argument was positioned to address the argument between the emotional sell and the informational sell, jingles versus actual product demonstration. Heads were shaking. Seats were emptying. My Northwestern professor shook his head in dismay.

Worse, my attempts to find financing merely ate up time. I had a product. I had a message. I had evidence. I could open doors. But finding investors proved futile. On a trip to New York City, at dinner with friends, I met the president of Seagram's, Jack Yogman. He was a marketing guy. He understood the Home Shopping concept. He said he'd introduce me to Stan Shulman, a long-time partner in H. Allen & Company notable in the years that followed for its timely investments in media. Mr. Shulman gave me five minutes. He fought the concept, parrying my replies to his questions like a combatant in heavy armor. "How can you run a television show with no programming," he asked? "Just commercials." He eyed Jack warily, and we were out of there.

The hurdles facing me appeared insurmountable. A buyer or an investor had to accept 1. A new delivery system called cable; and 2. A new programming concept called Home Shopping; and 3. That viewers would actually buy featured products. Further, the timing was off. The technology had yet to be understood. The value of more channels carrying more news and entertainment appeared questionable. A common criticism: "We got three national networks already. And a couple more local channels. We need more? No way." Turner had only the technology to sell. His programming was old movies and baseball games. I had to sell both the technology and the programming. And I was running out of money.

Judy made clear her assessment. She said, "Stop."

I said, "No." I had my reason. "We have developed an equitable position in an emerging market," I explained. "And we're not about to throw it away."

Judy expressed her skepticism. "You're expecting something to happen, a stroke of luck."

"I'm not looking for luck," I said, "I'm making a reasonable assumption. Cable is getting a lot of press. We're getting a lot of press. The networks are making programming investments. We're somebody's programming investment." We decided to continue our money losing business.

Looking back, days later, everything quickly changed. And as luck would have it...the phone began to ring.

A call from John Lack at Warner-Amex in New York. "We're evaluating whether we should develop a cable shopping network. Can we talk?" John would be the initial driving force behind MTV. I met him and Gus Hauser, Warner-Amex's CEO, at their offices overlooking Rockefeller Plaza. Lack promoted the idea of a collaboration. Hauser, also Chair of the National Cable Television Association, saw me as a competitor and showed his indignation as well as the door of his office. He made his money as a cable operator, selling a system he constructed in Alexandria, Virginia, a high growth market abutting Washington, DC. He had no programming experience. I was learning of the great divide between systems operators and programmers

A call from MSN. An introduction to Ray Joslin at Hearst. A meeting in New York with Ray, a former cable systems operator, and ABC's Herb Granath, a sports programming sales veteran. Together they had been assigned by their respective companies to create a cable programming partnership. "We'd like to talk to you about

By Way of Luck

running it," they said. They were under pressure to get something going.

A call from the "office" of Jerry Levin, then heading HBO and later the CEO of Time Warner. I was asked to send him a proposal. I sent him a Home Shopping Show brochure and a note suggesting we discuss the joint development of a Home Shopping Network. There was no further contact.

Aside: Levin rose to the Chairmanship of Time Warner and was later gulled into a merger with AOL that cost him his job.

I called Ray Joslin. We agreed to meet in New York on my way from Boston where I had a meeting with Gillette's Vice-President, advertising. Ray suggested we get together at Herb's office at the ABC building at 54th and Sixth. When I arrived there, I learned they had talked to several Home Shopping Show clients, confirming at the same time that I actually had met with the Gillette people. I was amused. Even before meeting me, I could tell by their telephone manner they had decided to offer me the job. Hearst was comforted by my magazine and book publishing experience, ABC by the nerve I'd exhibited in starting a television programming venture with no prior experience. The tapes I'd sent them were of acceptable quality.

Partnerships, I don't like, specifically a one on one partnership, like the one Ron Bernstein and I had, the kind that Hearst and ABC had entered into. To make it work, one has to give in to the other and rarely is there an equitable balance. If there is a third party, one can always take the role of the negotiator, or take a side; the odd number leaves little room for hard-nosed or blatant disagreement. The breech showed itself early, before I accepted the job. What to do with the Home Shopping Show, its merits obvious? Ray said it was worthless. Herb Granath said ABC might consider acquiring it. Ray told Herb acquiring it wasn't logical. I would hear that argument from Ray many times.

I solved the disagreement. I sold Home Shopping to MSN, the Modern Satellite Network. I recovered my investment and over the ensuing three years, with a royalty of the gross as a kicker, I made some money. Problem solved.

Judy was not happy with the arrangement. She liked Chicago. She felt safe there. She'd never lived in New York City, the prospect of it daunting, the move disruptive. After my first meeting with Herb and Ray, before terms were discussed, I invited them for a late afternoon drink at the Berkshire Hotel, the same hotel where I'd been hired by Curtis nearly twenty years earlier. I brought with me Judy and her father, IBM executive Andy Holb. I wanted Judy's participation in a decision we'd have to make together. I wanted Andy's assessment of the two guys who would be my bosses.

Andy was an IBM heavy-lifter, with offices at 595 Madison Avenue, IBM's home office, across the avenue where Doubleday was once located. He handled large scale administrative assignments, like find us a location and build us an office complex for the 3,000 people we're hiring for our new personal computer business. Andy was an accomplished executor and an intimidating presence. He could feign grumpy.

Sitting across from at a table in the hotel lounge Herb and Ray appeared cowed, like funeral directors, solicitous, their smiles waxen, nodding as if in constant concern, an air of care and benevolence about them. Their discomfort showed. Who brings his wife and his father-in-law to a meeting thought to be part of an on-going job interview?

How I might interact with them, the meeting showed, would be dense with discord. Herb understood television, the cost and the reward, from production through sales. Ray was new to Hearst, coming from a cable conglomerate, hired specifically to acquire cable systems for Hearst in much the same way that Hearst had acquired television stations. Neither Frank Bennack, Hearst's CEO, nor Ray fully understood that the two businesses were unrelated.

A television station has but one channel; a cable system would in time have countless channels. The investment in programming for cable, as well as the costs of a build out, were fiscally daunting. Finally realizing that, Frank had quickly backed off his original reason for hiring Ray, a cable system guy, warehousing him until something "came along." When I first met Ray and before the part-

By Way of Luck

nership came together, he was doing busy work, shuffling stacks of paper on a desk in make-shift space in a remote and empty room. Ray had no job.

Further, Ray had no pertinent experience. Which he understood. And which undoubtedly unsettled him. He was anxious, thus, to bring the partnership together and claim a role in co-managing it. Ray would in time understand the process of making investment decisions and become an important asset at Hearst. But after many months of tutoring, it was evident he could not comprehend the management of creative decisions or the people who made them.

The day after our Berkshire Hotel meeting, with Judy's concurrence, I agreed to a contract with the newly legalized Hearst/ABC venture to become its Chief Operating officer reporting to Ray and Herb.

Nonetheless, setting aside my misgivings, the job was attractive. I would be back east, again in New York City, and taking on a very visible assignment.

The President of Hearst's Magazine Division insisted that the programming should appeal to women and its content derived from its leading magazines, notably *Good House Keeping, Redbook* and *Cosmopolitan*. Ray's delivery to me of the President's edict was, for me, an Oh, No moment.

What is it about magazine publishers who assume their editorial materials have great value in other media? When Doubleday's Jerry Hardy went to Time, Inc. to start its book division, the editors of *Time* and *Life* magazines assumed their filed materials would sustain the growth of the book division. Not a chance. One or two hardcover books burned through a decade of previously published art and copy. Curtis had come to the same conclusion: its resources, the editors felt, would emerge as bestselling books that would save the corporation. But a handful or two came out of their files.

Magazine content cannot compete equitably with electronic content, by the manner in which material is prepared and presented and by its timeliness. Printed magazine material is most often extinguished before it's published. The medium is the message, not the content. Kindly, it can be said, magazine editorial copy has ephemeral qualities. There are exceptions. *National Geographic* is one. Magazines with small, niche interest is another. Books are another matter altogether.

How to Handle the Magazine Division's Demands

First, I wrote a précis for a programming a channel that would be of interest to women. Herb and Ray bought into it, sort of. Ray thought it important to circulate among Hearst's editors, as did I. Ray nor anyone else either approved nor disapproved it.

Secondly, I retained a Public Relations professional, Jackie Markham, whom I'd met a decade earlier when she was handling PR for the Norton Simon Company. A demure lady with egg-shaped cheeks that appear ready to hatch and a hoarseness in her voice, she now headed her own firm, Markham Novell, and had become a spokesperson on women's issues. She knew what to do: build the validity of our programming as a service to women. She staged a one-day seminar for women editors. The city's top editors came, from magazines, from newspapers, even from on-the-air radio and television news shows. Many, their careers banging against glass ceilings, sought a voice in how cable could be a liberating force for women. They asked that cable programming have honest, attainable values women could relate to. Tired of afternoon soaps, they insisted programming be information based, as service magazines were, on subjects that were openly directed to the needs of women, from health to homemaking, from children to careers. They asked that women be freed of their stereotypical portrayal in television advertising.

For the entire day, through lunch and end of day refreshments, the editors talked from personal experience, their recommendations bursting as if from a breech in a long dammed river. Had they ever, I wondered, been given the chance to express their professional interests so openly? In the companies that employed them? I didn't think so. Their recommendations for the kinds of shows we might produce would have filled to overflowing a giant suggestion box. Their good thinking fit comfortably with the direction our programming would take. The idea that magazine content might prove a valuable programming resource was pooh-poohed by strong willed women who knew what pooh was all about. Hearst editors sitting in agreed.

Having just a few afternoon hours of satellite time available to us, but five days a week, we called our show *Daytime*, its producer: Hearst/ABC. I began assembling the assets we'd require to go on the air, so to speak. But first, I had to confront what I was faced with.

The Hearst Legacy

Hearst Corporation is a newspaper and magazine conglomerate founded and driven by a ferocious egoist and warrior, William Randolph Hearst. Through the late 1880s and into the late 1940s, he created fear among his competitors, fought gun-fire battles for circulation dominance in more than a dozen major newspaper markets from San Francisco to New York City, and triumphed in nearly everything he undertook, from the public banning of marijuana to pushing the United States into the war with Spain. To serve his own needs, he wrested from city planner Robert Moses, a powerful eminence himself, the plan for New York City's proposed construction of the Triborough Bridge and redirected it to a derelict site in the Bronx he owned, then held the project hostage until Moses bought it from him for a substantial gain. He both played and acted the emperor.

For a first time meeting, entering Hearst's corporate headquarters building at the corner of 57th Street and 8th Avenue, a gray and bunker-like fortress, I could feel Mr. Hearst's hovering presence. The talk that ensued was cautious, words communicated as if in defense of the homeland. Frank Bennack, the corporation's CEO, spoke in short, inconclusive phrases, offering little substance, perhaps awaiting orders from a man dead since 1951 but still in the building. Ray solicited approvals from Frank with obsequious layering's of flattery, seemingly doting on Frank as Frank's predecessors had possibly doted on Mr. Hearst. The interior of the building had been redesigned not to effect a contemporary look, but to a look that prevailed during Mr. Hearst's era, an updating rather than a modernizing as if fearing Mr. Hearst's disapproval. In fact, the corporation had done little to advance the newspaper and magazine empire beyond what Mr. Hearst had built. The start-up cable television joint venture I was hired to manage may have been the Hearst Corporation's first attempt to break away from the lingering authority of the old man. I had to tread lightly, but deliberately.

I hired a financial guy, Sy Lesser, to build budgets and set up our accounting system; I hired Bob Fell a long time advertising executive to think through and manage a marketing and sales plan; I hired Kathryn Creech from the National Cable Television Association in Washington; her assignment: make nice with cable operators and make sure they distribute our programming. I hired Mickey Dwyer away from ABC where she was in charge of ABC's daytime programming.

Aside: One hire went quickly awry, a production manager from ABC who was more a network manager. I had to renege on a promise to keep him. He returned to his former job at ABC. I needed an experienced hand who could organize a shoot and manage edit. I found him at Channel 13, a New York City PBS affiliate: Marc Chalom, but 24 years old and brilliant. Without his ability to shortcut both process and expense, we could not have maintained our schedule. Nor our budget.

New Office Space in a Derelict Building

We looked for office space while squeezed into an empty storeroom in a 57th Street building owned by Hearst and awaiting renovation. When I gave Ray and Herb our requirements, Ray said we'd have to wait for space to become available in some other Hearst Building. He knew a wait would not sit well with me or ABC. Hearst, I could tell, would push for dominance and, I guessed, would attempt to

By Way of Luck

derive revenues from the partnership outside the sharing agreement. I was correct on both counts.

Needing approval of both companies to sign a long-term lease, I sought options. The certitude thing coming alive and merging with my now compulsive behavior thing, as offices I leased month-to-month one-and two-bedroom suites in the Mayflower Hotel just off Columbus Circle facing Central Park. The hotel had fallen into disrepair and suites were cheaply available. At one point I had eleven suites under lease at costs far less than rent in a commercial office building. Word was circulated by a couple of wags that Perkins was putting young women to work in hotel bedrooms. My response equally waggish, I circulated an office memo that found its way into the trade press announcing that each of our luxury hotel office suites had private baths and a conference room and were available for private parties. Mickey loved it. Ray said Hearst was concerned by my behavior.

Eventually I found offices on East 45th Street in a non-Hearst building and with Heart's grudging approval — the rent was cheap — moved everyone there. I set a deadline for our "on-air" debut, nine months out and offering only original programming. With but four daytime hours to fill, I could act boldly. When time came for a breather we had produced 270 hours of informational television for somewhat less than $7.5 million. Our direct costs averaged $26,000 per production hour. We were ready to go "on air."

Hearst balked at sourcing a 24/7 transponder position. Until the programming showed its worth and until we attracted national advertisers, Hearst saw our organization as foreign to its interests. Obviously, and without courtesy, it chose to treat us as a minor division within its jurisdiction and subject to its whims.

Hearst's requirements were burdensome. The executive assistant to the CEO demanded that we sell time by rate card, that is, as magazine space was sold. He did not understand that air time was perishable. What one could sell was what one could get.

Helen Gurley Brown, editor of *Cosmopolitan*, a Hearst magazine, insisted on having her own show and was told by Hearst she could have one. In a well-produced segment, she was awkward on camera. After seeing herself in a trial interview with Bob Guccione, her choice, she smartly informed us she did not have time for cable TV.

Hearst's chief financial officer rejected our preliminary budget because of a single line item: the purchase of word processing equipment. He had not an inkling of what "word processing" meant. When he was told, he drew a red line through the request, remarking, "That's work for the girls." Dinosaurus Rex occupied a seat in Hearst's executive suite.

Leonard Goldenson, who founded ABC and was its Chairman and CEO, attempted a rescue. He asked for an early look at our programming and invited an assembly of Hearst's senior people as well as his own senior staff to a demonstration. Mickey Dwyer and I cued perhaps thirty 3/4-inch cassette tapes featuring talk shows, cooking shows, style shows, audience participation shows, and so on. When we paused, as if suggesting we'd perhaps shown enough, Leonard said, "Let's see more." He was impressed by the quality we'd achieved but questioned the costs.

"How much are you spending to produce an hour of programming," he asked.

"Less than thirty thousand," I told him.

Leonard appeared stunned, his momentary silence telling. "That's extraordinary," he exclaimed. He was anticipating, even at the low end, a six figure number. "That's truly good."

"Too good," ABC's president Fred Pierce interjected. "What we've just seen is directly competitive with our day time network shows."

Herb Granath grinned a happy grin. Ray and his Hearst colleagues felt the pressure, nodding their agreement as well.

(In an aside, after the meeting, Fred told me the Hearst people we're "Cheapskates. They don't know how to invest in content. At ABC," he said, "We write off $100,000,000 a year on pilots that don't make it.")

Weeks later, at Hearst's headquarters, a gathering for lunch and further discussion regarding the partnership, Leonard stood up and argued in favor of "getting Jim a 24 hour transponder." His words

By Way of Luck

were met with indifference. Frank Bennack said, "We'll consider it." There was no further discussion.

Argument would be futile. Frank and Leonard had a personal relationship that superseded their common business interests. Leonard was a founder of the Multiple Sclerosis Foundation and on its board of directors, as was Frank Bennack. ABC and Hearst were sustaining donors. The idea of jointly investing in cable television programming arose after an MS board meeting, Herb told me, as the two men were sharing a ride home. It started with a casual remark by Leonard, asking, "What's new at Hearst, Frank?" Frank told him he'd just hired Ray Joslin to look for opportunities in the emerging cable business. Leonard, Herb said, suggested "Why don't we put your guy together with my guy, Herb Granath, and see what they come up with." However casual, it was the inaugural of a partnership that continues to thrive.

That four of Hearst's six television stations were ABC affiliates supported the relationship.

It was clear that Hearst wanted control. ABC was willing to give it to them. In the greater scheme of things, what I wanted and what I might have done to enhance the partnership was of little matter. Hearst's baseless concerns and inexplicable actions were characteristic of old-line publishing companies, my experience with Curtis told me. I'd live with it, for the benefit of the people I'd hired, the goals I had been given, and the asset I was charged with creating, and managing it as an acceptable irritant.

By contrast, ABC made life easy for me, various executives offered support, at luncheons introducing me to the network's key sponsors, with instructive tours of their production facilities, and with advice evaluating prospective on-camera personalities. I was also reminded ABC had a box at Shea Stadium that was available to me.

Hearst/ABC launched *Daytime* on schedule, celebrating its inaugural at an industry wide party at Windows on the World atop the North Tower of the World Trade Center, the event and the programming generating valuable trade publicity. Fifteen hundred people came looking for a party, and they got a memorable one.

Daytime's programs were better than adequate. As examples, we featured Julie Childs, taped live, in a series drawn by excerpt from her heralded shows at WGBS, Boston, interacting animatedly with our hosts and showing herself masterfully in unrehearsed dialogue. Another feature, a first, drew extensive criticism, a segment on breast cancer, with an oncologist demonstrating how his patient could exam herself for early signs of breast cancer. On camera the segment showed a bared breast, to Mickey Dwyer's knowledge a first time TV event. At ABC, the office in charge of compliance was aghast. Mickey was advised to abandon the program or "cover her up."

Mickey responded evenly, pointing out that the feature was purely educational and hardly prurient and reminding the compliance folks that without FCC oversight, cable had the freedom to produce and televise whatever cable might assume to be in the best interests of its viewers.

I believe it to be cable television's first challenge to its First Amendment rights. Hearst/ABC and *Daytime*, of course, prevailed.

On the street, Madison Avenue in particular, good things were being said about *Daytime*.

While Kathryn Creech lobbied the cable industry, enlisting systems to carry *Daytime* and racking up a laudable record, I focused on advertising sales. While Bob Fell made the sales calls, I connected with the upper echelons of the larger New York City agencies. Weekly, at the Lotos Club, usually on a Thursday, by agency, I conducted informational lunches, cocktails at noon, an appropriate meal, and an open conversation on the future of cable television and its impact on advertising agencies and their clients. I had no trouble attracting the top people I sought, the high ranking media buyers in the agency business: I was ABC, I was Hearst, our programming was in the news and given my experience with the Home Shopping Show, I was seen as a credible advocate.

When *Daytime* launched, 11 big-name advertisers had signed on for our inaugural week. But the dollars were small, little more than rounding errors. We had visibility but not much else.

By Way of Luck

The first advertising buy of any size came from General Foods. The buy was for under a thousand dollars. Given the crumbs cable was getting from marginally interested advertisers, it was a step-up for *Daytime*, and we made a big deal of it. Without disclosing the details of the contract and with the cooperation of the senior people at General Foods, we hosted a press conference at the Lotos Club positioning the buy as an example of the prospects cable could soon be seeing, and acting all along as if we'd scored a multi-million dollar commitment and offering no evidence that it might have been any less than that. We made small news into big news. Like igniting a jet's afterburner at take-off, *Daytime* leapt respectably into the air.

But between the partners, a nasty argument arose. ABC had been nursing a programming concept called ARTS. One show had been developed at great expense, "Swan Lake Minnesota." Herb asked that I take it over as a Hearst/ABC project and build a network of comparable, artistic programming. Hearst agreed with the idea but rejected Herb's proposal that Hearst/ABC acquire the programming at ABC's cost. Ray balked, so did Frank Bennack and for several weeks the once comfortable hammock strung between the partners rocked uneasily.

In time, ABC relented, ate the expense and gave me "Swan Lake…" and ARTS. But the partnership had turned sour. Had ABC not backed off, the partnership could have foundered.

The cost of programming ARTS at the artistic level ABC had established would be unsustainable, even if ARTS sold out its entire available advertising inventory. ARTS had but three hours of original daily time on an MTV satellite, from 8 PM to 11 PM, repeating for another three hours beginning at mid-night. Because I'd produced *Daytime* for small dollars, Hearst expected me to make a network out of ARTS just as cheaply. Everything, Ray professed, can be done less expensively if you know how to negotiate. Describing himself unabashedly as a talented negotiator, he assumed the needed qualifications to evaluate most anything, television creative and production costs included. He ignored taking advice from his partner, ABC, as if its long time experience somehow did not apply.

"Logic tells me I can do what you do," he said.
"That's a joke, right?" I said, thinking his remark deliberately comical.
"No, it's not a joke," he said, his smile confident.

Cable. Just Another Fad?

Hearst restricted further investment. Ray spoke gloomily. He assured his colleagues at Hearst that expansion was unwise, that no more than three cable networks would survive the cable crash to come. For a while, Ray's prophesies played out. CBS Cable, like ARTS, committed to cultural programming, collapsed in a matter of months. The Cable Health Network, a Viacom venture producing a 24/7 programming lineup, weakened. It sought, as did ESPN, to lay off late night and all-day Sunday broadcast time and making it available for independent producers. Panic was building.

Herb proposed that *Daytime* and ESPN merge, splitting ESPN's transponder day in half, ESPN from 6 PM to 6 AM, *Daytime* having the day time hours.

Cable Shop, a joint venture of J. Walter Thompson and a Boston area cable system, needed resuscitation almost before it went on the air.

The Entertainment Channel, a pay TV joint venture of RCA, NBC and Rockefeller Center, was short lived.

ABC and Westinghouse took a long look at producing a news channel but bowed out fearing the competition from Ted Turner's Cable News Channel, CNN.

"It's on," Turner had burbled at CNN's inaugural moment, "and it ain't ever turning off."

Many thought Turner a braggart, but nearly four decades later, CNN isn't yet turned off. There were more failures than successes and for a while Ray's prediction appeared prescient.

But for MTV, the growth of cable may have dragged on for years. MTV was hot, new, and original and had a beat that vibrated among youngsters. Its resounding slogan, "I Want My MTV," sent a message of hope to the cable system industry. New build-outs sprung up in major markets.

By Way of Luck

I pressed for better distribution, believing that what we had so far accomplished with *Daytime* gave me and Hearst/ABC's staff credibility. We were stonewalled. I looked outside for possible joint programming opportunities. I met with Arthur Taylor, a former CBS president, and CEO of the *Entertainment Channel*, discussed the possibilities of a merger with ARTS. Arthur said his financial backers were uneasy with the status quo and might favor a consolidation of the two services. He had acquired the cable rights to BBC's programming, a source of material that by itself could support a 24/7 network. In any event, he finally said, I'm leaving. He became President of Muhlenberg College.

Sadly, Hearst ignored the possibility. ABC looked the other way.

Viacom gave signs it was ready to bow out of the Cable Health Network and looked to Hearst and ABC as buyers. Herb and Ray shook their heads. Television networks and publishers had long been competitors and were reluctant, if not afraid, of talking merger among themselves if even on a tentative basis.

MSN, after a year of spotty success with The Home Shopping Show, gave it up. Inexplicably, they thought it would be a "turn-key" operation and put scant effort into its management. What could the company have been thinking of?

MSN sold The Home Shopping Show to people who had the resources to develop it along the lines of my original plan: Bud Paxson, a Florida broadcaster who was selling overstocked merchandise on his local UHF channel; and Roy Spear, an investor with the big bucks that allowed Bud to acquire a satellite transponder and build a state-of-the-art broadcast studio and an order processing and shipping center. They soon discovered that Bud's ability to sell deeply discounted merchandise gave them bigger margins and a faster return on their investment than my original premise would have. Within three years their sales were approaching a billion dollars and in less than six years both Roy and Bud were boasting publicly of their personal, newly gained wealth.

In later years I met Bud at a New York City gathering of media investors where he graciously introduced me as the father of the

Home Shopping Network, referring to me as an "original."

Nice, Bud. Many thanks.

Today, viewers can find The Home Shopping Network on most cable systems listed as HSN. It is a part of Barry Diller's media conglomerate.

There was no clear indication, even in mid-1980s, whether cable television — cable programmers and cable systems and their investors — would ever achieve an acceptable level of audience or advertiser popularity, whether cable would be part of a mixed bag of radio, over-the-air television and video cassette rental or, like a passing fad, would wither from indifference if not boredom. Having bet personal money on cable, broken up a rather splendid apartment in Chicago to move to New York City, taken peanuts for a job a monkey would have rejected, and gripped by certainty, I hoped to win over Herb and Ray to a course of action.

I could not engage them. They discussed easily the minutiae of the business I was building, but turned to stone on the larger issues. Frustrated, I once blocked them both in a narrow hallway outside a Hearst conference room where we'd been meeting. Being seen as an uncommitted cable programmer, I told them — emphasizing my every word — hurt Hearst/ABC badly among ad agencies' reluctance to promote us to their clients and among cable systems from whom we were seeking distribution. Herb and Ray pushed past me and walked away. I recall seeing only the backs of their suits.

Herb had no intention of rocking the boat. He had risen steadily, though sometimes precariously, within the ABC empire, promoted by the network's legendary sports producer Rooney Arledge.

What followed may have saved Hearst/ABC from itself, events that could not be influenced by executive decision, events that would sustain ARTS until it could become ARTS & Entertainment (A&E) and *Daytime* until it could become the Lifetime Network. And eventually until ABC could acquire ESPN.

1982-1984

Advertising expenditures among all media were in a trough.

By Way of Luck

Hearst was impatient. Its frustration showed. Frank Bennack's executive assistant in an informational meeting told my key employees that Hearst might have to shut down the venture. "At any minute," he said. "If things don't get any better." His remarks, totally unconscionable, rippled through the company. *Daytime* was just months old. I lost good people to competitors.

Ray Joslin accosted Bob Fell at a cocktail party, threatening to fire him if sales did not improve — immediately! A big guy, six four with ample tonnage, Bob was a pro, respected both by agencies and their advertisers. The threat cut him deeply, emotionally immobilizing him. I redefined his job as our new marketing director and gave him three months to make it work. Hearst was furious I had not fired him outright.

Whether prompted by his peers at Hearst, Ray proposed that I produce infomercials as I had for The Home Shopping Show and insert them in *Daytime* and ARTS. That way, he said, should our current programs fail, we'll have something to fall back on. He was not making small talk. He saw infomercials as a quick fix, ignoring that their production required a very different business model. Patently, he was afraid. Or was he pushing me into an untenable position in order to take my job? It was a "logical" assumption.

I hired John Silvestri, a Chicago ad salesman, to replace Bob Fell. Silvestri became perhaps cable's highest producing sales director and the best hire I ever made.

In the midst of the near suicidal chaos Hearst was creating, Marc Chalom, my 24 year old production manager, offered a proposition that could in part support us through the drought. Mickey Dwyer, our programming director, bought into it. So did I.

With so few cable systems in operation, Marc said, with but a few hours a day of non-prime time satellite distribution and with no published programming schedules, how could we ever prove that anyone was watching?

"Maybe," Marc said, "NO ONE!"

Marc always spoke with humor, his ever present grin offering hope. That he dressed badly and doused himself with a cheap cologne that could empty a room in seconds was overlooked. Marc worked in survivor mode: no wasted time, no wasted energy, no wasted people. During the 1967 Israel-Egypt war Marc's family fled Cairo, their long time home, found temporary refuge in Greece, lived through marginally better times in France, and finally found permanent residence in the United States. For homeless Jews it was a murderous era. Marc, then a child, learned to live at the edge.

That *Daytime* hit its announced on-air date with a full programming schedule was due in large part to Marc's determination, editing brilliance and his commitment to making do with less.

"So...," Marc announced to me and Mickey. "Let's stop producing original programming." He had a thesis. Most of what we had so far produced for *Daytime* had "legs," that is, it was neither timely nor dated.

"We can rotate our programming through different time slots week by week," Marc explained, "with no repetition within a week, and only occasional repetition within a month, and in the next few months we can begin the rotation all over again, loading in fresh inserts where we see they're needed.

"Further," Marc went on, "we won't need a studio, just an edit suite. Edit suites are over built and we can buy time…Cheap," he emphasized.

"What about ARTS," Mickey asked? Marc had an immediate answer: Between New York City and Los Angeles, in studios, production companies and public relations agencies, he told us, there's a sea of programming: stills, film, video tape even magazine pages. We can edit shows from that inventory and add minimal original material and a voice-over to pull it together. "Just as we did with the Julia Childs' shows," he reminded us.

Consider, he said, an ARTS series called *Biography*. "Can you imagine how much celebrity footage is in storage just waiting to be used? We can lease it, edit it and put it on the air for next to nothing." And another series called *History*. "Same thing," he said. He went on to explain how he could source the material. The whole effort could be assembled, Marc concluded, with a senior producer and interns, retaining readily available free-lancers when necessary. Ray Joslin, still sensing cable's coming collapse, was quick to endorse Marc's proposition.

Marc had another proposition. Citibank owned two satellite communication transponders, one for voice and data communications, the other as a back-up to the first. "Let's see if we can lease the back-up," he said. "It's a redundancy Citibank doesn't need. Data transmission uses very little band width. If Citibank's primary transponder goes down, for whatever reason, the bank can always find room on the sideband or on some other transponder on some other satellite utilized only for broadband. Sidebands are plentiful." Marc had done his homework. He was right.

Herb and Ray authorized us to explore the possibility. If there was any interest at Citibank, Ray said he would oversee the negotiations. He delayed action until Citibank shut down discussions because talk between the negotiators was taking "too much time."

Coming to the End...of my Second Year

Despite the stream of contradictions, the stops, the starts, the harshly delivered critiques, and the limiting resources Hearst/ABC had to work with, I felt satisfied with what it had accomplished. Ray and Herb agreed. Although, what they had agreed to was unclear. At a meeting at Herb's office, Ray offered me a bonus the partners concluded I deserved. He gave me a number verbally. It was substantially less than I expected, or I thought appropriate, and I told them that. Ray went into negotiation mode, but as he did so I could read his notes on a sheet of paper he held in his lap. He had penciled in an identical bonus for Kathryn Creech, the very same dollar amount for a staffer reporting to me.

Now we were both in negotiation mode.

Ray claimed she had the tougher job. Ray said there wasn't enough money available to go around. Ray said she had the greater experience. As a senior vice president of the National Cable Television Association where she'd worked for five years, she was a valuable asset and, besides, he said, she deserved the money. His explanation was ludicrous, his logic twisted.

Cable people side with cable people. Was Kathryn Ray's back door into the company? For her own ambitions, was she courting Ray? Was Kathryn undermining me? Only years later did I learn that my suspicions were correct. She wanted my job. Knowing that, Ray had played her off against me, using her to serve his own ends.

Meantime, as the dialogue between me and Ray went on, Herb had drifted off to the other side of his spacious office, picked up his telephone and pretended he was talking with someone. It was a ruse. He did not, would not, be involved in an argument that was about to ensue. He stood apart from me and Ray, looking vacantly through the window of his corner office toward a building across Sixth Avenue and engaging in a make-believe two-way conversation. He was abandoning me to Ray.

I cut the argument short. Ray, I said, "Give me one dollar more than the bonus you're giving Kathryn."

In an honest negotiation the issue would have quickly dissipated.

Ray said, "No." He was unrelenting. In a demonstration of his negotiating prowess, he said Hearst "had lost confidence in me." I shrugged, tossed Herb a good-bye and left the office. I was done with Hearst/ABC, and Hearst/ABC was done with me.

Two days later, Frank Bennack, Hearst's CEO and Ray's boss, asked me by phone to meet him for lunch at the Metropolitan Club on Fifth Avenue opposite the entrance to the Central Park zoo. Frank was a newspaper man, ascending to his senior position by his remarkable effort rebuilding the San Antonio Express-News, a small newspaper in a big newspaper market and facing bankruptcy. Frank retired twice from Hearst, called back from his first retirement to replace his successor who'd fallen out of favor with the Hearst family.

Frank made a friendly effort to be supportive, asking that I stay the course. He shared with me his assessment of Ray whom he liked, he said, and would grow into his job. That said, he gave me warning. The people at Hearst, he told me, had found me "disagreeable."

By Way of Luck

So accused was not a surprise. Managing a start-up, particularly in a new industry, an entrepreneurial spirit has to prevail, the vision has to be seen, the leader has to lead. If he's constantly seeking approval and having to lurch back and forth between non-responsive partners, as I was, the partnership would be mired in mud. The business, I told Frank, was my first responsibility. I had to keep the partnership in balance. I could not always satisfy the partners' divergent interests. Being disagreeable brought them together.

Frank appeared puzzled by my explanation. By his posture alone I could see he had no interest in striking a balance with ABC, the partnership, to him, demanded on-going negotiation, his objective to contribute the least and come away with the most. In his concluding remarks, he suggested I had an obligation to Hearst as it was through Ray and because of my publishing experience that he and Ray had decided to hire me.

On a walk from the Club along Central Park South, Frank said he understood my position. My misfortune, I understood his as well.

Disagreeable Me

Before my next meeting with the Hearst/ABC board, I dwelt long on who I was, where I'd come from, what I'd done professionally, and what might lie in store for me. My self-assessment showed, wherever I'd been, whether as a raw Air Force officer at the bottom of the heap in the Pentagon or an early promoter of cable, I was not one of the gang. My abilities were apparent, employers were eager to hire me, but once my assigned task was completed, and when a guy in a corporate suit could take over, consistently I was disposable.

Yet I felt comfortable doing what I was doing and how I was doing it. Impatient, yes. Abrupt, yes. Too direct in my evaluation of others, yes. A team player, no. Zipping my lip, no. Willing to stand in line, no. Wait and see, no. Frequently impolite, yes. Occasionally given to stupidity, yes. But dammit, I got things done, good things, creative things usually ahead of time and beating expectations.

Could I change, no. If I wanted to, no. If I tried, no. Did I care, no. I succumbed to the beast inside forbidding me to say yes. Thank you, Mary Astor.

At the next meeting of the Board, principally Herb and Ray, each joined by two fellow directors, I ignored the agenda and asked for an explanation from Hearst and the "loss of confidence" remark Ray made in Herb's office. Ray confirmed what he'd said. His fellow directors, Harry and Ben, said they, too, had lost confidence in me. Herb's fellow directors, Jack and Larry, surprised by not having been earlier consulted, yet without hesitation — and somewhat defiantly — together supported me.

Pretending shock, Herb looked toward the window.

Ray had used our contentious discussion of my bonus as an opening to jettison me. That his colleagues had without further discussion supported Ray was proof of that. I stood up and walked away, opening the door as I left, and closing it behind me.

Larry, an attorney, was assigned to settle my contract.

Within days, Ray settled into my former office at Hearst/ABC to manage *Daytime* and ARTS.

Ray's self-serving actions would in time cost Hearst dearly.

In the meantime, Ray had an agenda he could follow. Mine. Ray was a logical guy, depending on his perception of what might be logical, what might not be, drove him to reconsider my earlier urgings to either acquire or merge The Entertainment Channel with ARTS and bring *Daytime* and The Cable Health Network together.

Herb concurred and let Ray do the work. Arts and Entertainment (A&E) emerged as did Lifetime.

16

Call it Luck

My resignation caused not a stir. Amidst a flood of firings, reassignments and down sizing's hitting cable programmers, news of my departure was swept into the dust bin, unnoticed and unimportant. Or so I thought.

Arnie Semsky, executive vice-president, media at BBDO, found me at home. BBDO was the first agency I entertained at the Lotos Club, Arnie joined by his key buyers and a believer in cable's future, although he was doubtful cable would ever matter as much as network television. "We'd like to talk with you," Arnie said. "We" was Arnie and Jack Thorne, another BBDO executive vice-president and head of the account management group.

Arnie and Jack had cleared with the agency's president, Allen Rosenshine, an idea they wished to discuss. Can you stop by for a chat? Their offices were in the same building as Holt, Rinehart.

The idea was a big idea. BBDO had major clients: Pepsi, Gillette, GE, Dodge-Chrysler just a few of them. Among independent agencies they boasted the biggest billings in television advertising. 'I don't want our clients to learn about cable from the trade press," Arnie said. "We want to establish a cable presence here at the agency. We want our clients to learn it from us. If there's a proprietary position for an ad agency to be found in cable, we want it."

Arnie and Jack talked broadly and creatively, their vision refreshing, about advertising content and about co-production with their clients. "We want to bring back 'Texaco Theater'," Jack said, and 'the Colgate Comedy Hour,' " his reference the long-ago tight tie-ins between producers and advertisers common in the days of black and white TV. "There are big changes coming in television," Arnie and Jack agreed, "and we hope to influence those changes."

"How do I fit in?" I asked, thinking that Arnie and Jack were hoping for some casual advice.

I was wrong.

"We want you to headline it," they said. "To produce the argument and take it to our clients."

BBDO had given a good deal of thought to this, they assured me. They were not hip-shooting. They saw the proposition as core to the agency's future growth.

I had left Hearst/ABC just a week or two before, barely time enough to leave behind the dodge-ball game Herb and Ray were playing. Like a meteoroid crashing in my lap, the offer came too fast, too soon. I'd need time and thought to assess it. Give me a few days, I said.

Was there a director off-stage playfully juggling the script and amused by my confusion? Would I emerge from a darkened theater, seeking sunlight and an explanation of the offer I had just been handed? And someone there to tell me what to do?

Except for CNN, MTV, premium channel HBO and a struggling Financial News Channel — that would in time be acquired by NBC and reconfigured as CNBC — the cable business was idling, there was still little hiring. At an industry event featuring a panel discussion, six cable channel chief executives sitting awkwardly on metal folding chairs, the moderator guessed aloud that within a year none of them would be holding their jobs. Close. One CEO survived.

I asked Judy Perkins for advice. While I was putting Hearst/ABC together, Judy was free-lancing as a producer, her principal

By Way of Luck

client ad agency J. Walter Thompson. Although seen from a different perspective, what she'd learned there, along with my daily front-line reports from Hearst/ABC, Judy had stored enough industry savvy to be a trusted counselor.

"For what BBDO wants," she said, "You're the best guy available. Maybe the only guy." She went on. "They're smart. They've seen you in action at the Lotos club." Without trace of a smile, she concluded: "Besides, I don't see many companies standing in line to hire you. Take the job and decide afterward whether you've made the right decision."

She spoke so deliberately, I had to agree. But wasn't her conclusion pretty much how I'd managed my career all along?

"I'll need your help," I said. "Work with me on this." I reminded her how well we teamed up to produce The Home Shopping Show. "OK," she said. "Just until you get this thing off the ground."

Arnie and Jack, two agency guys who didn't drink at lunch, an anomaly, joined me mid-day at the Lotos Club. Perrier was the beverage of choice. We agreed I'd prepare a plan — with their participation and for their approval — a summary of how cable television would evolve, from a programming perspective as well as an advertising perspective, and how BBDO clients would benefit from the change. I asked Arnie and Jack that Judy join me in the effort and my Hearst/ABC secretary, Molly Gelb, be hired by BBDO and assigned to me.

A pause, Arnie eyeing Jack, Jack's eyes widening. "Does that mean you're accepting our offer?"

"If you're accepting mine, Yes."

Arnie taking the lead said, "We're thrilled you'll do it. And for adding Judy and Molly. We're comfortable with that."

Jack added, "You're the guy, the experience we can't do ourselves, you're the futurist, we're just the spear carriers." Jack, every bit a salesman, was given to overstated remarks.

BBDO gave us adequate offices, Judy, Molly and I moved in, and over the next four weeks we produced the plan, running a bit longer than we'd expected, but full of good stuff that ad guys should know and their clients would find compelling. Final copies went to Arnie and Jack who'd done some of the heavy lifting along the way. And an extra copy for Allen Rosenshine.

BBDO people were not hesitant to smile, I learned right away, wanting to be liked and eager to excel, acting as if the entire agency were performing before a box seat audience in a sellout show. Turf was understood, who owned what and how it was managed — the goal clear, do good work and make the client happy — and incentive driven. The average age of the people I met was easily ten years below my counterparts at Hearst and at ABC, I usually the eldest in BBDO meetings, both refreshing and sobering.

At my first face-to-face with Allen, he jumped from his chair, his greeting scarily enthusiastic. "I read the plan," he said in a near shout. "How did you know about *The Macaroni Journal?*"

"I made it up," I said.

A section in the plan dealt with the fracturing of audiences. Readers and viewers, because of the coming technology, could be identified more exactly, by taste, by habit, and by need, giving marketers greater efficiency in their delivery of both entertainment and information. I had written a line, "offering content as finite as one might find in *The Macaroni Journal*," never thinking that such a magazine might exist. Well, it did.

Allen thought it hilarious.

"At the beginning of my career, when I decided to be a writer," Allen said, "the only editorial job I could find was with *The Macaroni Journal*. It's no longer published. I never put it on my resume." He shook his head in disbelief. "I can't believe you made it up of out of thin air."

Allen complimented me on the plan, but mostly on the writing, still bubbling he said I might be the most creative person in the building. As he did so, BBDO's creative director, Phil Dusenberry, overhearing us as he walked into the office, shot us both a sharp look of annoyance.

By Way of Luck

Allen was a man apart, difficult to assess whether serious or social, leaving me wondering where the suit ended and the man began. Abruptly, at this first meeting, though, making quite clear what he wanted, he said, "Let's work together on this."

So began the meetings with BBDO's top clients, Gillette's CEO in New York, and Pepsi's EVP Marketing in Purchase, New York, for starters, coffee and muffin informality the norm. After introducing me, Allen tossing me the ball and I balancing it seal-like on my nose, so to speak. Satisfied by my performance, Arnie and Jack became my schedulers and accompanists.

Between these meetings, Tom Clark, BBDO's president and head of the account group, and Allen's equal, kept me occupied, inviting me to meetings and urging me to participate, and in several instances bringing me along on calls to his "constituents," people of influence who could help him pitch new clients or reinforce his relationships with current ones. Tom was the constant observer, his eye on every interaction, however subtle, client or staff, committed to consistency and intolerant of any deviation from what he deemed acceptable. Sitting in on the rehearsal for the introduction of a new campaign for an established client, Tom challenging the words, even the nuances, bore out my assessment. Like a Marine drill instructor, top-kick Tom drilled his account managers mercilessly, his criticisms sharp, often demeaning, and unending until he was comfortably satisfied he had gotten from his people the best they could give him, at this point becoming a grateful and accepting boss.

What to do, though, about the flip side of my assignment, encouraging clients to invest in programming? My evaluation of work in progress among cable and network television producers revealed few credible prospects for co-production. Unless a specific opportunity arose, I had nothing to promote, or so it seemed. A news item in the business pages of the NY Times, reporting that Texaco was to acquire Getty Oil, changed all that.

Reading about the acquisition, I connected the dots. Years earlier, at a time when diversification, even among the oil giants, was a raging corporate goal, flush with cash Getty acquired fledgling network ESPN, taking 85% for itself and selling ABC 15%. Texaco, I immediately surmised, would have no interest in owning a cable television network and would likely choose to spin it out. Why wait for the spin out? Why not step in and buy it? All of it? Part of it? Who would run it? I called Herb Granath at ABC. Though he had but thinly supported me at Hearst/ABC, this was not a time to ignore the possibility of a play for ESPN.

Herb, I said, are you at your desk reading what I'm reading about Getty?

"Yup," he said. "The paper's open to the business page."

"Are you figuring what it might take to buy it?"

"Yup. Looks like it might be too expensive."

"Write down a number," I said. "What it will take," I urged. "Got it down?"

"Yup."

"Two hundred million," I said.

"That's the number I wrote down. Good guess."

"I can help you find the money," I said.

"Can you come over?"

Before leaving the BBDO offices, I convened a quick meeting with Allen, Arnie and Jack, gave them a briefing on what I was up to. Suggesting there might be an attractive position somewhere in the mix to come for Gillette, a long time sports advertiser, I got their ok, not an ok, ok, it was an enthusiastic OK!

I walked the ten blocks to the ABC building on Sixth Avenue, imagining what I would say and how I would say it. It came to me as I crossed Fifth Avenue one block away

Herb showed me the note pad on which he'd written: $200. "Just to show you I wasn't making it up."

Herb lit his pipe, told me an unrelated story he found amusing, a personal style, and said, "Well?"

"How about buying from Texaco what ABC doesn't own of ESPN... the 85%...for nothing?"

Herb's pipe hadn't taken the light. He lit it again, puffing away

By Way of Luck

until a crown of smoke leapt out of the bowl. "How," he asked?

"How to you, too," I said. "Put down the peace pipe, and I'll tell you how."

Herb liked joking. I had his attention.

My proposition went as follows. Bring together advertisers who buy sports advertising...sell them a percentage of ESPN for $200 million...offer them a deeply discounted insertion rate to be debited against their investment...and at the end of seven maybe ten years, an estimate of the time required to zero out the investment, pay them a "kicker" — the appreciation of their original investment multiplied by a negotiated factor of, say, eight to ten. ABC now owns the full 100% for a lot less than $200 million.

My suggestion was not altogether original. To finance ABC's purchase of the rights to NCAA football, ABC's Sports impresario, Roone Arledge, pre-sold a sufficient amount of advertising time to finance the deal. The difference: it was a straight media buy.

"Can BBDO find enough advertisers to participate in this?" Herb asked.

If BBDO says it can, I said, it can. Before I proceed further, I need to know whether you can get your guys on board with this.

He'd talk to Leonard and Fred, Herb said. They'll go for it.

One more thing: Your relationship with Hearst.

ABC and Hearst had a gentleman's agreement that the two companies would partner equally in the development of cable television programming. They had already done so with ARTS and *Daytime*.

I cautioned Herb.

I reminded him of the slap Hearst had given him at the start-up of ARTS, the foot dragging and the serial negotiation on just about everything that followed. "ESPN is still a baby," I said. "A sports programmer in ABC's wheelhouse its management should be ABC's to control.

Soon after I returned to the office and readied myself to brief the BBDO guys, Herb called. Fred and Leonard and Roone Arledge liked the approach. They were less than sanguine regarding Hearst.

The progress was swift. I had opened an idea and closed on it in the same day. No one had committed to anything, but I'd made plausible progress.

BBDO's next moves were impressive. Arnie and Jack caught the attention of two clients: Stroh's Brewery, which had just acquired Schlitz, and safety razor company Gillette. Their interest is genuine, Arnie said. For both companies, sports programming is where they spend their advertising money. There are few other efficient media to reach their primary audiences, adult men.

Meantime, Allen and BBDO's CFO had found a potential funding source, should it be needed. Steve Gilbert, formerly a managing director at Morgan Stanley, was head of a venture capital unit at Chase Bank. The CFO told me Steve "Will put the whole $200 million into ESPN at prevailing interest rates plus one point." Steve was known for making smart, serious plays.

A good start, I thought, but too early to assess, whether the entire two hundred would be required, what other funding sources might be available, the extent to which the participating advertisers might wish to invest, and what position ABC might take, giving up a point, though negotiable, a hurdle, and so on. Yet, a positive beginning.

Herb was impressed BBDO had moved so swiftly. So was I.

What followed next:

A lunch meeting at ABC, Herb, Larry and Jack hosting; myself, Arnie and Jack from BBDO, and two wrong choices from Stroh's and Gillette, senior media buyers with no understanding of the financial implications we'd be addressing. They kept asking, What's the cost per thousand? Herb had welcomed their attendance, he knew them both, and was patently disappointed. The meeting ended on a flat note: Let's stay in touch, Herb told them. They left. We offered one another apologies.

BBDO suggested Pepsi and P&G as candidates. Allen said he would make the appointments.

Until he had something substantial to report, Allen had put off briefing BBDO's Chairman, Bruce Crawford, about ABC and ESPN and the working proposition of bringing advertisers and programmers together. It was time we brought him into the loop, Allen

By Way of Luck

said. Was he hoisting a red flag? I thought so. I took his remark as a warning.

As an adjunct to his post at BBDO, Bruce was also Chairman of the Board of the Metropolitan Opera Company. Thus it was no surprise when we arrived at his BBDO private dining room for lunch that we were grandly greeted by waiters and kitchen staff alike, most of them out of work opera singers. There are as many as 5000 opera singers living in New York City, Bruce said, seeking jobs in the Met and the Civic Opera companies. He shook his head sympathetically. I employ as many as I can. For the next few minutes, he told stories about the Met.

Now, what is it you two want to talk about?

Allen's recitation was brief. On hearing ABC, ESPN and sponsor supported programming, Bruce cut him off with a stern rebuke. "Stop! he said! "You're breaking the rules."

Allen showed pain. He had just been stepped on by the gargantuan in the room. What transpired next, I cannot faithfully recount. As colleagues and friends, Allen and Bruce had a lengthy history. They spoke to one another in short, familiar bursts, their references common history and foreign to me, yet each of them apparently understanding fully what was being said. I was ignored.

But I do recall specifically how the lunch meeting ended. "An agency's responsibility," Bruce declared, "is to make the ads and buy the media. That's it!" He told Allen to shut down all discussion of direct co-operation with network programming. "You're crossing the line," he said.

I doubt Bruce understood what his stern command implied. Like wadding a paper towel, he had crumpled the agency's grand vision of itself and tossed it aside. Where Allen saw big, Bruce saw small. Or was his ear tuned to Carmen, the operatic tragedy, Bruce playing the role of Don Jose and dramatically plunging a gilded dagger into Allen's heart? The rebuke was painful. Yet Allen had to respect Bruce's order. His objectives for the agency would have to be postponed.

In the following year, Bruce Crawford resigned from the BBDO board to devote himself full-time to the Met as its general manager.

In transit, he had up-set BBDO's entry into television programming and possibly crippled its later efforts to produce internet advertising. But he had not deterred Allen.

Further Words About Allen

Allen and I got along easily. He regarded me as an equal, and said so, acknowledging my skills as a writer, as a marketing guy, inventive, he said, and as someone who could "take a few blows and always bounce back." Allen was a deliberate thinker. During quiet moments, in a comfortable chair, his back to the door and left open — his posture signaling "Do Not Disturb" — he set aside time to think. Just think. He was sometimes assessing, I learned, how BBDO could become a global advertising and marketing company. Within a year of our first meeting in the late 1980s, and after Bruce Crawford had relinquished his role as Chairman, Allen made a bold move. Gaining the support of BBDO's board, he founded Omnicom, a corporation that would acquire ad agencies under a single management umbrella, yet allow them to maintain their creative independence. By way of merger, Allen had concluded, a conglomerate of agencies acting not as "shops" but as "businesses of consequence" would be seen as legitimate entities and would deservedly be given major roles in the global buying and selling of products and services.

Beginning with BBDO, he acquired TBWA, which included Chiat/Day, Needham Harper Worldwide and DDB (Doyle Dane Bernbach). Other acquisitions followed. Given the impetus Allen provided, Omnicom, now a public, New York Stock Exchange company, succeeded in doing just what Allen had envisioned. Easy to say, Allen had the right idea, but he also had discipline and a gutty instinct that served him and his colleagues well.

Allen has been characterized, deservedly, by *Advertising Age*, as "one of the most influential people in advertising…over the past century."

By Way of Luck

Postscript

ABC bought the 85% of ESPN it did not already own from Texaco for $188 million plus $14 million for the production and uplink facilities in Bethel, Connecticut, still ESPN's headquarters.

Ignoring Hearst, ABC sold 20% for $60 million to RJ Reynolds. ABC financed the balance of the acquisition with debt.

Two years later, when ESPN's success appeared more certain, ABC acceded to Hearst's purchase of RJ Reynolds' stake for an estimated $175 million. ABC defined Hearst's holding as a passive investment. Hearst would have no say in the management of ESPN.

Reader, please note. Hearst paid a premium of $115 million for what RJ Reynolds had bought for $60 million.

Capital Cities Broadcasting acquired ABC. Within 20 months, Cap Cities was sold to Disney.

Along the way, Herb became Chairman of the Board of ESPN and for the next 18 years, his history as a number two guy shaken off, he guided ESPN's world-wide growth and made it television's most profitable network.

A question I've often asked myself since: was Herb playing me when I gave him the $200 million number? I think he was. Unknowingly, I had set the price of the ESPN purchase and sale. I'm sure of it.

Ray Joslin, following the mergers of ARTS and The Entertainment Network, hence A&E, and *Daytime* with the Cable Health Network, hence Lifetime, returned to his desk at Hearst. Over the next twenty years, ensconced in the same office, in the same chair and at the same desk, he negotiated an increasingly larger position for himself, admirably I say, retired wealthy and not long after died of stomach cancer.

My value to BBDO was over. The presentations to key clients had been completed. Allen and Tom wanted to keep me around, asking me to take up some of the management slack. We tried that for a while, I operating as a general corporate executive. But it didn't work. Coming in from the outside to a tightly knit group and taking a high level job, I could sense the resentment of the longer time employees who thought of themselves as more deserving.

With blessings from Allen and Tom, and a fair reward, I moved on.

More than 30 years had passed since taking up a civilian career. Financially, I was in good shape. My Uncle Peter, during my Doubleday years, coached me on investing in publicly held corporations and from that time forward, whenever I had more cash than I needed, I put it into blue chips. I caught rises in the eighties and in the nineties, and developed a long-term, sustaining portfolio. Augmented by the proceeds from the sale of Perkins Bernstein and The Home Shopping Show and from various other investments, I've since enjoyed the financial flexibility of sorting out what I wanted to do, what I could do.

Leaving BBDO, I put money into a newly organized production company specializing in infomercials, but found it a step backward. I took up skiing again and joined a golf club, got involved in not-for-profits, organized and chaired a municipal Wetlands Commission in Connecticut and promoted the rebirth of an area wide conservation organization. I thought, perhaps, I might reroute my career and devote myself to environmental projects and for a while partnered with a local mayor addressing landfill issues, acquisition of open space and broadening a town's recreational inventory, succeeding but disappointed by the politics of it all.

Lady Luck Comes Calling, Again

A phone call. Jim Cornehlsen, a Dartmouth alum and able executive recruiter said he had a proposition for me. His call led to still another high profile assignment I could not possibly turn down. My potential employers were eager, he said. After my first interview, I was offered a rare and compelling assignment.

17

Not One, But Three Employers

Often overlooked, yet fundamental to the creative arts, in fact, to creativity itself in the broadest sense, is the "getting it done" part. An artist, a painter, say, must know how to source and mix his paints, stretch and mount canvas, board or paper, choose when to use a brush or a palette knife or his very own fingers. Writers have embraced pencils, pens, and typewriters, the QWERTY keyboard designed conveniently for them, word processors and computers, and employed the software that makes them usable and productive. The makers of books have made a steady advance from wood and lead type, to monotype and linotype, to photo type and electronically set type. Cameras have been revealed, too, as part the creative process.

There is an art to the construction of art and I have been drawn to it, encouraged, looking back, by my earlier reported encounter with the purple moose and the clack, clack of a letter press bringing him to life and giving it purpose.

My creative side is pleasurable. It moves me to construct things to be read or seen or heard, and giving me room enough to move them along from ideas to their eventual manifestations. What I do, Herb Granath described best. "He makes things happen," he said.

Unsurprising, then, as from my first bout with an IBM electric typewriter and hearing myself in the 1990s referred to as a "user," that I should bolt from my inkwell generation and find a landing in the emerging interactive community...all that co-ax and fiber buried in the ground delivering mega-tons of information and entertainment and the buying, and selling of hard goods and soft, and the management of people and money and the instantcy of it captivating and clinging to me like cobwebs, I should be looking for a way to be involved, to making it happen. I did not have to look long.

Banks and Telcos, the Techs and Mass Marketers

Jim Cornehlsen, flashing his Dartmouth green tie, was waiting for me in the 23rd floor dining room of the Yale Club where our college has privileges. He was the male half of a power couple; his wife Carol was the Executive Director of the Multiple Sclerosis Society. Jim appeared masked, his intentions hidden, a questioner, serially evaluating and assessing people. And why not? He was a skilled and practiced head hunter. He sourced people for a living, sometimes to fill a specific assignment, as often posting in his diary for future reference casually amassed names and impressions. I asked myself whether behind the mask he acted differently.

Are you on top of what's going on with the interactivity stuff? he asked. How would it develop? And what would the services look like? Tell me about the technologies.

I told him what I knew about the business segments that would be involved.

The banks had already gone interactive, their ATM cash machine networks expanding rapidly. The Justice Department's decision in 1983 to break up AT&T created seven local, independent telephone companies US West, NYNEX, Ameritech, Bell South, Bell Atlantic, Pacific Telesis and Southwestern Bell, the seven off-spring of Ma Bell known as the Baby Bells. AT&T continued to own long distance and International traffic. It was seen as an anti-trust victory by the administration, but it left the Bells roiling in confusion. The major techs, IBM and, Microsoft, were taking vaulting leaps in both hardware and software development, but how readily would users adopt

By Way of Luck

personal computers and how large could the market become? Other roles by other potential participants were still difficult to foresee. My reply raised doubt.

But I understood, from a marketing perspective, what the end game should look like. Marketers, in particular direct marketers, I told Jim, had the clearer vision, of interactivity accelerating what they were already doing, at faster speeds, offering more responsive customer service and having more efficient product management tools. They were also more nimble.

Consortiums were forming, small gatherings of industry leaders asking themselves the same questions and having few answers. A major event changed the dialog. IBM, CBS and Sears announced their formation of a partnership called Trintex to create and manage a national informational and transactional interactive network. It would be named Prodigy.

Have you heard of Prodigy, Cornehlsen was asking me?

I had.

What do you think?

Pretty early, I said. I don't believe the technology is far enough along. It will take a while and a whole lot of money.

I've got a client with both the patience and the money.

Who?

Cornehlsen, as was his habit in busy dining rooms, lowered his voice to a confidential whisper. I can't say, he said, unless you sign a non-disclosure.

Consider it signed.

Tentatively, Citibank, NYNEX and RCA have agreed to a partnership that could challenge Trintex, Cornehlsen went on. They've retained me to find the right person to run it.

Is this a social conversation or do you think I'm the right person?

You may be the only person. Frankly, I haven't found a credible guy who fits the bill. You have no conflicts, no history to suggest you might favor one partner over another, you've already done most of what they're looking for and a reputation for getting a job done.

Like making things happen?

Citibank's HR people would be managing the interviews. Representatives from each of the companies would join in, each taking a position, I surmised, that reflected the culture of their respective companies. Could I find a topic that might be common to all? That we could argue to a point of solidarity? Yes, it arose immediately, Videotex, a recently developed interface, i.e. moving pictures on a computer screen and deliverable by wire to other screens. It had gained acceptance, mostly from engineers, and was considered break-through technology, sufficiently "good enough" to build a market around. Or so the whole industry thought.

Coincidentally, some weeks before, at a meeting of the Videotex Association I was introduced to Hilary Thomas, a vibrant Welsh woman new to the United States, and the Association's president. She had been a software developer for a British R&D company for four years. More than that, she was considered an "architect", a designer of multiple computer programs that must eventually and logically come together to produce one or more desired functions. She was now an employee of France Telecom (FT), the national French telephone company, its representative in New York City, her assignment to identify strategic partnerships in interactive media.

The word "internet" was yet to be in vogue.

After the commentary and chatter had subsided, attendees crowded the open bar leaving me and Hilary a chance to talk. She had her own take on Prodigy: the people involved aren't experienced enough to know whether they're on the right or wrong track… it will take them time and money, and lots of it, before they find out. And on Videotex: it's the best technology available…but until a better piece of software comes along, it will only be of interest to the techies who'll want to play with it…it's too slow, too expensive and not ready yet for prime time, she said. We moved into a small computer room where she could give me a demonstration, on the screen, lines flitting back and forth and moving slowly downward, in time filling out the screen, yet taking 10 or more seconds per frame. My take? Unusable.

By Way of Luck

Minitel

France Telecom implemented in 1981 a national, interactive network called Minitel. It was simply designed. At the user end, there was a "dumb" terminal, a mini, non-computational computer, a keyboard and a screen costing no more than $100 to manufacture and ship, with little storage and but a handful of features. At the other end of the network lay the brains, communications hubs, an array of distributed processing centers that provided storage, applications, software development and maintenance. The two ends were tied together by radically new, wide band, high speed telephone lines. To jump-start usage, in its home country of 55,000,000 people, FT sold or gave away 6,000,000 Minitel terminals in its first two years of operations. Minitel was speedily embedded in French homes and offices and immediately useful. Its architecture was amazingly similar to what today in 2014, over thirty years later, is referred to as the "Cloud."

Arguably, FT had built the horse ahead of the carriage, while elsewhere in the world, primarily in the United States, the carriage was built first. The carriage was called MS-DOS which stands for MicroSoft-DiscOperatingSoftware. It required a customer — a user in Telco lingo — to purchase an expensive machine, load it with Microsoft's software even a nerd would have trouble deciphering, and then spend hours searching through an underbrush of coded, alien symbols to find something useful to do. Yet in the United States putting the carriage, as clumsy and leaden as it was, ahead of the horse prevailed. Outside of France, Mintel was ignored.

How did this happen? While FT at the time had the more efficient technology, Minitel was government operated, short on innovation, and lacked competitive spirit. Further, it was indifferently supported by the French government. Minitel was seen as an engineer's plaything. Eventually it gave way to Microsoft, IBM, Intel and Apple and to the massive deployment by cable systems and the Telco's of broadband fiber and wireless networks. Minitel's horse never got out of the barn.

Over the years, thus, the Internet emerged sporadically in slow, jerky very expensive bursts and continues today a patchwork of over built, dithery, dependent technologies that could collapse and bring world commerce to a standstill. Evidence of this lies in the ease by which WikiLeaks founder Julian Assange and whistleblower Edward Snowden, with relative impunity, could hijack a billion pages of classified United States government documents and distribute them to interested parties around the world. With no one aware of what they were up to until news of the theft hit the newsstands.

Indicative as well, is the proliferation of international cyber-attacks, us against them and them against us, that are made possible by huge holes in the networks and their vulnerable data bases, too many to count and too much to manage.

Should the shift from the personal computer to personal digital assistants such as the iPhone and the iPad, already an exploding phenomenon, continue to drift more and more toward a communications model similar to the French Minitel "cloud", both voice and data networks could become safer and more efficient than the Internet we know today. Cross your fingers.

CNR Partners is Organized

The four interviewers, one each from their parent companies, fluent in business and engineering, plus a Citibank Human Resources coordinator, appeared to be civil, knowledgeable people. Yet the interview got underway like a ground breaking ceremony, each participant grabbing a shovel and digging a hole in which to plant his or her own partialities. Apparently there had been no prior agreement as to how the interviews were to be conducted. The conference room heated up.

Citibank's HR person barked, Let's all look at the video. It was a demo of a technology they had all seen and agreed would highlight the yet-to-be defined network. It would be a good place to start. Nervous, I was concerned it would not be a good place for me. Putting the focus on technology, for which I was then but marginally

By Way of Luck

equipped to discuss, would be challenging.

Lights down, computer up, bands of light slowly scanning the computer screen: Videotex!

Thanks to Hilary, I was well prepared for the discussion that ensued.

Two days later I was offered the job, subject to agreement on compensation. There had been no other interviews, I was told. My guess: a good many people, more experienced than I, had been approached and had walked away, either failing to understand the Partners' goals, were involved in less speculative activities or failed to see the excitement in tackling a yet-to-be-defined business.

I was thoroughly vetted, calls made and questions asked of ABC, Hearst, *Playboy*, and Times Mirror. (Canvassing of this kind had happened to me once before, when arriving at the Pentagon with no security clearance; back then an investigator actually travelled to my home town in New Hampshire, his questioning causing quite a stir among my neighbors and leaving them worried I might be in trouble.)

The Citibank HR people were rushing to contract. Here are the benefits, the office, and so on. Whoa! I wanted to meet the guy in charge. He was Rick Braddock, Citi's president and — should I say it? — a Dartmouth alum, class of 1962.

Braddock appeared the perfect boss, relaxed, engaging, sincerely affable, knowledgeable and dismissive of the expansive suite designed just for him and Citi's CEO John Reed, and staff. Their space, in one of the world's largest banks, took up an entire city block and featured a fully equipped gymnasium. We moved quickly to a resolution of goals and responsibilities and funding. There would be a lunch meeting where contracts would be signed committing RCA, NYNEX and Citibank to the venture and where I would be introduced.

I was not prepared for what occurred at lunch. Rick conducted the meeting, Jim Johnson, a Citi executive vice president joining him. Representing RCA, executive vice president and chief financial officer Richard Miller (another Rick) and senior vice president and technologist Jim Alic. And from NYNEX two executive vice presidents from a core of four EVP's who pledged their involvement. In the aggregate, they would comprise my board of directors. Each brought house counsel.

Following a meal of handshakes and happy talk, the contracts were parceled out and serious discussion followed to a point of common agreement. Signatures were readied. Rick Braddock asked that all parties turn to page 33 where a blank space had yet to be filled in, the amount each party had to commit to the project. In an offhanded yet practiced manner, he suggested as a starter they each put up $50 million, and without encouraging discussion he wrote that amount in the Citibank copy on the table in front of him. The others withheld comment, nodded their agreement, and filled in the blank space in their respective contracts. A Citi attorney quickly gathered the documents and sped away.

After lunch, everyone scattered, leaving me and Rick together. He had promised me $15 million as a starter with more available as I needed it. The $50 million number had not been discussed. I was surprised and actually feeling foolish. His response was in character. Had to be serious money, he said, or the partners would not take the project seriously. Citi issued a press release. Advertising Age ran an article headlined: "Perkins to Head $150 million Interactive Network." My phone rang for days.

For a long while I avoided doing the usual: hiring, leasing offices, putting together a timetable and plan, and so on, instead educating myself on what I might need to know and the right direction to take as I moved ahead.

During the weeks that ensued, I went on the road becoming hands-on familiar with the fast emerging communications technologies — not only the here-to-there linkages, but the development rate of hardware and software, semiconductors and processing speeds, satellite and wide-band deployment. Not surprisingly, I spent much of my time in the San Francisco Bay area finding companies willing

By Way of Luck

to talk to me: Intel, Hewlett Packard and Cisco among them. But I received the more valuable tutorial from the video game developers and most of all from Activision and its founding CEO and friend Jim Levy, formerly of GRT. (Hello, Levy. Perkins here.)

The reason: The technologists, with few exceptions, were building machines that offered unlimited promise yet limited purpose. Video game developers, on the other hand, were designing user content and user controllers, interactive games that captured the interest of the young and the curious who felt at ease talking to a machine. While Microsoft and Apple were slow to gain acceptance of their desk top computers, the larger market was drawn to Pong! Nintendo and Activision, all three today still in business and flourishing.

Levy and his crew made themselves generously available. What emerged from our two day chats was less the understanding of hardware and software, but more the observation of collaborative thought processes, the definition of problems and their solutions, unbounded free-thinking and the eagerness of the developers to push and push again, not just to attain the good or the better, but to revel at being the most creative and the best at what they were doing.

I promised myself I would bring that kind of attitude home with me.

On my return, even before finding office space, I hired three key people: from RCA, Grant Reusch for his financial management skills; consultant, Denis Manelski, a Venezuelan with a Ph.D. in electrical engineering from Northwestern University and expert in electronic funds transfer; and from the Hearst Syndicate, Allen Priaulx, a newspaperman and reporter who once headed the Associated Press Paris Bureau, as my content guru. Their varied experiences blended with mine and served to make a flexible team. We called ourselves CNR Partners.

We set a goal: to design and build an interactive communications platform that would give an individual the free choice to see anything, hear anything, read anything, write anything and enter into transactions of every kind from anywhere in the world.

Rick Braddock applauded our approach. If you're able to bring this off, he said, with or without the partnership, Citi will fund it, whether you need $30 million or $300 million.

Next, I met individually with the partners. I had to know who they were, their perspectives on what I might be doing. They had vetted me. I was vetting them, their personal experiences, their resources and the depths of their commitments. They represented a club I had been invited to join, but I was obliged to take charge of the initiation.

Rick told me RCA and GE were talking merger. There might be changes. Jim Alic, I learned, had managed a $600 million debacle betting on the wrong approach to the development of DVD. His wounds were not healing. After the two companies came together, Rick Miller moved to GE and Jim Alic resigned, his replacement a lower level GE marketing executive.

Jim Johnson, responsible for Citi's retail business, gave me a vote of confidence, all I'd get, he said, the "crocodiles are snapping at me. I'm swamped." He smoked in an office where no one smoked. In a few months he left Citibank to become CEO of R.J Reynolds Nabisco. I did not see him again until he appeared on television with six other tobacco company presidents at a Senate Committee hearing, their hands raised and avowing that smoking was not addictive. Larry Weiss, one of Citi's top 35 executives, replaced him.

At a one-on-one lunch with Jim Hannafin, a NYNEX EVP, he said he was astonished I had not heard of him. "I'm the father of the ten cent phone call!" He went on to explain that New York Telephone, a subsidiary, was determined to raise the price of a public telephone call from a nickel, where it had been for over forty years, to a dime. He said it took him eleven years, fighting New York regulators and the Federal Communications Commission, to get it done. His pride shone. My curiosity rose: surely, elevation to one of the highest ranking positions in a major telecommunications company had to derive from something more than a ten cent phone call.

In less than eight months, the partners who'd approved my

By Way of Luck

hiring had been reduced by half and the new half was a distanced assemblage that had no skin in the game. I understood at once the quandary I was in and disappointed I had been slow to realize it. RCA and NYNEX (a merger of the New York Telephone Company and the New England Telephone Company) were crippled companies and the moves they were about to make would cripple them even further. Further, Citibank would be equally wounded, miscalculations in part responsible but largely, there's no other way of saying this, because the company got greedy. I chose to not think further about what I had concluded. My commitment came first.

I will expand on the above "critical" comments later.

Making Things Happen

CNR plotted two directions: one labeled *Mousetrap*, building on present infrastructure and making it better; the other, labeled *Looking Glass*, its architecture entirely new and relying on satellite retransmission to ground based antennae for wireless broadcast directly to both desk top computers and telephones with screens.

From there we outlined the hurdles that lay before us, starting with user loading and transmission speed. Switching from analog to digital was essential. Analog was too limited. Yet digital ate too much band width; could we compress it? We invested in the research and found out how. Already we were ahead of possible competitors. Next we designed the architecture for a wireless network with sufficient speed and band-width to support video. We did not appreciate at the time that these efforts were a gateway the entire interactive community would one day pass through.

Engineers at NYNEX winced at the first mention of wireless, as too new and not practical. Hardly. Guglielmo Marconi was granted a patent for wireless in 1897, laying the ground work for the invention of ship-to-shore communications, wireless radio and wireless television.

Our resources appeared formidable. We had access to the RCA Labs and, by way of NYNEX, the Bell Telephone Labs, yet the more profound technology lay with Citibank. Unlike RCA and NYNEX,

Citibank's research had a specific, on-the-table business need: cementing its consumer base by making banking transactions easier and faster. It had pioneered the ATM machine, had engineering and manufacturing facilities in Los Angeles and Long Island, and had in development the various pieces of a network that could offer banking services directly to home and office. Citi's engineers had already developed the model of a "screen phone" which CNR would later build on by adding the concept of portability, a palm-sized phone that a user could carry in a pocket or brief case.

Further, Citibank was a retailer that valued its customer base, and sought to understand it, nuance by nuance, in a research laboratory of its own making. Several street floors beneath the Daily News Building at 42nd Street and Second Avenue Citibank maintained a unique test site. It developed and evaluated customer interfaces, that is, what screens and keyboards could offer in graphics, text and voice to assist an individual in making an electronic banking transaction. Randomly, passers-by were lured off the street to participate in monitored 30-45 minute sessions, quizzed and debriefed, and given a gift certificate in exchange for their time. The value sought was gained experience that could be integrated into Citi's ATM's and, for CNR, how *Mousetrap* and *Looking Glass* could interact with its eventual user base.

Larry Weiss was in charge of the street lab and of ATM development. Short, bearded and balding, with a bruising temperament, he was a brilliant though controversial manager who pushed his people with angry outbursts and physical threats. Were he not the bad guy to Braddock's good guy, the two of them former colleagues at General Foods, Citi's management might have deemed Weiss an embarrassment and barricaded him from having direct contact with its employees. On my first visit to the Los Angeles facilities, managers looked past me, as one, fearful I might have Larry in tow.

At the time, the mid- to late-eighties, the question looming among developers was "adoption." Were an interactive network designed and made practical, what was the "killer" application that what would most likely be adopted by users? To our small CNR

By Way of Luck

group, and to those of us with direct marketing experience, the answer was obvious: financial transactions, the buying and selling of products and services. Much of the infrastructure was already in place. Credit card use was widespread and growing. UPS and FedEx were emerging as competent overnight delivery systems. Digital tape as a storage and retrieval medium was acceptable for the management of inventories and customer accounts. Yet to be developed, the network, and the software and hardware to support it. Cisco was at work on it as was HP and Sun Microsystems. Yet to be understood: the time and the investment to create it. The promise appeared great.

RCA and NYNEX were not as sanguine. RCA was now in the hands of GE which stripped it of its television manufacturing business, swapping it out with Thomson Electronics, a French company, in an exchange for its medical imaging business, and restructuring the famous RCA labs as an independent, not-for-profit engineering facility, later merged with not-for-profit SRI, Stanford Research Institute.

Understandably, NYNEX had reason to reject the whole idea of wireless, its embedded network, endless miles of twisted copper wire in the ground a mammoth asset. It faced the prospect of either replacing it with wide-band cable or building out a wireless network, at the time neither options financially attractive and, to a staid and aging management, unnecessary. Except for Caz Skrypczak, NYNEX's chief scientist, and an up and coming young vice president, Ivan Seidenberg, then managing NYNEX's Washington, DC office, I encountered few NYNEX executives who expressed any interest or enthusiasm for accepting what so many of us saw as inevitable change.

As a result, in spite of commitments made, upheavals were early in coming at CNR. NYNEX withdrew from the partnership, citing a conflict. That CNR was pushing the notion of phones with screens, in fact, had by then a functioning working model, NYNEX might be in violation of a covenant embedded in the AT&T break-up agreement that forbade the Baby Bells from designing and building telephony equipment. NYNEX paid the partnership a break-up fee of $3,500,000.

I sought GE's support as a way of keeping the partnership together. Rick Miller, former Executive Vice President of RCA, with the sale of RCA's television business would soon be out of a job. (In time he became Executive Vice President and Chief Financial Officer of AT&T.) In the interim, he held my hand, bringing together a GE evaluation group to assess what CNR had so far accomplished, which was considerable. The group included one GE vice chairman, two Executive Vice Presidents, Miller, and Bob Wright who had just been appointed CEO of NBC. The assemblage was so top heavy with GE's senior executives, I wondered who back in Fairfield, Connecticut, was available to help Jack Welch run the company. An EVP, a Dartmouth alumnus, spoke for the group.

Denis Manelski and I had prepared a presentation, but during the introductory chatter I realized my audience was well out in front of me, totally knowledgeable and apparently of a mind to withdraw from the partnership. The meeting was a courtesy. I treated it as an opportunity. Instead of the facts and figures that had been expected, as I did with Serge Semenenko and the Bank of Boston, I talked about futures, defining for my audience where interactivity was heading and of its importance to companies like GE. I expressed my opinions coolly, I thought, yet with passion and detail. My remarks, I felt satisfied them. Perhaps they might continue as CNR partners. The very next day I got feedback.

Rick Miller called. Nice try, he said. Everyone impressed. But no sale. I've called Rick Braddock, he said. GE's attorneys will be in touch with Citibank. Miller then told me, following the swap with Thomson, his "release" was certain.

A second call came from the GE vice chairman who'd attended the meeting and to whom GE Aviation reported. Could I meet him at his New York City office in GE's building on Lexington Avenue? I knew the building well, one of the few surviving deco towers in mid-town. Tomorrow would be fine.

"Call me Fred," he said, immediately foreclosing any greater

By Way of Luck

formality. Less remote than he had been two days earlier, he was nonetheless a wee bit stiff and ostensibly cautious. He offered me "a coffee," pointed to a seat, and talked. He had papers on his desk, and appeared to read aloud from them, but never looking at them directly. There were no questions: just remarks.

He thought CNR's goals, though too early too ambitious, foretold the future. Quite "adequately," he added. Citibank's financial processing systems appear sufficient for the domestic market, he said. GE has a comparable global network. He understood, he said, how I had come to define CNR's direction, my background "oddly" making me "fit for the job."

What CNR is doing and what it proposes to do, he went on, establishes a conflict for GE. Knowing GE in part from the inside, but largely from 10-K's and Annual Reports, the only possible conflict I could see was between Citi and GE Capital. But the two bankers were in very different markets, the potential conflict minor and of small importance.

How to respond to Fred? Where was he going with his monologue? With GE leaving the partnership, there was no longer a partnership, just Citi. I was not troubled by that, my head steeped in the project, the design of the network, the resources employed, continuingly tinkering with the architecture Denis and I had drawn, and the management of personal and the investments made. The network was my larger picture. I had not contemplated a lesser one. I was certain it would go on.

Fred's next comment unsettled me. We'd like you to join us at GE, he said, and talked to that possibility. I was soon smothered by sincerity.

GE is a multi-national, technically diversified company, with outposts throughout the world. GE Capital aside, the company builds machines: locomotives, turbines, pumps, compressors, aircraft engines, medical imaging equipment, nuclear plants, generators and so on. Except for light bulbs, dishwashers and refrigerators, big stuff. It does not operate what it builds, yet its products are integral to over half the US commercial economy. I did not see the fit. Joining GE would be like taking residence on another planet, alien and distant, where my experience would have little relevance. And my skills, perhaps, of no relevance at all.

We've got a network, Fred said. It's functional. It serves us well. For now. But the requirements will grow and change and how we go about change will require leadership. Fred stopped there. He was talking then about what, in 2010, became a reality, GE and its many partners tying machines together in one global loop, whether located in Germany or China, Pittsburgh or Buenos Aires: a girdled connection that would allow users to manage, up-date and recommend local maintenance and parts replacements world-wide. As an example, currently GE knows where every aircraft engine it has ever manufactured and still in service is located, its status and its maintenance record, and ready to issue advisories to local owners and maintenance facilities regarding service and parts replacement. The very same network, an industrial network, as it was then described, can now effectively and economically engage electronically with machines throughout the world. The network has a name: The Internet of Things. GE has since added to the network a "Data Pool" from which it can draw solutions to new problems.

Fred was asking at the end of the 1980s whether I'd be interested in taking the job. What Fred may have had in mind was much too vague. Was he expecting me to fill in the blanks?

Except for my assignment to the Pentagon decades earlier, I had never been in a job where I considered myself essential, that is, where success was demanded and where I might be involved in a broad dependency. Had a book not been published, an article not read, a dress not manufactured, or a TV show not produced, whether a loss of significance was actually incurred would be questionable. Disappointments perhaps, but not failures leaving deep tracks. But when a locomotive does not perform, a jet engine does not survive its anticipated life, or an imaging machine is made obsolete by a competing technology, the outcome can result in the loss of jobs, if not the loss of companies, and be awkwardly memorialized in an annual report. GE has been, and continues to be, a company of great

By Way of Luck

consequence. What it does or doesn't do affects thousands if not millions of people, sometimes positively, sometimes not.

Moreover, in an organization where accountability, the kind GE is known for, is as integral to production as labor and materials, individual creativity, freedom of expression and the cultivation of ideas — my only skills, my only tools — could be marginalized. I would be the odd man out. I chose then to cut short my meeting with Fred.

Fred expressed no surprise when I excused myself. I have a contract to run CNR and for as long as it exists, I intend to honor it, I said, a satisfactory excuse for my real reason: disappearing into a maw of 300,000 GE employees, given a desk, a phone and a paycheck…and spending a good portion of my time explaining myself.

Thanking Fred, I left.

GE withdrew from the partnership, at what price I did not ask. Citi folded CNR and absorbed its balance sheet.

Just the two of us in his office, Rick asked me to join Citi, to continue with the project, and offered me an attractive bonus and a three year extension of my contract. The goals were to be unchanged as was the promise of funding. Just do for Citi what you were doing for CNR, he said.

There was a contingency: I had to report to Larry Weiss.

The offer was attractive. Test the proposition I told myself. I would call Weiss.

I'd had an outside the office, one-on-one encounter with Larry. We'd met late one evening on the sidewalk at Citi's Third Avenue exit, each of us walking north from 54th Street on the way home. Larry talked non-stop, about children and family but mostly about himself. With one block to go, he readied to cut east on 57th Street, I ready to proceed north to 74th Street, lights about to change, he gave me a brief moment to answer: what are your kids up to? I raised an arm and pointed to a movie theater marquee high on the corner of 57th and Lexington Avenue. In bold letters it read ELIZABETH PERKINS in BIG. I thought Larry would be amused. Apparently not. The light changed to green and Larry strode off in an apparent huff and without a parting gesture, feeling, I am sure, deliberately up-staged, as if the episode had been a plot to embarrass him.

Learning that Rick and I had met, Larry called me. "I know what you're doing," he screamed. "You're trying to build a wedge between me and Rick." His words asputter, I could hear the furor boiling in his lungs. "I won't let you get away with it." Drawing a deep breath, all at once whishing and threatening, he said, "You're dead if you try."!"

I held the phone silent and decided not to challenge or even understand his pathology. I hung up and the following day wrote Rick, whom I deeply respected, and thanked him for his generous offer.

The future would show itself.

The Cripples — in Retrospect

AT&T: Ma Bell, an affectionate nick-name for AT&T, was a direct descendent and benefactor of Alexander Graham Bell's late 1800s invention of the telephone and the business it spawned. From its early days and over time it built a national voice and data network that extended to every state in the country, to every town, and to every household that wanted a telephone. It was a gem of a company with two unparalleled resources: Bell Labs, a forward thinking research laboratory whose always advancing technologies were made readily available to its operating companies; and Western Electric, a designer and manufacturer of communications equipment that distributed telephones at little or no cost to both homes and businesses. AT&T was highly regulated by the states and by the federal government, subject to over-sight by both the Senate and the Legislature and to regular audit by the Federal Communications Commission (FTC). Clearly, it was a monopoly. It should have been nationalized.

Instead, the Justice Department decided to screw with it. It took AT&T to court in 1974 and by1983 had forced the break-up of the Bell System, the final edict handed down by Judge Harold Greene in a Washington, DC, Federal Court. It was seen as an anti-trust victory by the administration, but it left AT&T and the seven Baby

By Way of Luck

Bells adrift, and without clear direction they went into mourning. It took nearly an entire generation of management, stripped of its familiar relationships within the Bell family and emotionally wounded, to adapt to the changes brought about by the ruling.

During that time, and for nearly a year, CNR had a partner attempting to determine — Judge Greene's conclusions lacking specifics on the question — whether NYNEX could design but not manufacture a telephone, either by itself or in partnership. Meetings were inconclusive. Memoranda were ignored. Caz Skrypczak's technical team, overstaffed in anticipation of a regulatory reversal and with little to do, waged a war against CNR. Whether real or not, NYNEX felt shut out from its core business. Challenging every technical detail possible, from the effects of ambient static and its influence on wave-length propagation to the probabilities of CNR's wireless architecture, the team could do no more than plot fanciful war games, shout out in frustration, and flood conference rooms with sweaty anger. Their behavior, apparently sanctioned by management, was distracting and expensive. Why NYNEX, knowing this, had committed to the partnership and allowed this to happen was puzzling then and is still puzzling today.

But things change. Ten years later, Ma Bell came bouncing back. Convinced that a restructuring proposed by the Baby Bells could provide an acceptable competitive balance, both the FCC and Justice approved Bell Atlantic's merger and acquisition of NYNEX, Bell South, GTE, and Southern New England Telephone (SNET) pulling them together in a company named Verizon. For its long distance services, it bought MCI.

Meantime, Southwestern Bell was allowed to merge the remaining Baby Bells, bought AT&T as its long distance carrier, and in the aggregate became known as a newly formed company called AT&T.

The regulatory ease by which this was accomplished was seen as an admission by Justice that its 1974 — 1983 break-up of the original AT&T was an over-reaching decision that gave credence to the old saw: "If It Ain't Broke, Don't Fix It."

Verizon and AT&T, however, have only given the appearance

of being competitors. In quiet understanding, the two companies, eschewing competition, have since stayed out of each other's local land line markets. Only later, exclusively with their respective wireless networks, have the two companies become nationally competitive.

But consider what had a happened during the interim: with the biggest producer of telephones banned from the their design and manufacture, the Bell technology quickly migrated to Asia and Europe, consequently limiting emerging local companies — Apple, Microsoft, and Google among them, all designers of telephones — the right to the jobs and business opportunities of manufacturing telephones in their own country — the country that had invented the telephone in the first place.

RCA: Radio and TV. In 1912, Italian engineer Guglielmo Marconi, inventor of wireless communcations and a supporter of Great Britain's entry into World War I, extended the license for the use of his invention to the British. At the outbreak of World War I, the Brits extended the license to its ally the United States as a way of easily sharing communications between one another. At the end of the war, in 1919, the U.S. extended the license to four American companies with the idea they might do something with it for the public good: GE, AT&T, Westinghouse and the United Fruit Company.

Why United Fruit? It ran "banana boats" between Central America and Eastern U.S. ports and was a logical ship-to-shore test bed for the newly formed Radio Corporation of America, shortened eventually to RCA.

A young engineer, a 28 year old Russian émigré named David Sarnoff, was put in charge of the testing. Unwittingly, RCA's four parents most likely hired the first guy who walked into the room with an engineering credential. There was no way they could know that Sarnoff would become one of the great media developers of the 20th Century.

Ship-to-shore Sarnoff handled with ease. In order, he invented the radio, a name derived from a technology that "radiated" a signal. Realizing that the signal simply radiated to someone or something

By Way of Luck

had little value (by themselves banana boats were not an audience) Sarnoff invented programming. He retained conductor Arturo Toscanini to produce hours of classic symphony to be received by RCA's radios. Thus was born the entire concept of commercial broadcast. Sarnoff would sell radios to appreciative listeners. The more programming he had, the more radios he could sell. He called his radio enterprise the National Broadcasting Company, NBC. He went on to invent the Victrola, also called a phonograph, and there found the inspiration for RCA's trademark, a short-haired terrier named "Nipper" sitting next to a Victrola with a large broadcast horn and listening to "His Master's Voice."

In 1939, the first commercial television receiver was introduced by RCA, its black and white signal delivered direct by wireless from NBC, followed 14 years later by NBC's world-first, all-color television broadcast. When I visited RCA in Princeton in the mid-1980s, walking along a corroder of the Sarnoff Building I saw through an open door the first HD television set ever produced. The picture quality snapped my head around. What was that? I exclaimed to a companion. I stood transfixed by the color and depth of the video frames rolling by.

RCA and David Sarnoff went on to produce VCR's and Direct Broadcast Satellites, and contributed mightily to America's Distant Early Warning system known as the Dew line, its purpose, to provide early warning of a Russian air attack coming from over the Arctic Circle. With his retirement, Sarnoff passed control of the company to his son Robert. Invention slowed. Far from being a technical genius like his father, or a genius of any kind, Robert was not equipped to run RCA as his father had. He sought to diversify RCA into other businesses.

RCA bought Hertz, the auto rental giant; it bought Random House, the publisher; it bought a carpeting company, a frozen food company, and engineered an alliance with Whirlpool to sell its appliances. RCA was clearly out of control. And even after Robert resigned from RCA and was replaced as its head by three successive CEO's, the fourth of whom was Thornton Bradshaw, the company continued its erratic operations. Bradshaw, blessed as he was by education and experience, barely slowed the bleeding. He was a teacher and a consultant, a former CEO of a major oil company and a professor at Harvard, his alma mater. But for all his credits, he was as flummoxed as were his predecessors.

What many regarded as a "private" sale of a public company, he sold RCA to GE's Jack Welsh for $6.3 billion — without negotiation or seeking other potential buyers. Stockholders, if not the entire investment community, were outraged. In succeeding years, GE totally dismantled the company, the final piece, NBC, sold to Comcast in 2012.

Warning: if you see RCA on a new product today, it is not Sarnoff's RCA. It is a trademark, its license owned by Sony and a host of other non-competitive licensees.

Bradshaw could have done better, but I believe he did not have the energy to do it. I met him for the first time at the West 34st Street heliport at the Hudson River. I had booked the RCA helicopter to take me to Princeton for the day. I waited long past the plane's scheduled arrival. On landing, Bradshaw and his wife together disembarked. She was on a shopping trip. Bradshaw waved me aboard, apologizing for the delay. Women, you know, he said, suggesting he was not responsible for the delay. The noise of the rotors precluded conversation. Bradshaw said meeting me was a treat. We'd have lunch later, he said. He held his promise.

So what did we talk about? Nothing. Our meeting could have been the inspiration for NBC's Jerry Seinfeld Show which was, as co-star character, George Costanza declared, "About nothing, absolutely nothing." Bradshaw gave me a synopsis of his career, a long lament. He asked where I had attended college, nodding knowingly when I said, "Dartmouth." He left no openings for questions I might ask, except "How's the salad?" His manner was drear. He deflected however I might engage him. It was 1986. By then word of RCA and GE was around. The sale was a given. In his eyes I could see defeat, this proud and humble man, yet his smile was constant. Two years after RCA's sale to GE closed, he died at age 71.

By Way of Luck

Sandy Cole, Boy Genius

Less than a few hundred yards down a hill and across a street from my home in Littleton lived one of my boyhood pals, Sandy Cole, he and I joining up when we were about ten or eleven. Sandy did not play baseball; he couldn't swim or ski; acne pocked his face; he was ignored by girls; and without bottle-thick corrective glasses he was functionally blind. Further, he seemed not to be good at his studies. Yet he went on to become a senior engineer at RCA, credited with gaining multiple patents for the company and on his retirement honored by his peers for his contributions to science and to the development of modern communications. Learning how his career turned out, our entire town was astonished. How could this have happened?

Sandy could read. And one day in 1945, in our local library, he read an ad in *Popular Mechanics* magazine that promised a career in radio. He tore out the ad and mailed it in and within two weeks, a speedy reply in those days, he received a packet of promotional materials featuring more promise and asking for a $9.95 check. Sandy's mother Louise was a housewife of the thirties: she cooked, she made beds, she did laundry, dressed and sent the kids off to school, and relaxed toward the end of her along day with a slug of gin. Sandy's father Sam and his uncle John owned a hardware store on Main Street and sold propane in hundred pound tanks, a small town business that could barely support two families. There would be no check.

Sandy figured it out for himself. Rummaging through a local junkyard and other people's basements, he unearthed busted radios, casings cracked, tubes broken, electrical cords worn bare, wires loosened from their soldered roots and out of the wreckage managed to assemble a radio that worked.

And he read some more, from free radio equipment catalogs. And by setting aside ice cream money and movie money and the occasional dollar bill his grandmother would slip him, he had cash enough to buy parts by mail. By the time he was sixteen and had passed a Federal Communications test for a limited broadcast operator's license, he had constructed in the attic of the Cole house, amidst a hoard of abstruse objects of metal and glass — he discarded nothing, saved everything — a reasonably sophisticated though rubble-strewn communications suite. He had become adept at Morse code, proficient in producing short wave signals, and by both voice and code was part of a world-wide network of "ham" operators. He stood on that mountain of accumulated junk like a king.

I was there, to cheer him on, to run errands, to sort through stuff, to squeeze Sam or Louise for dimes and quarters, and to explain why Sandy seemed never to sleep: only at night could his attic-originated signal bounce cleanly off the tropopause — a lower level of the atmosphere — and make its way to other parts of the world. Then together we'd talk to "ham" operators in Australia, Mexico, Brazil and countries in Western Europe and even South Africa. Sandy was the engineer; I labored as his assistant. While I understood the whole of his mechanical scheme, I could not grasp the parts. The complexity of it all eluded me. My value to Sandy changed when we decided to produce a radio program, a Bob and Ray WBZ comedy before there was a Bob and Ray. We played it to small audiences — locally and distantly — and got appreciative responses from our listeners.

I tell this story because Sandy was at the vanguard of a revolt, of kids just like him who did not fit the social standards of the 40s and 50s. Promoted by magazine and television advertising that featured creamy-cheeked children with dimpled smiles, primly aproned mothers, and smugly successful dads, how families were expected to look, dress, eat and sleep was steeped in bliss and totally fanciful. Worse, it set an unacceptably high bar that Sandy's kind of kids could not hurdle. They were assigned back row seats in the class room, got beat-up on the way home from school, and rarely received invitations to neighborhood birthday parties. Derisively, these kids were called mean and cutting names: losers, queers, girlies and shit heads just a few. "Nerds" did not come along until later.

Yet these kids have changed our world. Set apart in the class-

By Way of Luck

room and jeered on the playground, they found relief in the pursuit of the tough courses, the studies that challenged most other kids: engineering, math, physics and chemistry, the science courses that demanded deep study and hard work and where they could attain a level of excellence their detractors could not. In one gigantic 50-year leap, from Marconi and Sarnoff, Edison and Tesla to Jobs and Gates, Moore and Bushnell, the nerds of their day, the technologies that emerged from their persistence and brilliance have led to a better, safer, more inclusive world, the talk of inequality notwithstanding, we as humans are more equal than ever before. The technologies that Sandy and his kind developed have allowed us to see each other closer, to recognize differences more readily, to be more tolerant of one another and regardless of our varied religious beliefs, to share a greater faith. For in the end we are one.

Citibank: Over a period of 40 years beginning in the 80s, no financial institution put on as many false faces as Citibank. Whether it was a legacy of master banker Walter Wriston, or his successor, John Reid, or his successor Sandy Weill or Weill's successor Charles Prince, or his Chairman Richard Parsons, is moot: to isolate the blame for what went wrong, or how wrong was done, there were too many fingers, too many pies. A reader can easily Google for himself or herself to learn how two decades of utter turmoil tore apart an American institution and left thousands of employees either broke and on the street or rich beyond reason.

The bank's deeper troubles began in 1999 with the attack on the Glass-Steagall Act which, since 1933, to avoid the obvious conflicts, forbade the mixing of banking and investing. Pushed by Treasury Secretary Robert Rubin and his deputy Lawrence Summers, and with Congressional support from both sides of the aisle, it was repealed. Its deconstruction brought on mischief. Bankers could now act as investors, investors as bankers; the wall of separation between them designed to protect consumers was brought down. Bank customers were left vulnerable. And they still are.

Going back 200 years — Citi's claimed heritage — Citibank has long been the scoundrel among the big American banks. It has cheated its investors, lied to its customers, bribed clients, knowingly sold bad paper, mis-stated its earnings, side-tracked careers, paid off politicians, and used its clout to extort favors and intimidate competitors. In early 2000, when home-owner loans ballooned, it hesitated not at all to originate and sell toxic mortgages, offering them in massive bundles too thick to assess and under names that cloaked the thievery hidden within them. One such bundling was called Auction Rate Securities. For a time I owned bundles of bundles.

In 2007 I sold my house, the one I promised my wife we would live in for the rest of our lives. I sensed a teetering market. It bore no promise. The sale closed on August 1, 2007. We'd rent for a time. I had cash. My brokerage representative at Citibank's subsidiary, Smith Barney, a smart, conservative lady, suggested I put the cash into ARS's, defining them as good as treasuries, never as mortgages, offering a point or more, and telling me that ARSs had long been available only to commercial clients and for the first time management had made them available to retail customers as well. She sent me the literature. They would roll over every Friday at which time I could renew them or cash them out, giving me the flexibility I needed. I had no reason to doubt her representations. We had worked together profitably for several years and we still do, but she was clearly duped by her employers. I parked a big chunk of money in ARS's.

Though the market crash was upon us, for a few months into 2008 the roll-overs worked as advertised, but on one Friday in mid-February they did not roll over. I was assured by the end of the following week, they would. They didn't. Don't worry, she said. Her managers had told her there was a blip in the transaction processing procedures.

I worried.

Immediately, I wrote a complete summary of my ARS transactions, with dates and serial numbers, in a letter asking for help.

I sent the letter to our two Connecticut Senators: Chairman of the Senate Banking Commission Chris Dodd; a note from him

By Way of Luck

written on my letter and returned to me said, "Call the Connecticut State Consumer Protection Bureau. A put off. Once a vice-presidential candidate, Joe Lieberman did not reply.

I sent the letter to my home state's Attorney General, Dick Blumenthal; I got no reply.

I sent the letter to Ben Bernanke, Chairman of the Federal Reserve Bank. I received a pleasant call from his office informing me that the Bank had no authority in the matter. Good luck, the pleasant voice said.

I sent the letter to Hank Paulsen, Secretary of the Treasury; I got no reply.

I sent the letter to Andrew Cuomo, then New York State's Attorney General. My phone rang. A voice said: "Jim, my name is Bruce Brown. I'm an assistant attorney general in Attorney General Andrew Cuomo's office. I have your letter. It is perfect. With your permission, the AG wants to use it as testimony in suits we're filing against all those bastards. In fact," he added, "It will be the number one piece of evidence we'll be offering." I gulped. Wow, I thought. Can this be real? I gulped again. "OK," I said. He thanked me, told me he'd stay in touch. Which he did.

Two days later, my Smith Barney agent called. "I've just received a subpoena," she said, "ordering me to appear in Court in lower Manhattan."

"Wow," I said again. (Obviously, I am not reluctant to let the child in me surface.)

"What does that mean?" she asked. Her voice trembled. I felt sympathy.

"It means," I said, "there's a good chance I'll get my money back."

Bruce, as promised, called me several times with progress reports. Within three months, checks started hitting my account, most of them from Citibank and Pimco, and did not stop until my Auction Rate Securities were fully redeemed. I vowed then, if Andrew Cuomo ever ran for governor and asked for my vote, I would move to New York State to cast it. He made no promises. He asked nothing of me. He did his job. He restored my faith in government.

Judy, my wife, hearing the news gave me a long hug. "I'm beginning to believe," she said, "you are one lucky guy." Later she amended her comment. "You make your luck. You put yourself in positions to be lucky." She shook her head. "I don't know how you do it."

I don't either.

The untold story: the holders of ARS's who didn't worry and took no action, easily thousands of them, are in 2015 still owed billions of dollars, their hope of redemption slim if not gone.

18

Postlude

On leaving CNR, Denis Manelski and I formed a partnership, incorporating ourselves as U.S. Tel, Inc. We had many commonalities, a robust resume, a proven work ethic and a wish no longer to be involved in corporate management. Whether by choice or by circumstance, we were outliers, respected but perceived by employers as undeserving of the collegiality enjoyed by more committed institutional employees, good to have around when needed, but easily offed at the conclusion of an assignment or the unfulfilled promise of opportunity. Jokingly, I told Denis we were among the hoboes of corporate America who were either abandoned by management elitists or who chose not to work according to corporate dictum. We were a good pairing.

Denis was born in Vienna, Austria, in 1937 of Jewish parents, doctors both, who, before Denis was two years old, fled to Venezuela, escaping the holocaust they could see coming. Denis was raised in Caracas, grew fluent in both Spanish and English, and while still a teenager was a member of the Venezuelan National swimming team. He attended Northwestern University, graduated *Summa Cum Laude*, earned a doctorate in electrical engineering, never went back to Venezuela, spoke little of his father, not at all about his mother nor any siblings he might have had. He was a private man. Whether he had humor, or suffered indignities, felt cheated or ignored, one could not tell. He had a single genius: down to the last string of code, he understood electronic funds processing, the architecture and the requirements to support it. He knew how to employ the "killer" app!

We based U.S. Tel in Greenwich, Connecticut, at a posh address and convenient to where we both lived, together swam several times a week at the Greenwich YMCA pool and lunched afterward at a diner across the street. We promoted ourselves with a few phone calls. We were known and had credence

Unsurprisingly, we were engaged by France Telecom. Hilary Thomas had orders from Paris: Retain the key people who left Citibank and CNR, she was told. FT was negotiating a relationship with US West to bring Minitel to the United States. Were it to be realized, they wanted a local team to step in and handle it. How many guys? Hilary asked. Talk to Perkins, he'll know. A handful to start. Hilary handed us a check for $150,000, stand-by money she said. No strings. We stood by. Denis and I put three former CNR "key" people on hold while they looked for jobs elsewhere. The negotiations took longer than expected. US West was not as nimble as FT had hoped. We released the three.

There was no movement. FT and US West were merely talking. Negotiations had not begun. So Denis and I took the initiative. We defined what needed to be done, a proposal with costs attached that both US West and FT could crunch and possibly agree upon. It worked. We structured a test of the Minitel system, locating it in Minneapolis, outlining both the technical requirements and a marketing plan. And there began an extended relationship with US West and FT, financially beneficial, but intellectually and emotionally unrewarding.

For Denis and me, Minneapolis wasn't New York City. France Telecom wasn't NYNEX. And US West wasn't anywhere it could match up with some other company or easily located. Spread over 14 states from Minnesota and the Dakotas to the Rockies and the

By Way of Luck

Pacific Northwest, with incursions into Arizona, New Mexico and Nevada, it was then a deadening sprawl of left over, small market telephone companies with but three metropolitan mother-ships: Minneapolis, Denver — US West's headquarters — and Seattle. Corporate management spent half its time traveling, half its time deciding where it was traveling to, and the rest of its time attempting to engage in something productive. Its employees felt distanced. Corporate culture was an anomaly. Visiting a US West outpost could be an upsetting experience. We had no idea what to expect.

A corporate vice-president asked me to address the Seattle managers. Speak to them about futures, what the coming technologies will mean to them and to their careers. Can you do that? he asked. It was an easy assignment.

In a hall in a US West building in Seattle over 300 company employees, casually dressed and lounging in their seats, were assembled on a late morning to hear what I had to say. I was introduced. Applause followed. I opened my talk with a common salutation; "Ladies and Gentlemen…"

I was promptly cut off. A man in one of the up-front rows had jumped to his feet. Pointing a persistently jabbing finger at me, he hollered, "We're not ladies and gentlemen here, Mr. Perkins." He paused momentarily and looked about the auditorium as if seeking consensus. I could see heads nodding. "We are men and women!" he shouted, like a bomb going off and with it an approving roar of approval that was slow to die down. In what seemed like minutes but was only seconds, I restarted. I said, "Men and women, boys and girls, and the little critters running about under your feet and eating your lunch, I'm happy to be here. Mostly because I was paid in advance." I got laughs. I talked a good talk, but I was shaken. What conceivably could have prompted the interruption? Back in Denver I got an answer. Out there, a highly placed executive told me, they don't think they're part of the United States. Wait till you meet our people in Arizona. It'll be worse.

Denis and I were otherwise trusted and respected, but maintaining US West's interests was difficult. Its employees seemed always to have more important tasks underway, a common dodge in overly-layered workplaces, and frustrating to FT. So, on speculation, that is, at our expense, we continued originating comprehensive proposals for their review and upon their acceptance we became third parties to the projects we would manage as well as vendors. On our part, the personal investments we made were considerable, but with FT's endorsement we made it work.

Unfortunately, our practice led to a disturbing discovery. US West was co-opting our proposals, those they did not accept, but found informative and possibly of value. One such proposal was repackaged by a US West vice-president — removing all evidence of our proprietary interest in the proposal and labeling it as his own — and presented it in its entirety to senior management as an internally produced document. We found out about it when management asked us to evaluate it. US West apologized for the obvious theft of US Tel's property. Embarrassed and acknowledging our proprietary rights, US West paid us a substantial fee.

US Tel took on other projects.

We represented FT in its management of a relationship with Sprint.

For MasterCard and a consortium of banks, we designed and produced the software for a funds transfer network to move money efficiently between the United States and Mexico.

For Western Union, we earned a contract to up-date its electronic funds transfer system; anxious to keep us, we surmised, they paid us in advance.

We introduced FT and NYNEX to a proposal for a joint venture and got the assignment to deliver a business plan.

For Ameritech, the Baby Bell located in Chicago, we jointly explored a basket full of propositions that so excited the company's CEO he insisted we move to Chicago and work exclusively for him. What impressed him, he said, "You're talking what I've been thinking."

By Way of Luck

For Toshiba, a software development assignment that Denis managed.

For Lotus and Phillips Electronics, a joint venture that had acquired the rights of Citi's screen phone and sought support for its development. This latter assignment found me and Denis in conflict.

The joint venture, located in Cambridge, Massachusetts, was managed by a former Lotus employee, an ego-centric software developer, a sloven who farted uncontrollably driving people out of meetings if not out of the building, who habitually picked his nose, his right forefinger generally buried deep in a nasal passage, and humorlessly reminding his employees that he was "In charge of saying no!"

At startup of the venture, its President alienated a long time Phillips engineer who'd moved to the United States — having been told by a most senior executive in Eindhoven, the Netherlands, Phillips principal offices, he would manage the venture. With Lotus's backing, the President told him otherwise and excluded him from meetings, setting in motion a conflict that grew more venomous as the days went on. The venture was doomed.

Too much rancor around here, I told Denis. We should give up the assignment. Denis said it was premature. I disagreed. Denis stayed on until the Philips-Lotus partnership collapsed. We never again worked together.

For a while, I managed myself. Possibilities came and went, interesting assignments all. Yet, only one grabbed my attention: the Thoroughbred Racing Associations, a trade organization that represented the major thoroughbred race tracks in the United States. Its newly appointed Commissioner, Brian McGrath, needed help. Previously, Brian had been commissioner of a European Football League, living in Switzerland and, as he explained, the titular head of a game he did not understand. He did not know much about horse racing either. He was the affable Irishman with an unsullied past who told a good story.

Joslin Surfaces...Again

Hearst's Ray Joslin was promoting an internal proposal to create a horse racing cable television channel. Hearst could not possibly bring it off without the involvement of the Associations. Moreover, starting something was not Ray's strength which lay in taking over existing projects from somebody else and making them better. Ray chose not to call me. Instead, embarrassed I believe, he recommended that Brian retain me as a consultant. Which Brian did. For the next two months, nothing much happened. Ray assured me the project would proceed. His Board had approved the plan, he said. There was but one hurdle left to clear.

Meanwhile, I was introduced to the many disparate parts of horsing racing: the Thoroughbred Breeders Association, the Jockey Club, the trainers and the jockeys, Autotote, one of two tote suppliers that manage the electronic betting machines at the track and calculated the betting results, the Jockey's Association, the auctions in Lexington, at the Keeneland track where thoroughbreds are bought and sold, the New York City and Philadelphia OTB (Off Track Betting) parlors, the professional gamblers and the handicappers, and the cameramen who shoot the actual races and the up-link suppliers who distribute them live to other tracks and, separately, those who shoot the photos taken at the finish line and are responsible for capturing the "photo finish."

Thoroughbred Racing operates as one large, integrated corporation, yet there is no entangling corporate structure, just letter agreements and handshakes, each of the above entities running pretty much independently although, by practice and preference, and by state regulation, they are dependent on one another, the informality not unlike a family business. Yet, there were different opinions on how the participants in the "industry" saw themselves. The president of the Thoroughbred Breeders Association explained its commitment to 'improving the breed." She told me that racing was of less importance, that "commercial" race tracks were unnecessary; "If we want to race our horses," she said, "we have tracks of our own."

By Way of Luck

I was taken by the people I met, the business concerns they expressed, but most of all I was taken — still to this day, the picture in my mind — by a thoroughbred brood mare put up for auction at Keeneland who struck me romantically almost as deep as had my wife Judy at our first meeting. The mare, hosed and groomed, a large animal, her coat cinnamon brown and sleek, walked hesitatingly into the half-moon auction pit. She did not wish to be there, her dignity stripped. As the bidding began, she looked disdainfully at the shouting buyers, her eyes messaging, "I am a queen. You're using me. I resent you." She looked at me for confirmation and, I swear, as an ally. My heart reached out to her.

The bidding stopped: "Sold for two million eight hundred thousand," a record price. The buyers roared their approval. Sensing the value she had wrought, she raised her head dramatically and walked away, as much the operatic diva exiting a theatrical stage, her ample hips rolling, her tail tossing the bidders a final message: "You've had me once. You'll never have me again."

There are fabled tracks, classic in their antiquity and their distinctive architecture, like Churchill Downs, Santa Anita and Saratoga, and warm weather tracks like Del Mar in Southern California, and Gulfstream in Florida. And there are the down-market tracks, the few in number distinguished by lingering, acrid cigarette smoke, the litter of discarded betting slips and crumpled Racing Forms with scribbled notations, by the pervasive odor of a chlorinated floor wash of mixed green and gold and by the ragged appearance of unemployed, mid-week bettors looking for a win if only to recover what they had already lost.

Bringing my friend Harold Hansen up-to-date on my latest endeavor, he took issue with my regard for American tracks and American thoroughbreds. Harold was a publisher of directories, an exacting business, for their accuracy had to be precise. One wrong phone number, street address or corporate description could result in a cascade of subscription cancellations severe enough to make marginal the many profits he earned. He was by nature a cruel critic of most everything which, editorially, served him well. Yet he was an excellent travel companion. He jumped to make reservations, hail a cab, open an umbrella and order the wine as if he had just been released from a long incarceration and had to make the most of time lost. Until you've visited the European tracks, he said, Your evaluations of America racing are unacceptable.

Coincidentally, Harold said this as he and his wife Bobbi Hansen, Judy and I were booking a trip to London and then to Paris, the women to shop and, Harold added to the itinerary, for the men to visit a few tracks. Off we went.

The meet at Newcastle was comparable to an up-scale race day in the U.S. But Brighton, on the ocean, was a disaster. We ate in a building that could have once been an auto repair shop, pushed through a sweatered and coat-less mob to place our bets and out to a grandstand enveloped in dense, swirling fog.
Harold was unperplexed. He had little interest in watching the race, he said. He was a bettor with a system, what we today call an algorithm, by calculation alone evaluating how a horse might win or lose, his joy coming not from the thrill of a race but solely from his anticipated winnings.
Fog or not, the race course manager apparently approved the running for we could hear the alarm at the opening of the gate, the sounds of the hooves beating past us, and the race caller calling a race, we were sure, he also could not see. Yet the results were posted. The fog lifted by the fourth race, but by then Harold was certain the meet was fixed: in the first three races, he had neither won, nor placed nor showed. He was ready to move on. To Paris, he said.

Longchamp, the famed Paris track located along the Seine, is a wondrous, elegant place, lengths ahead of American tracks. It speaks to a visitor of France's culture, its food, its wine, its architecture and of its sweeping gardens, of women fashionably gowned and men clad

By Way of Luck

in reflection of their political and economic rankings. We were there to watch the running of the famed Prix de l'arctriomphe, heralded as the most important race in all of Europe. Harold and I in coat and tie, walked freely among the stands, lunched on linen, sipped sturdy brews and at the walking ring — what in the U.S. we call a paddock — assessed the favorites as they began the parade that would lead eventually to the starting gate. On our day of glittering sunshine and glamourous sight-seeing, the winning horse was Irish-bred Sinndar, owned by the Aga Khan, the fourth of his line, and one of the world's largest equine breeders. By afternoon's end, I was exhausted if not a bit sotted and ready to leave, but Harold said, There's more.

Back to the walking ring we went for the trophy presentations to the day's winners, no ordinary event, but a celebration. Instead of the usual hoisting of a cup and a round of applause, there was the marching of the guards, the Irish and the Welsh Guard, honoring Sinndar's equine heritage, and the French Republican Guard honoring everyone else. The Aga Khan and his retinue, accompanied by the marching Guards, were brought by horse drawn carriages to the walking ring where, from a portable stage, and amidst the arcing sparkle of flash bulbs, they acknowledged the plaudits of appreciative race-goers and accepted gratefully the winner's cup. Harold shot me a knowing eye. I nodded in agreement. No American track could boast of such extravagance.

Brian asked me to accompany him to an annual Associations meeting in Washington, DC, to observe, he said, and to give the attendees an up-date on Hearst's Racing Channel. Before packing my bags, I called Ray for a status report. Appears we're good to go, Ray said, pending contract negotiations with you and Brian when you're back from Washington. Certain? I asked. Certain, Ray replied. The "hurdle" to be cleared," he assured me, was no longer a factor. Which is what I reported to the Associations' members.

Ray had failed to come clean with Brian and me on the "hurdle." Victoria Hearst, daughter of Hearst's Chairman, Randolph Hearst, and granddaughter of William Randolph Hearst, the company's founder, according to Ray, was an avid horse woman. She had indeed expressed interest in how the channel might be programmed. Which was correct, but Brian and I were led to believe her interest was positive. Undoubtedly, hoping that her position might not be taken seriously, Ray hid from us that Victoria was against Hearst being involved in any way with horse racing. Or perhaps he did not know.

Victoria was on a morality tear, first attacking *Cosmopolitan* magazine as pornographic, demanding it be sold or closed down, and later condemning the proposed racing channel as being supportive of gambling. Both, Ray was told, were denigrating the company's reputation, in particular horse racing. Everyone knows, she was to have said, the tracks run a scummy business.

Cosmo editor, Helen Gurley Brown, had a platform from which she could adequately defend herself. The magazine was Hearst's most profitable publication. Ray, with but a business plan, had no platform at all. The proposed racing channel was DOA. Ray delivered the obit apologetically, by phone, his call our last encounter.

The Luck Goes On...

Mid-June, 2008: Driving from Shelburne Falls, Massachusetts, home for my daughter and her family, I headed south toward Kent, Connecticut, where Judy and I live, a journey I've made countless times. But on this one trip, unthinking, I took a very different route, passing through rural communities where streets are like cow paths, where roads are not well marked and where the likelihood of making a wrong turn is a constant. Irked, I complained to myself, why had I ignored taking the familiar highways I knew so well. A change for the sake of change, I finally assumed.

I was not in a hurry. In another few miles I'd swing on to a US highway that parallels my usual route, and make up the time I'd lost. Which I did, eventually coming to an intersection that would take me directly to Kent. Inexplicably, I passed it by and continued on. I approached still another intersection leading to Kent, passing it by as well. And another and another until there were no further alternatives. By then, obviously coming out of deep

By Way of Luck

denial, I admitted to myself what I was up to. I was heading toward the New Milford Hospital, now just minutes away.

For unaccountable reasons, over the last several weeks I suspected I might have pneumonia. The thought had been nagging at me, yet I was not ill. I bore not even a sniffle. Nonetheless, having driven this far I was determined to go on, planning what I would do when I arrived at my destination. I would drive onto a ramp that led to the hospital's emergency entrance. Once in the ER, I would ask for an X-ray. I think I have pneumonia, I would say. Clearly, I was a child acting out or an innocent who had been slipped a hallucinogen.

A reader may think this recounting bizarre. At the time, without question it was for me as well. I am not immune to social antics, nor to mindless suppositions, but my erratic behavior, even for me, was outlandish. As I stood before the receptionist, I actually feared I might be accused of perpetrating a hoax.

X-rays were taken by a skeptical radiologist, my expressed symptoms apparently unconvincing. I waited for his return, confused and angry at myself for what I deemed silliness and readying an apology. "You don't have pneumonia," the radiologist said. Whew, that's a relief, I replied, anxious to leave.

"But," he added, "there's something we should look at." Together we walked to the x-ray room where he mounted on a light box the film he'd taken of my chest. Microscopically small — I squinted to see — there was a barely perceptible black dot on the upper lobe of my left lung.

Several days later, a biopsy revealed I had a malignant tumor. I did not know whether to laugh, cry or just bang my head against a wall, my astonishment so great. The actions I thought silly were made real.

While my make believe fears were allayed, a new and existing fear lay ahead of me. My local go-to doctor and friend, George Barth, said, Let's not screw around with this. I know the right guy at Sloane Kettering. He made the appointment for me with Dr. Bernard Park.

We sat across from one another in an examining room at 160 East 53rd Street in mid-town Manhattan. "I'm having a hard time believing this," Dr. Park said. It's a tumor all right, and malignant, but it can't be, at most, maybe three months old. Or even less, he added. I then told him of my errant drive from Shelburne Falls to the New Milford Hospital. He shook his head in disbelief.

No treatment could be prescribed, for the tumor, a K-Ras mutation, would not respond to either radiation or chemotherapy. Instead, the lobe was excised. Three years following surgery, by a consensus of Sloane-Kettering's doctors — each of them saying redundantly, It's good we got it early — I was declared free of lung cancer, its possible return 99.5% unlikely. An additional six years have passed and I am still clean. I do not breathe as sumptuously as I once did. But I breathe freely.

I am still bewildered by having driven an unfamiliar route that June day, pushed aside reason, and conducted myself with such spooky sureness. Eventually. I concluded, I had once again been in the arms of lady luck.

And...On

On December 22nd, 2014, Judy and I were in New York City, there for several days to enjoy the holiday merriment, making the familiar rounds of theater, museums, shopping, music, food and at mid-night on Christmas Eve worshiping at the Cathedral of St. John the Divine. We had a schedule laid out, places to be, at times that did not conflict, and with all reservations confirmed. We had worked it all out flawlessly, or so we thought.

Walking to theater — on our way to see Glenn Close and John Lithgow in *A Delicate Balance* — a heaviness slowed my steps, the result of a disappointing meal, I thought at first. But in an instant, the heaviness engulfed me, pain coursed the left side of my body and radiated down my leg and into my toes. I am in trouble I said aloud, frightening Judy. We were on West 45th Street between Sixth and Seventh Avenue approaching the heart of Times Square. The sidewalks were bustling with sight seers and theater goers, workers were coming and going; automobile traffic in the street was jammed, fender to fender, moving slowly or not at all.

By Way of Luck

If I did not find help, my immediate reaction, I would worsen. Then what? In the midst of perhaps a half million swarming people, my mind whirled. Where can I go? How do I get there? I can barely move. Even if I could, walking was impossible. Judy pointed. Why was she pointing at me? No, she was pointing past me. She yelled above the city's noise, "Turn around." I did. I was not five feet from a New York City Fire Department ambulance parked parallel to the curb. Had it just pulled in? Was it about to leave, on a call or some other emergency? I lurched against the driver's side door. A window rolled down. What can I do for you? said the driver. I think I'm having a heart attack, I said.

All the experience and all the training a couple of EMTs could possibly muster came together in one mad though practiced rush. I was trundled onto a gurney, an aspirin shoved into my mouth, a voice saying chew on this, a siren sound, an EMT preparing syringes of nitro-glycerin that would stabilize me, EKG pasties stuck to my chest, and in spite of the crowds, the jam-up in the streets of people and machines, Judy and I were on our way to 114th Street and Amsterdam Avenue to St. Luke's Hospital that the EMT told me was one of the best — and nearest — cardiac centers in the city. We made the 70 block run in less than ten minutes.

How is it that the ambulance was there? Were it not, where would I have gone, how would I have gotten there? As I've talked to the doctors and seen the records, I know now that I could have died that night. My heart was strong, functioning at 100% the surgeon said, but my arteries were worn ragged and mostly closed, my blood barely moving, the heart straining to keep me alive, but eventually having to give way if relief did not come and the flow of blood shut hard. A close call someone in the intensive care unit said.

As I write this, I am but seven weeks removed from surgery, grateful and forever beholden to the ambulance team, whose names I did not get, and St. Luke's Chief of Cardiac Surgery, Dr. Sandhya Balaram, whose surgical skills brought me back to the living.

And how do I now reflect upon the absolute luck of an ambulance standing ready at my side, as well as all the instances past when luck stood by me?